The Story of Appleby in Westmorland

Martin Holdgate

HAYLOFT

First published, 1956 by J Whitehead & Son (Appleby) Ltd
Revised edition, 1970
Reprinted by Dalesman Publishing Company Ltd, 1982
This edition completely revised and largely rewritten, 2006

Hayloft Publishing Ltd, Kirkby Stephen,
Cumbria, CA17 4DJ

tel: + 44 (0) 17683) 42300
fax. + 44 (0) 17683) 41568
e-mail: books@hayloft.org.uk
web: www.hayloft.eu

Copyright © Martin Holdgate, 1956, 1970, 1982, 2006

ISBN 1 904524 35 4

A catalogue record for this book is available
from the British Library

The right of Martin Holdgate to be identified as the author of this work has been asserted by him in accordance with the British Copyright Design and Patents Act, 1988.

Apart from any fair dealing for the purposes of research or private study or criticism or review, as permitted under the Copyright Designs and Patents Act 1988 this publication may only be reproduced, stored or transmitted in any form or by any means with the prior permission in writing of the publishers, or in the case of reprographic reproduction in accordance with the terms of the licences issued by the Copyright Licensing Agency.

Printed and bound in the EU

Papers used by Hayloft are natural, recyclable products
made from wood grown in sustainable forests.
The manufacturing processes conform to the
environmental regulations of the country of origin.

To the memory of James Faulkner Whitehead MBE JP
16 May 1890 - 17 August 1974

Councillor, Alderman, Honorary Freeman and
six times Mayor of Appleby

For 44 years a Governor of Appleby Grammar School
Who first made me interested in the history of the Borough
and gave constant encouragement during the
preparation of the early editions of this book

Map 1 (endpapers) - The burgage map prepared for the Parliamentary Election of 1754. It shows the pattern of mediaeval burgage plots very clearly. Note the numerous abandoned plots along Doomgate, Scattergate and the Sands. Reproduced by kind permission of Lord Hothfield.

Contents

	Illustrations	6
	Preface	9
1	The Beginnings of History	11
2	A New Appleby	35
3	Prosperous Borough	54
4	Decline and Fall	79
5	Depressed Area	107
6	Appleby's Great Lady	134
7	Busy Market Town	161
8	Into the Modern World	202
9	If you require their Monuments…	228
	Some notable dates in Appleby's history	237
	References	241
	Index	251

Illustrations

MAPS AND PLANS

Map 1. Appleby burgages in 1754   End papers
Map 2. Roman and Romano-British Westmorland   17
Map 3. The development of 'New Appleby'   41
Map 4. Appleby Friary   77
Map 5. The original site of Appleby Grammar School   128
Map 6. Historic monuments in Appleby   188

Plan 1   Appleby Castle, ground level plan   37
Plan 2   St. Lawrence's Church   73
Plan 3   Appleby Castle, east range   164

         The de Goldington family of Appleby   71

PRINTS AND DRAWINGS

Frontispiece	Appleby Old Bridge	8
Figure 1.	The Appleby hog-back tombstone	31
Figure 2	The development of Appleby Castle Keep	51
Figure 3.	Appleby from the Sands	75
Figure 4	The Countess' Pillar	138
Figure 5	Margaret, Countess of Cumberland's tomb	141
Figure 6.	Appleby Castle in 1761	167
Figure 7.	Bongate Church and Appleby Castle in 1773	201
Figure 8	Appleby's old and new Coats of Arms	225

Photographs

1	Aerial view of the castle	91
2	Appleby Castle Keep	91
3	The Great Picture	92
4	Lady Anne Clifford, aged 15	93
5	Lady Anne Clifford, aged 56	93
6	The memorial to Lady Anne	94
7	St. Lawrence's Church	94
8	Lord Thanet's mansion	95
9	Lady Anne's Hospital	95
10	The Cloisters	96
11	The church organ	96
12	The old Grammar School	97
13	The old school doorway	97
14	The new Grammar School	97
15	Bongate Mill and Victoria Bridge	98
16	Appleby Bridge	98
17	Appleby Assizes	173
18	Appleby Assizes	173
19	The Shambles	174
20	The Moot Hall	174
21	The cheese market	175
22	Market day	175
23	Queen Victoria's Diamond Jubilee	176
24	Boroughgate	176
25	Market Square	177
26	Proclamation of King George V	177
27	Appleby New Fair	178
28	Appleby New Fair	178
29	Battlebarrow in 1900	179
30	Appleby signal box	179
31	River Eden in flood	180
32	HM the Queen's visit in 1956	180

The Story of Appleby in Westmorland

Frontispiece - Appleby old bridge as drawn by Thomas Girtin in 1793. The gatehouse which formerly stood on the right had been demolished by this date.

Preface

OVER fifty years ago I was talking to the late Alderman James F Whitehead – six times Mayor of Appleby, Honorary Freeman of the Borough, and a man so dedicated to his town that some nick-named him 'Mr Appleby'. He had just published a revised and extended version of a history first written by Canon William A Mathews, Vicar of St Lawrence's Church from 1883 to 1896. With the arrogance of youth, I told him I didn't think much of it. 'Write me a better one, then!' came the riposte. Mr Whitehead duly published the result, in 1956. In 1970 I was able to expand and improve on this first text, and this version was reprinted by Dalesman Publications in 1982.

Since then, many publications have added to our knowledge of Appleby, with the result that my juvenile efforts have become thoroughly out of date. Living in Westmorland, within ten miles of the town, I have been able to take up the subject again, and this new text is the result. It follows the same pattern as the original book, but the list of works to which I have referred is more than twice as long, and I have had the time to do some research into questions which have puzzled me. I have also had the benefit of advice, and would like in particular to thank Dr Angus Winchester of Lancaster University and Mrs Margaret Shepherd and Dr Charles Moseley of Cambridge for commenting on the text and steering me in the direction of relevant literature. I am also most grateful to Mrs Mary George of Appleby (Mr Whitehead's daughter), Mrs Margaret Gowling of Brough Sowerby, Mr and the late Mrs Thwaytes of Appleby, Lord Hothfield, the Rt. Hon. William Hague MP, Mr R. Hawkins of Penrith and staff of the Record Office in Kendal for advice and help.

Despite my research, the book depends largely on information that was originally published by others. And like the earlier version, it tells the story of Appleby itself, not of Westmorland as a whole. But a small town exists only in the context of its locality and region. Appleby in Westmorland, now absorbed in the modern amalgam that bears the ancient name of Cumbria, has depended throughout its history on its setting, and that setting lies close to the western march of the ancient

Border. During the first three centuries of its existence, Appleby lay alternately in Scotland and in England, and even when it became irreversibly English it was never remote from northern threats. As I wrote in 1956, "the politics of England and of Scotland are as relevant to the history of Appleby as the properties of two millstones are to the grain that is ground between them." I have paid rather more attention to the millstones in this new book.

Martin Holdgate
Hartley, Kirkby Stephen, 2006

CHAPTER 1

The Beginnings of History

THE history of Appleby has been greatly influenced by its setting. The upper Eden Valley is surrounded on three sides by high hills; the Lakeland mountains on the west, the Pennines on the east and the Howgill fells to the south. Although these hills have been crossed by trade routes from early times, they have formed a kind of separation zone: a ring of waste land which has divided the culture of the Eden Valley from that of the fertile lowlands of Lancashire and Yorkshire. On the other hand, the valley lies open towards the north, and this fact is also reflected in its history. While England and Scotland were separate and warring kingdoms the Eden Valley had to meet a persistent threat of invasion from its unguarded northern side; indeed for several centuries the possession of the valley alternated between the two countries. In this 'debatable land' it was difficult for any town to accumulate and retain wealth, and the history of Appleby has resembled a game of snakes and ladders, periods of prosperity and expansion alternating with downfall.

We usually begin what we call the 'history' of a place with the appearance of people, and especially people whose records have come down to us. Pre-history in the Eden Valley began after the ice finally retreated from the Lakeland fells and the North Pennines some 10,000 years before the present time.[1] Tundra was followed by open forest of birch and pine, and then, about 7,000 years ago by a denser vegetation of oak, ash, alder, hazel and elm. The weather became warmer and wetter, peat bogs expanded on the higher plateau lands of the Pennines, and the rising sea level cut Britain off from the rest of Europe. This was the time when hunter-gatherer Mesolithic (Middle Stone Age) people using flint-tipped arrows began to roam the countryside.

These Mesolithic hunters reached Cumbria 6,000 years before the first Appleby came into existence. They found the Eden Valley clad in woodland, but the lowland forests were probably neither continuous nor impenetrable. Peat mires spread on the floors of soggy valleys, and glades were kept open by the grazing of wild cattle, deer and wild boar.

Human impact soon made itself felt, for the Mesolithic people began to clear patches of forest and the pressure intensified in the Neolithic (New Stone Age) period that followed, around 5,500 years ago. Neolithic farmers kept livestock and grew cereal crops, although they also hunted deer and other wild animals. Pollen preserved in lake sediments and peat provides a record of vegetation change, including the beginning of forest clearance at this time. Quite early on, there was a dramatic decline in elm, possibly because it was cut for fodder but also perhaps because of the introduction of an early form of what we now call Dutch Elm Disease.[1; 2; 3; 4; 5]

There must have been several thousand Neolithic people in Cumbria, and some of them lived high among the mountains. Between 4,500 and 5,000 years ago there was a hive of industry among the crags of Pike of Stickle in upper Langdale, chipping axe-heads from the fine-grained volcanic rock. Other stone-axe factories existed on Glaramara, Great End and Scafell Pike. Over 2,000 Lakeland stone axe-heads have been found, scattered throughout Britain from Dorset northwards to the Firth of Forth and eastwards into East Anglia. Finds in the Isle of Man and Northern Ireland prove that some were distributed by sea.[2; 3; 5; 6; 7]

The oldest surviving human monuments in our district are the long barrows (burial mounds) built by the early Neolithic farming people. There are eight to ten in Cumbria, most of them in the Eden Valley.[5] One, crowning the summit of a low hill called Rayseat Pike near Ravenstonedale, was excavated in 1875 and found to contain burnt bones in a cremation trench. This suggests a cultural link with northern Yorkshire and Northern Ireland where similar structures also occur. A second, rather similar, cairn (not yet excavated) lies not far from Crosby Ravensworth.[8; 9]

The Lakeland stone axe industry probably ended around 4,300 years ago, when a different kind of axe, made from a different kind of rock, came into use among Bronze Age people. As the name implies, those people made bronze weapons and implements as well as characteristic beaker-shaped pots. Like the late Neolithic people, they buried their dead in round cairns or mounds.[4; 5] Sir Mortimer Wheeler, writing in 1936, recognised about 140 of these in the former county of Westmorland alone, and many more have been found throughout Cumbria since then.[8] They are abundant on the limestone ridge which runs from near Kirkby Stephen northward and westward by Shap to

Brougham.[8; 9] This ridge, like other English limestone and chalk uplands, probably attracted settlers because it was well drained, had light soils and bore a cover of ash forest which was easier to clear than the woodland on the heavier soils of the valleys. However the concentration of remains in these uplands may be partly an artefact, because many prehistoric monuments must have been destroyed in the more intensively cultivated lowlands.

Many Bronze Age cairns are surrounded by small stone circles, while Cumbria has several greater circles that were probably used for public ceremonies and rituals. The earliest of these date from Neolithic times, and may well have been built by the same people that chipped the axes of Langdale. Some stand not far from the routes along which the roughed-out axes were taken from the fells for finishing and polishing in the lowlands.[5] The most impressive of them all is Long Meg and her Daughters, at Little Salkeld by the Eden, where there are 69 stones arranged in a ring over 100 metres across. The magnificently-placed circle at Castlerigg near Keswick has 38 stones in a ring 30 metres in diameter, and it is curious that a line running from its centre to Fiends Fell on the distant Pennine skyline also passes through the centre of Long Meg and for both marks the sunrise on the day of the ancient spring festival of Beltane.[5] Near Eamont Bridge, the amphitheatre of Mayburgh has a rampart of piled stones six metres high, within which a stone circle once stood. It looks towards the nearby but slightly younger earthwork known as King Arthur's Round Table, which does not appear to have contained a stone circle. Lesser circles stand close beside the M6 motorway near Shap, at Gamelands near Orton and on the moors above Crosby Ravensworth.[5]

Although there are no stone circles near Appleby, there is a cluster of Bronze Age burial mounds a few miles away on Brackenber Moor, the only large tract of nearby land to have escaped cultivation.[8; 9] Finds of axes and spear heads indicate that a trade route for Irish bronzework passed from the Solway up the Eden Valley and crossed Stainmore long before the Romans built their road there. In the middle Bronze Age this trade may have passed onwards into Scandinavia.[5; 10]

Bronze Age graded into Iron Age, and Iron Age into the Romano-British period. This is the first era from which we have numerous remains of the buildings in which people once lived. They are marked on the Ordnance Survey maps as 'Settlements' and they are abundant on the limestone ridge between Shap and Kirkby Stephen.[9] There are others along the foot of the Pennines east of Appleby (as at Castle Hill above Flakebridge Woods and on Brackenber Moor). Many more must have been obliterated by mediaeval and modern ploughing. The settlements appear to have been farms, housing a family or small group of families, with their livestock. Today they are marked by banks and depressions – the foundations of huts and small enclosures, built of dry stone walling and turf. Many of the most obvious small enclosures were probably stock-pens, and they are sunk deep into the ground because manure was dug from them in springtime to spread on nearby cultivation terraces. Excavation has discovered very few articles, presumably because most household goods were made of perishable wood or leather, and even cultivation tools were of wood.

The huts and stock-pens cluster within an enclosing wall, but the perimeter is often irregular and they are not usually surrounded by a ditch or rampart.[8] Shallow banks – all that remains of walls enclosing small fields – adjoin many of the settlements, and in a few places like Severals above the Smardale valley the prehistoric landscape can be reconstructed fairly readily. By the time they were built the ancient 'wildwood' had been stripped from much of Cumbria[11] and the landscape would have been an open patchwork of cultivation plots and pastures, the remnant woodlands banished to ravines, valleys and slopes unattractive to settlement but still important for timber, firewood, herbs and as hunting-grounds.

Some of these farm settlements were certainly inhabited in Roman times because Roman objects have been found in them. Moreover, the Roman Road that runs past present-day Crosby Ravensworth bends distinctly as it passes the big settlement now known as Ewe Close, as if acknowledging its presence.[8] We can deduce, therefore, that these upland homesteads were the dwellings of the Celtic tribe known as the Carvetii, who lived here when the Romans arrived in the first century AD. By then, the Eden Valley and Solway Plain west of Carlisle were densely inhabited (see Map 2).[12; 13]

The Carvetii were probably a sub-group of the great tribe of the Brigantes, whose lordship extended from sea to sea across northern England. Clifton Dykes near Brougham may have been the home of the Carvetian chieftain Venutius whom the Romans pushed into marriage with the eastern leader, Cartimandua, making them joint-rulers of a

The Beginnings of History

client-kingdom of Brigantia.[12; 14] The idea was to keep the north peaceful and save the Romans the trouble of conquest. But it went wrong when Venutius and Cartimandua fell out in the late 60s AD (the Roman writer Tacitus says she got tired of her husband and had an affair with her armour bearer). Whatever the reason for the breakdown, in 69AD Venutius chased his ex-wife from her lands around her large and heavily fortified settlement at Stanwick, near Scotch Corner.[13] The Romans rescued her, and clearly decided that the only solution was to occupy the unruly region. They seem to have mounted a two-pronged attack on the Carvetii, one force under Gnaeus Julius Agricola marching up the Lune valley from Lancaster and the other, led by Quintus Petillius Cerialis, coming from the east across Stainmore after reducing the Brigantian stronghold at Stanwick.[12; 14] Cerialis was Governor of Roman Britain at this time, though Agricola was to succeed him in 77AD: relations between the two are said by Tacitus to have been frosty, but he is not a dependable historian and was biased towards Agricola who was his father-in-law.[12]

It seems likely that the two Roman forces converged on Clifton Dykes, where they doubtless impressed their authority on any of Venutius' followers who lingered there. The temporary camps at Rey Cross on the top of Stainmore and at Redlands Bank near Appleby (now almost obliterated by ploughing) may well have been thrown up during the campaign of conquest and later occupied during the construction of the permanent Roman road that the modern A66 largely follows. At over 20 acres both are big enough to accommodate a full legion plus four auxiliary cohorts.[15] The earliest fort at Brougham (Brocavum[1]) close by Clifton Dykes probably also dates from the campaign, which reached Carlisle and the Solway shore by 71AD.[12; 14; 19]

By 79AD the Roman hold on Cumbria had been consolidated by the creation of two main military roads (Map 2).[8; 15; 16] The first crossed Stainmore and passed north-westwards by Brough to Brougham. Judging from the large number of forts, fortlets and signal towers along its length, it was regarded as of special importance. There were probably three reasons for this. First, it followed an ancient and well-

---

Note 1 - In this book I use the Roman names that tradition associates with places. Most have been deduced from 'itineraries' listing the forts along the main roads. A few identifications, like Luguvalium (Carlisle), are confirmed by inscriptions. Others are uncertain and may even have changed during the Roman period.[12]

established trade route. Second, it linked two major Brigantian centres at Clifton Dykes and Stanwick. Third, it was the nearest crossing of the Pennines to the Tyne Gap and the Roman frontier, when the latter was set at Hadrian's Wall in around 120AD. Permanent forts were built a reasonable marching distance apart, at Bowes (Lavatrae), Brough (Verterae) and Kirkby Thore (Bravoniacum). The top of the pass was defended by the smaller fort of Maiden Castle, while there were watch towers on Stainmore, on the descent towards Brough, and by the road across Brackenber Moor. There was a fortlet at Castrigg, on a ridge top a mile north of Appleby. This Roman road has remained important ever since, and it must have been a factor in the decision to build a Norman castle at Appleby over a thousand years later.

The second main Roman road crossing the upper Eden Valley converged with the first at Brougham. It was the chief route on the west of the Pennines, running from Burrow in Lonsdale northwards through the Lune gorge to Low Borrow Bridge (just south of Tebay) and thence over the limestone scarp and down the west side of the valley of the Lyvennet to Brougham. Here it crossed the Eamont on a bridge and cut across the flanks of Penrith Beacon to old Penrith (Voreda), and then northwards to Carlisle. The modern names 'Burrow', 'Borrow' and 'Brougham', like 'Brough', speak of their Roman history, for they are derived from the Old English *burh* – a fort – a natural description of a Roman structure whose defences would certainly have been quite formidable in the seventh or eighth centuries when English-speaking peoples arrived in the district.

There must, of course, have been a much more extensive network of minor roads in pre-Roman and Roman times. It is not altogether surprising that routes along which the roughed-out Neolithic axes were carried in the Lake District are still used by walkers today.[5] Some of the Roman roads that crossed the high hills can still be seen – like High Street that ran from Brougham southwards along the fell tops to Ambleside (Galava) and Watercrook (Alauna), south of Kendal, and the so-called Maiden Way that ran from Kirkby Thore over the shoulder of Crossfell and down to the strong fort of Whitley Castle in the South Tyne valley. The Maiden Way and Whitley Castle were probably built to give Imperial security to the lead mines of Alston Moor.[8; 17] Another hill road ran west from Low Borrow Bridge and climbed over the Whinfell ridge before dropping through Moorbank, Patton Bridge and Mealbank to Watercrook (see map 2 opposite).[16]

The Beginnings of History

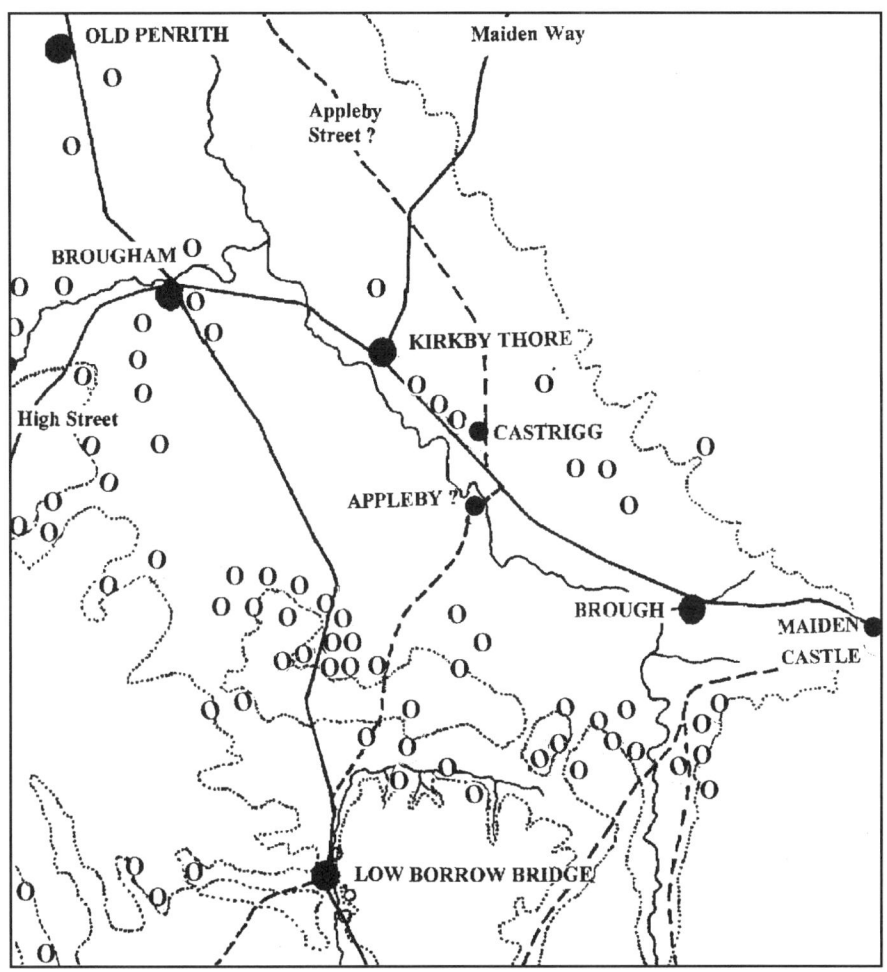

Map 2 - Roman and Romano-British Westmorland.
Large solid circles = Roman forts.
Smaller solid circles = Roman fortlets.
Open circles = Romano-British sites, mostly farm 'settlements'.
Solid lines = confirmed Roman roads.
Broken lines = possible minor roads.

Based on Royal Commission on Historical Monuments (reference 9) and D. Shotter (reference 12).

Other roads have probably been obscured by cultivation or embedded in later highways. One, known as Appleby Street in the fourteenth century, diverged from the main Brough to Kirkby Thore military way near the Castrigg fortlet north of Appleby and more or less followed the line of the modern road from Long Marton to Milburn, continuing along the foot of the Pennine escarpment past Renwick towards the Wall.[18] Yet another may have run from Stainmore to Kaber and Winton, near Kirkby Stephen, there dividing with one branch going southwards beside the upper Eden to the fort at Bainbridge (Virosidum) in Wensleydale and the other south-westwards past the suggestively-named Street Farm to the main Lune Valley road south of Sedbergh.[16] It seems most probable that there would also have been some kind of east-west route beside the upper Lune, linking Low Borrow Bridge to Brough.

But what about Appleby? It was certainly not a major Roman station. The similarity of name to Aballava, a place named in the Antonine Itinerary, is fortuitous: Aballava is most likely to have been the Latin name of the fort at Burgh by Sands on the Solway.[19] Only a few Roman remains have been found in the town, and those may easily have been carried in by passing travellers. Appleby does not even lie on the main road, which runs straight past the town half a mile or so to the east. However in 1967 a well that had once been square and lined with timber in characteristically Roman style was discovered under the floor of a basement room in Appleby Castle.[20] Most unfortunately, no samples of the timber lining were taken for dating, but it has been inferred that the well lay within a Roman guard post, built on the Castle hill to watch over the traffic across the Eden at Bongate ford. This ford might well have lain on another minor road, running from the military way to cross the river and pass by Hoff and Drybeck towards the cluster of Carvetian farms in the upper Lyvennet valley, and over the scars to join the west coast main road near Tebay. Street Farm in Orton stands beside Street Lane, which might have been part of such a minor road (see map 2, page 17).

The Roman occupation of what is now Cumbria used to be thought of as predominantly military, and maintained by repression: in words put by Tacitus into the mouth of the defeated Caledonian chieftain Calgacus, "they create a desolation and call it peace!"[12] In fact, as the leaders of invasions have found right down to the present day, a durable occupation is impossible without the willing co-operation of most of the occupied, and the trick is to persuade them to govern themselves in accordance with your policies! And although north-western Roman Britain lacked the wealthy villas and towns of the south, there were substantial civilian settlements and many productive farms, indicating a large population.[12; 21]

The farm settlements of the Carvetii probably increased in number and productivity under the *pax Romana,* supplying meat, hides, wool, hay and corn to the army and the civilian settlements. Barley and wheat (including bread wheat) were grown. Beef seems to have been a staple food of the Legions, though a lot of the bones found in excavations were of old cows, suggesting that the troops only got them when they were past producing calves and milk. Modern soldiers will not be surprised to learn that there are signs that the officers did better![22] Increased demand is likely to have boosted arable production in the lowlands, while the higher settlements (for example on the limestone country around Waitby) concentrated on stock raising.[12] The pollen record shows that there was considerable forest clearance in the second and third centuries AD, probably reflecting agricultural expansion and the need for building timber.[1; 12]

A substantial part of the Brigantian territory was granted local self-government by around 150AD.[12] Soon after 200AD the Carvetii achieved the same status, with Carlisle (Luguvalium, the city of Luguvalus), as their administrative centre. By then Luguvalium was a mainly civilian town, the military stronghold being at Stanwix (Petriana), across the Eden on Hadrian's Wall.[19] Carlisle's importance is shown by the numerous carved and inscribed stones it has yielded. It had several large houses and a piped water supply.[12] Civilian villages or even small towns also grew up alongside most of the forts. They were the base for craftsmen like metal-workers and potters, who lived there with their families. Butchers supplied meat, and no doubt leather-workers made things from the hides.

Brough, where the existence of a civilian settlement east of the fort was proved by excavation in 1971-72, also had a bath house and a substantial cemetery.[23] It was the centre of a flourishing local industry engaged in the manufacture of bronze brooches,[8] and was clearly also the base for a controller of Imperial trade, for over 130 lead seals used to mark goods in transit have been found there. The seals indicate that one of the classes of material transported was metal, almost certainly lead from the mines on Alston moor.[24]

There was also a fair-sized township at Brougham, flanking the roadsides leading from the fort. It seems to have been the centre for the cult of a local deity, the horned god Belatucadrus 'the fair shining one' whom the Romans identified with Mars.[25] One of his altars has also been found at Kirkby Thore where the fort was flanked by another extensive civilian town.[21] Even Low Borrow Bridge in the centre of the Lune Gorge, long regarded as little more than an isolated military station, is now known to have had a substantial settlement nearby, and a burial ground along the road to the south.[14; 21] Taking the forts and their associated civilian townships together with the fortlets and signal stations along the roads, the mines in the hills and the many native farms in the countryside, we get a picture of a well-populated and prosperous district that, long before the end of Roman rule, administered its own local government.

In 382AD Magnus Maximus ('Great Greatest') withdrew the legions from the west of Hadrian's Wall and marched south to try to make himself Emperor (with a name like that it must have seemed a foregone conclusion!) He lost, and was executed in 388 – but the troops did not return. Although Roman soldiers remained in parts of Britain until around 430, it seems likely that the defences of the north-west were entrusted to a local militia, no doubt headed by local rulers.[12; 26] There are indications, moreover, that they defended their lands effectively. For during the Roman period the original fortified frontier along the line of the Antonine Wall between Forth and Clyde had been threatened repeatedly by alliances of Picts (from Fife and the eastern Highlands) and Scots (from Ireland and subsequently the western Highlands) and invaders from the north had from time to time swept down on Hadrian's Wall. But in the century following the Roman withdrawal the Picts seem to have been driven back by the Britons, and by about 550AD the British kingdoms extended north of the line between Forth and Clyde.[27; 28]

There has been a lot of speculation about how Britain was ruled after the link with Rome was broken. Legends speak of Vortigern (the name simply means 'great overlord'), accused of propping up his position by importing treacherous Saxon mercenaries,[38] and his opponents Ambrosius, Uther and Arthur. The heroic tales of Arthur have, of course, entered into the mainstream of western myth. What are we to make of it – especially for our region?

It does seem clear that in the immediate post-Roman period Coel Hen ('Old King Cole') ruled a broad area of the north and was the ancestor of several major dynasties.[34] The connections with Arthur are much more tenuous: Uther Pendragon, his supposed father, is commemorated in the

The Beginnings of History

(much later) castle at Mallerstang; there are Arthurian tales about the Carlisle area; some of the battles attributed to him may have been in southern Scotland; and the final battle of Camlann 'in which Arthur and Medraut fell' has been put by some at the Roman Camboglanna, probably Castlesteads on Hadrian's Wall.[19] The hollow hill in which Arthur and his knights sleep until their coming again has been set in Northumberland – but this is to move from history into romance.

What we do know is that after the Legions withdrew people went on living in the Roman towns and Christianity was the established religion. The Roman centres of Carlisle, Lochmaben in Dumfries, Great Chesters, Brougham and Papcastle (near Cockermouth) seem to have been particularly important.[29] Excavations have shown that buildings in Carlisle went on being repaired well into the fifth century – and some of the town's Roman water pipes were still working in 685AD when they were shown to St Cuthbert.[12] At Brougham, continuity is confirmed by a find of coins dating from around 600AD and by the dedication of a local church to the fifth century missionary, St Ninian (reflected in the modern name of the church, Ninekirks).[25] Crop marks indicate that it once lay in an enclosure amid a cluster of buildings, and these may have been an early Christian centre designed to supplant the local cult of Belatucadrus.[30] Ninian, who was a contemporary of St Patrick, may have been Bishop of Galloway, with his seat at Whithorn, the celebrated *Candida Casa* or 'white house'. Patrick was probably born of Romano-British parentage near Carlisle. Legends say that as a boy he was carried into slavery in Ireland, but returned to Strathclyde and served there before being sent back to Ireland as a Bishop in around 435.[28; 31] It was probably from Carlisle that he wrote a forceful letter to Ceredig (Coroticus), King of Strathclyde, objecting to his selling Christians captured in Ireland as slaves.[28]

The most immediate consequence of the end of Roman rule may well have been a decentralization of government. The Imperial rule and administration that had held the Province together had gone, to be replaced by a series of local war-lords.[30] Some of these joined together to build kingdoms like that of Rheged, whose chief centre was Carlisle, *caer Luel,* the former Luguvalium. Urien, its most famous king, and his warrior-son Owain, were descendants of Coel Hen. They are named in the ancient verses of the Welsh Book of Taliesin as 'lords of Llwyfenydd', linking them to the river now called Lyvennet.[29] Their royal manor may have stood somewhere near Morland, not far from Venutius' old base of Clifton Dykes, or among the cluster of farms around the present site of Crosby Ravensworth. But (like Venutius), Urien was lord of a place near Catterick called Catraeth (possibly the Roman Cataractonium, but also possibly Cartimandua's old stronghold of Stanwick).[29; 31] The best guess is that at its height Rheged encompassed Dumfries and Galloway, the Eden Valley, the Lake District and northern Lancashire, and extended across Stainmore into north Yorkshire.[29; 31; 32; 34] It was a Christian kingdom and a major centre for the Celtic tradition of the faith, led by fifth-century saints like Ninian and Patrick and carried northwards to Glasgow by St Kentigern or Mungo.[28] Glasgow lay in the adjacent kingdom of Strathclyde, ruled from Al Cluith or Dumbarton by a separate line of kings among whom Rhydderch, alternately nick-named *'hen'* ('the old') or *'hael'* ('the generous') was prominent.

In the mid-sixth century northern Britain was threatened by pagan Anglian[2] ('Saxon') invaders from what are now the northern Netherlands, north-west Germany and southern Denmark. These incursions began in about 547 under the leadership of Ida, who founded the kingdom of Bernicia in what are now Northumberland and the Lothians. His successes forced an alliance among squabbling British warlords. Rhydderch Hen of Strathclyde, Urien and Owain of Rheged, Guallauc of the upper Forth and Morcant who had been displaced from his lands around Lindisfarne by the new invaders formed a defensive grouping called 'the Men of the North.'[31; 32; 34; 35] Their chief campaigns were against Ida's successor, Theodric (572-579). Rhydderch Hen was victorious at Arthuret (*Arfderydd*) north of Carlisle in 573[33], but the sites of the other battles are lost and most of the detail we have comes from romantic poems in praise of Urien and Owain in the Book of Taliesin.[31] The climax of the campaign came when the Men of the North besieged Theodric's army in Lindisfarne for three days. But the successful alliance of the British chieftains was disrupted when Urien was assassinated in around 590.[31] Owain defeated and killed Theodric's successor, Aethelric, in around 593 but himself fell soon afterwards:

Note 2 - I use 'Anglian' as a collective for the peoples Bede (and others) called 'Angles, Saxons and Jutes'. If Bede is to be believed, the invaders of Northumbria were Angles from present-day Schleswig, at the base of the Danish peninsula.

The hero famed in song lies in a narrow vault;
His keen-edged spears were like the wings of the dawn!
Never again will be found the like
Of the brilliant Lord of Llwyfenydd! [34]

With Urien's murder and the fall of Owain the power of Rheged was shattered.[31] In around 598 the war-band of the Lords of Edinburgh tried to recapture Catraeth, and to get there without storming through the heart of Bernicia they may well have marched up the Eden Valley and across Stainmore. They were massacred, and their defeat is mourned in a lament for the fallen called the *Gododdin* which includes what is probably the oldest reference to Arthur in Welsh literature.[31; 34] Catraeth marked the end of British rule in the north-east and by 610 the Kingdoms of Bernicia and Deira (around York) were welded into a single Northumbria.

In around 613 Ethelfrith, King of Northumbria, defeated a British alliance at Chester and separated the people of Rheged from their kinsmen in Wales. His successor, Edwin, who ruled between 617 and 634, invaded North Wales and extended the Anglian conquests in Yorkshire and Cumbria. By 630 the Northumbrians controlled Carlisle, the coasts of the Solway and the Isle of Man, fragmenting Rheged. It was not all, however, a matter of blood and thunder. The invading pagans were being converted to Christianity by Celtic priests from Rheged and Strathclyde.[29; 36] In Northumbria, the Christian preachers were reinforced by Paulinus, said by Bede to be one of four priests sent by Pope Gregory to support Augustine's mission in Kent. He accompanied Ethelberga, daughter of the King of Kent, when she came north to marry Edwin of Northumbria in 625 and baptised King Edwin's daughter Eanflaed that same year and the King, his nobles and many of their people in 627³.[37] But Paulinus' mission in the north was brief, and did not dint the local dominance of the Celtic church.

Edwin's reign is described by Bede as a time of peace and prosperity for both his British and Anglian subjects. It ended in 633 when Cadwallon of North Wales defeated and killed Edwin and one of his sons and drove his heir, Oswald, into exile in Strathclyde. A year later Oswald

---

Note 3 - A version of Nennius' *Historia Brittonum* states that Rhun, son of Urien, baptised Edwin.[38] But this is hard to reconcile with Bede's detailed account, and it seems improbable that Rhun and Paulinus were the same man.

bounced back, killing Cadwallon and restoring the Anglian kingdom of Northumbria which he ruled between 634 and 652.[29] A devout Christian, he followed the teachings of the church of Strathclyde and Iona, and it was from there that he brought Aidan to be the first Bishop of Lindisfarne.[37] Oswald also established a dynastic alliance with the British by marrying his brother Oswiu to Riemmelth, great granddaughter of Urien of Rheged.[29] Their son was Alcfrith, thought by some to be commemorated by the wonderful cross at Bewcastle, though the inscription is now so weathered that this identification cannot be sustained.

It is impossible to be precise about the borders of Rheged, Strathclyde and Northumbria in this period. However by around 635 Northumbria probably extended across the Pennines to the Eden, and in a broad wedge to the Solway shores and the Isle of Man. A remnant of Rheged seems to have survived as a self-governing British kingdom of Cumbria, centred on the northern Lake District. Strathclyde had absorbed northern Rheged and met Northumbria somewhere around Dumfries.[32] But dynastic alliances and ties of Christian faith linked the Anglian and Celtic peoples.[29] In 664 the Synod of Whitby resolved the dispute between the Celtic traditions of Strathclyde and Iona and those of the Roman church, brought from the south by Augustine and powerfully supported by Wilfred, later Archbishop and Saint.[28; 37] By 670 the authority of King Ecgfrith and the Bishop of Northumbria extended to both Carlisle and Morecambe Bay. In 685 St Cuthbert, then Bishop, visited Carlisle and the king gave him the estate of "Cartmel with all the Britons" (*Britanos*) "belonging to it."[40]

The Synod of Whitby was a clear sign that the two branches of the Christian church were able to unite across the ethnic divide. The wording of the grant to Cuthbert and other evidence from Celtic place-names suggests that Cumbria and north-west Lancashire, the last parts of England to come under Anglian rule, retained a significant British population. In the Carlisle area leading members of the British community, linked as they were by marriage to the Anglians, seem to have adopted the Anglian culture[30] and around the edges of the region there was evidently substantial Anglian immigration. Monasteries at Dacre and at Heversham, near Kendal, had English abbots.[40] Nearer home to Appleby, it was almost certainly in this same late-seventh century period that the cluster of villages with names ending in *–ton,* such as Long Marton, Bolton, Dufton, Brampton, Murton, Langton, Hilton, Winton and Wharton were founded. They form a distinct group, west of the Pennine escarpment and (for the most part) east of the River Eden, and this pattern may imply some kind of concerted settlement under Northumbrian rule. Brough (Burgh) also has an Anglian name, meaning a fort.[43]

These settlers may well have been the *westmoringas*, 'people west of the moors' or (if the word was really *westmaringaland*) 'people of the western march' who gave their name to Westmorland. The name, originally applied only to the east side of the upper Eden Valley, obviously fits the perspective of someone living across the Pennines in Northumbria. But older names remained: Knock, for example, comes from *cnoc*, a rounded hill, aptly describing Knock Pike, and British communities almost certainly still lived west of the Eden and in the Lakeland hills, in what the English called 'Cumberland', the land of the Cumbri (*cymru).* This Celtic territory seems to have included Lowther and the Greystoke-Penruddock district, but part at least of the Lyvennet heartland had become an Anglian royal manor and Clifton and Brougham are Anglian names.[29] The Anglian occupation may well have extended to some areas later settled by Danish people – such as Appleby, close by the important crossing of the River Eden – although this can only be speculation.[41] And the pattern of settlement may have been perturbed by the first major plague epidemics recorded in Western Europe, which passed through our area in 550 and again in the 660s.[31; 42]

One unanswered question is how many of the Romano-British farms went out of use, and when. It seems likely that the high-level settlements along the Pennine flanks and around the Kirkby Stephen to Crosby Ravensworth ridge were already deserted at the time the Anglian settlers arrived. One reason may have been that their situation caught up with them – they were on the lighter land, most easily cleared but also most prone to erosion and soil degradation. In the Lake District a lot of soil cultivated by Romano-British farmers ended up in lake sediments between 200 and 580AD.[1] The Anglian settlers brought better tools, could work heavier lowland soils, and built stouter, rectangular, houses: their British neighbours would not have ignored these advances. In a few places later (mainly Nordic) dwellings were built on the sites of Romano-British settlements[11] and we can guess that the more productive of these were redeveloped either by 'in-comers' or the descendants of their builders. As the centres of occupation moved downhill the marginal

The Story of Appleby in Westmorland

farms would have been abandoned leaving their remains to dot the upland pastures, now used as summer grazings.

Northumbria remained powerful for about 200 years, its rule extending from Edinburgh to York and westwards to the Solway, the Eden Valley and Morecambe Bay.[40] It was in this period that the great crosses at Bewcastle and Hexham and lesser fragments at Kirkby Stephen and Kendal were carved. There was an Anglian Bishop at Whithorn in 720 and in 875 Bishop Eadulf of Lindisfarne was able to find refuge there when he fled west with St Cuthbert's body.[32] But in the late ninth century Northumbria began to decline, while Scotland, then centred on Scone north of the Forth-Clyde valley, began to thrust southwards, increasingly dominating Strathclyde. On the other side of our area, the Kings of England were also growing in power and clearly saw themselves as High Kings of the whole island.

The decline of Northumbria was partly due to the incursions of the Danes, whose descents on the eastern coasts of England had begun as piracy in around 790 and ended in colonisation, so that by 866 Northumbria had Danish rulers.[33; 39] Viking Northumbria, centred on York, came into repeated conflict with Scotland, whose King Constantine I was killed by the Danes in 877.[28] Strathclyde was threatened by Norwegian Vikings who had colonised the Western Isles and the coasts of Ireland and in 870 its near-impregnable stronghold and capital, Al-Cluith, on Dumbarton rock, fell after a four-month siege: 200 longships were needed to ferry the captives to Ireland.[28] In 875 an army under Halfdan advanced up the Tyne, burnt Carlisle, "and made frequent raids against the Scots and the Strathclyde Britons."[44] Not long afterwards, new raids began on the coast of Cumbria, where the invaders were Norwegians from Ireland.[39; 40] During the first half of the tenth century Irish-Norwegians occupied much of the county's western seaboard. Simultaneously, Danes who had won an important victory over Constantine II, King of Scots, at Corbridge in 918, spread into the Eden Valley from the north and east. British Cumbria and Anglian Northumbria were alike squashed in the Danish-Norwegian pincers!

It was the early tenth-century Danish incursion that led – we cannot say exactly when – to the foundation of the first Appleby along with many other settlements in the Eden Valley whose names have the terminal syllable *–by*. The name 'Appleby' – *epli-by* or apple-place[43] – suggests peace and fruitfulness in stark contrast to the savagery of conflict

The Beginnings of History

that dominates the Chronicles. It is quite possible that some at least of the new *–by* settlements like Appleby, Asby ('ash-place') or Colby ('Koll's place') took their land from Anglian or British predecessors.[41] Others may have simply fitted into gaps between pre-existing settlements – possibly including some depopulated by the seventh-century plague. However Crosby Ravensworth ('cross-place of Hravensvartr' or Ravenswart) stands at the head of the upper Lyvennet amid other Nordic names like Barnskew (Bjarni's wood), Gunnerskeld (Gunnar's spring) and Oddendale (Odlin's dale) and implies that the heartland of Urien's Rheged was no longer British. Indeed Nordic names dominate the country west of the Eden.[43] The existence of 'Kirkby' (church-place) and 'Crosby' (cross-place) names confirms that the new arrivals were Christian, but that does not prove that their occupation was peaceful!

At about the same time that the Danes spread into the Eden Valley, the English kings were taking an increasing interest in their northern marchlands. King Edward the Elder was progressively expanding his power and in 920 he was accepted as 'father and lord' by the King of Scots, the King of Strathclyde, the Norwegians and Danes of the north-west and Rognvald, ruler of Northumbria.[39; 44] This recognition was cemented in 926 when Edward's son King Athelstan (who had already made himself ruler of Northumbria) received the submission of "all the Kings in this island: first Hywel king of the west Welsh, and Constantine, king of Scots, and Owain, king of Gwent, and Ealdred Ealdulfing from Bamburgh. They established a covenant of peace with pledges and oaths at a place called Eamont Bridge on 12 July."[44] Owain, named in this extract from the Anglo-Saxon Chronicle, was *not* King of Gwent, in south Wales, but of Cumbria: he ruled from 915 to 937 and some chronicles make him heir-presumptive to the Scottish king.[29; 32] Eamont Bridge may well have been chosen because it lay on the border between Westmoringaland, the 'west march' of Northumbria, and the Scottish client-kingdom of Strathclyde.[28; 40]

Despite the ceremony, a Norse-Scottish-Strathclyde confederation soon emerged in opposition to Athelstan, who retaliated in 934 by invading Scotland "and harrying much of the country."[39; 44] Owain of Cumbria was one of those who fled from him.[29] Three years later, in 937, Athelstan and his brother, Prince Edmund "won undying glory with the edges of swords, in warfare around Brunanburh."[44] Despite its legendary fame, the site of this battle is uncertain, though some recent analysis favours a place in the Wirral. What is clear is that Athelstan was faced by an alliance of Norsemen from Ireland, Scots under Constantine and Strathclyde British under Owain, also called Eugenius, who may possibly have been the ex-King of Cumbria.[29; 32] The Irish Norsemen were led by Olaf Guthfrithson, "an imperious and ambitious Viking", who also claimed Northumbria and had married the daughter of Constantine II of Scotland.[39] Five young kings, seven Norse jarls and Constantine's own son fell. "Never before in this island, as the books of ancient historians tell us, was an army put to greater slaughter by the sword."[44]

Triumphs in these unsettled times were often short-lived. The great King Athelstan died in 939, and his brother and successor, Edmund, destined to be a strong king though a short-lived one, was only eighteen. Olaf Guthfrithson bounced back, secured York, raided into the English midlands and consolidated his power in a treaty that secured him all of Northumbria – only to die and be succeeded by a second Olaf, called Kvaran, from whom the midlands were soon wrested by a resurgent King Edmund.[39] In 944 the latter "brought all Northumbria under his sway," and in the following year he "ravaged all Strathclyde, and ceded it to Malcolm, King of Scots, on the condition that he would be his fellow worker by sea and land."[44]

Legend has it that it was during this campaign that King Edmund overcame Dunmail (Domnall or Donald) King of Cumbria, son of Owain of Strathclyde, in a battle on Dunmail Raise above Grasmere. With his victory King Edmund restored English dominion to what it had been after Brunanburgh, while the grant of Strathclyde to Malcolm emphasised its status as a puppet kingdom with Scottish connections but under England's ultimate authority. There were also personal dynastic links, for Malcolm was the younger brother of Owain (who had died in 943) and hence the uncle of Dunmail who seems to have survived the battle to be given rule over northern Strathclyde.[29; 32] Cumbria, therefore, 'stayed in the family'!

Olaf Kvaran also reappeared. King Edmund had ejected him from Northumbria in 944, and in 947 that province did homage to the murdered Edmund's brother and successor, Eadred. But in 948 the Norsemen of Northumbria broke their pledge and took Eirik Haraldsson called Blood-Axe, son of King Harald Fairhair of Norway, as their ruler. Eirik was "violent, pagan and un-English" and his wife Gunnhild had an international reputation as a sorceress as well as the nobler title 'Mother of Kings.'[39] On Eadred's insistence Eirik was chased out of York a year later. Back came Olaf Kvaran – only to be supplanted by Eirik in 952. Two years later came the epic battle in which Eirik "by the treachery of Earl Osulf was slain... in a lonely place called Steinmor."[39; 45] We cannot be sure of its exact site, but romance favours the bleak moor-top by the Rey Cross, within the ramparts of the old Roman fort. Eirik's entry to Valhalla is celebrated in an epic poem called *Eiriksmal* which some have attributed to his witch-wife Gunnhild. He is welcomed by the heroes Sigmund and Sinfjotli who demand to know who accompanies him from the battle.

> *'Five kings', Eirik said*
> *'Their names I will tell.*
> *I the sixth, at their head*
> *In the bloody fight fell.'*

After Eirik's death King Eadred seized Northumbria and England enjoyed many years of freedom from Norse aggression.[39]

We do not know what impact all these squabbles had on the upper Eden Valley. If the frontier then lay at Eamont Bridge, Westmoringaland may not have been included in the territory ceded to King Malcolm I of Scotland in 945. It has been suggested that Eirik Blood-Axe saw it as friendly ground for which he was making when he was waylaid on Stainmore.[29] If so, he might have expected hospitality at Appleby, for we can guess that it was established by 940. Equally, if as legend has it, Olaf Kvaran was Eirik's opponent, he may have marched down the old Roman road from Brougham to Brough on his way from Ireland. If so, he would have passed (and could have plundered) Appleby.

All that is conjecture, but we have one tangible monument of the original Danish Appleby – the hog-back tombstone dating from around 1000AD which now forms the lintel of the north door of the former St. Michael's Church (Figure 1). Hog-back tombstones were designed as conventionalised models of the houses of the period,[46] and the Appleby example, although battered and defaced, still bears a pattern representing roof shingles on its top, while below the eaves there is a system of interlacing strands thought to depict the interwoven framework of 'wattle and daub' walling. Below this there is a plain band indicating the stone-built lower section of the walls: some hogbacks (like two at

Lowther[9; 47] are ornamented by carving, but in the Appleby tombstone this has been worn away, if it ever existed. So here we have a stylised representation of an early 'long-house' and we can assume that the original Appleby was a cluster of this kind of dwelling. Moreover, since only fairly substantial people are likely to have rated a stone memorial, we can deduce that an influential family lived there – maybe grand enough to share a horn of mead with the King of York!

The presence of the hog-back in St. Michael's Church implies that the Danish manor and village were sited in the district we now call Bongate, possibly on either side of the old track down to the ford. They ante-dated the settlement in the loop of the Eden by at least a century, and this is probably why Bongate was referred to in mediaeval times as 'Old Appleby.'[48] In early charters, too, the Church of St. Michael is given precedence over that of St. Lawrence, supporting the idea that it was the earlier foundation. Although there is no evidence to support the claim that has sometimes been advanced that the Castle earthworks date from the Danish period, many later Norman lords chose places that were already of some significance as the seat of their Baronies and it is plausible that Appleby was a well-developed township and the centre of a substantial lordship long before William Rufus occupied the 'land of Carlisle' in 1092.[29; 79]

The see-saw of different people vying for supremacy in the upper Eden Valley may have eased after the battle of Stainmore, but it did not end. It is not easy to work out just what happened, for there are no contemporary local documents and only occasional references in charters and in national records like the Anglo-Saxon Chronicle. There is a puzzling entry in the latter for 966: "Thored, son of Gunnar, ravaged Westmorland, and the same year Oslac became Earl" (of Northumbria).[44] Thored was the son of an Earl but did not succeed to that rank himself until 979. What was he up to? There is no record of immediate reaction from Malcolm of Scotland, so presumably Thored kept out of the ceded territory of Strathclyde. Was he seeking to enforce his authority on a Northumbrian outpost west of the moors? Was it just a bit of private feuding? Did he sack Appleby?

Although there is no recorded response to Thored's foray, the Scottish chronicles do say that in 972 King Kenneth II, son of Malcolm I, raided into Cumbria as far as Stainmore and, with the consent of King Edgar, placed Malcolm the son of Dubh (possibly Donald Dubh, 'Donald the

Black') to rule Cumbria.[29] This could imply a 'tidying up' operation, possibly in response to Thored's raid, placing the international border at the Rey Cross on Stainmore and imposing unambiguous sovereignty on the upper Eden Valley. The arrangement appears to have been confirmed a year later, when King Edgar was rowed on the river Dee as a token of his supremacy by Kenneth of Scotland, Donald son of Owain, King of Strathclyde and Malcolm son of Dubh of Cumbria.[29; 32] It would imply that, under the Scottish throne, the Kings of Strathclyde and Cumbria together ruled territory extending from Stainmore northwards to the head of Loch Lomond.

The next reference in the English Chronicle is also odd. It states that in 1000 King Ethelred "marched into Cumberland, and laid waste very nearly the whole of it."[44] This would clearly have been in breach of the treaty with Scotland, and Scottish records suggest that he was indeed opposed by yet another Malcolm, the son of King Kenneth II (the Cumbrian Malcolm son of Dubh had died in 991).[32] But another chronicler records that Ethelred's enemies were the Danes, who had "a very great colony" in the district attacked.[49] It is quite true that by the time of the first millennium Danish and Norwegian armies were again descending on the coasts of England, and Ethelred's hatred is indicated by an order he issued in 1002 that all the Danish people living in England were to be massacred.[39] But Ethelred was far too weak and King Svein Forkbeard of Denmark and his allies too strong for most of the Danish

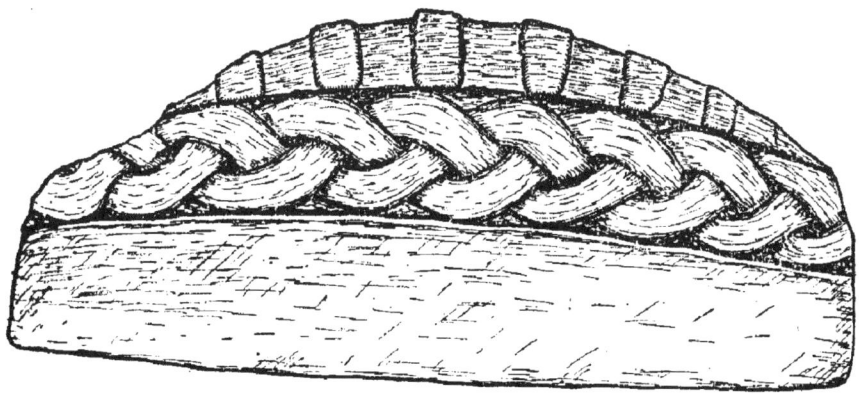

Figure 1 - Hog-back tombstone over north doorway of St Michael's Church, Bongate, Appleby. The pattern at the top represents roof-shingles: that below woven wattles and the plain lowermost section a smooth wall.

settlements to be at risk, and Ethelred is well remembered for buying off his enemies with 'danegeld'. In a fanciful historical novel Nicholas Size[50] suggested that the Norse settlers in the Lakeland valleys were the target, and that Ethelred suffered an ignominious defeat, but there is no hard evidence to back this notion up. It is possible that the Danes of Appleby (and of Asby, Crosby Ravensworth, Kirkby Stephen and the other *–by* settlements) were among Ethelred's victims, but this is also speculation.

The Border see-saw went on bouncing up and down. There was trouble between King Malcolm II of Scotland and Earl Uhtred of Northumbria sometime around 1015: Uhtred raided into Cumbria but was defeated near Brough and the booty recovered.[29] In 1018 King Malcolm and another Owen – Owen the Bald of Strathclyde – defeated the Northumbrians and secured the Lothians as far south as the Tweed.[32] In 1031 King Knut of England (and Denmark and Norway) went to Scotland to receive the submission of the three kings between whom the country was then partitioned – Malcolm II, Macbeth of Moray and the Lord of the Isles.[29] Knut is said to have agreed on that occasion to the transfer of Lothian to Scotland on condition that Cumbria – which Malcolm had granted to his grandson Duncan – was returned to England.[32] However the deal seems to have been short-lived for in 1034 Duncan became King of Scots and gave Cumbria to his eldest son, later to reign as Malcolm III and be known as Canmore from the Gaelic *ceann mhor* or 'big chief'.

People familiar with Shakespeare's plays may recognise this latest bunch of characters as the central figures in *Macbeth*. As the play records, Duncan was killed, although he was *not* an old man and he was probably not murdered. Macbeth added central Scotland to his own lordship in the northern Highlands, Duncan's younger son Donald Ban ('the white') fled to the western isles, and Malcolm Canmore took refuge with Earl Siward of Northumbria who helped him back to his kingdom in 1054.[28] From around 1058 Strathclyde and Cumbria as far south as the Rey Cross on Stainmore were firmly in Malcolm III's hands. Although the English chronicler Symeon of Durham says that this rule was "not by right, but by conquest,"[51] it is clear that by this period Cumbria had become a traditional possession of the heir to the Scottish throne. It was recognised as an integral part of Strathclyde, and Strathclyde was very much a Scottish fiefdom.[32] In 1070 the Scottish army used the Eden

Valley as a jumping-off point for a raid into Teesdale during which they wasted the lands beyond as far as Cleveland. And the Scottish rule was ecclesiastical as well as secular: the Eden Valley and most of Cumberland were now included in the Diocese of Glasgow, whose cathedral was the cult-centre of Cumbria's patron saint, St. Kentigern or Mungo.[33] This arrangement continued until the Diocese of Carlisle was created in 1133.

By the reign of King Edward the Confessor what later became the County of Westmorland was therefore split between the two kingdoms. The southern part, later to become the Barony of Kendal, including Kentdale and Lonsdale, was part of the Earldom of Northumberland. At the Norman Conquest it was English and as such was included in the Domesday Book.[40] The northern part, later to become the Barony of Westmorland, together with Lake District north of Dunmail Raise and the western and northern coastlands of Cumberland, was Scottish. When King William the Conqueror began to extend his authority over the north of England, therefore, the international frontier lay at the Rey Cross on Stainmore. There is a legend, perpetuated in a rhymed version of Hector Boece's fifteenth century chronicle, that the cross was set up by Malcolm Canmore and William the Conqueror to mark their frontier, and it is even described:[52]

> *Into Stanemure ane cors of stane was set*
> *Quhair the marchis of thir tua kingis met;*
> *And on the cors, as ye sall understand,*
> *Tua crownit kinges with sceptour in to hand*
>
> *The king of Scotland on the northmest side,*
> *The king of Ingland also on the uther,*
> *Haldand thair faces eurlik ane fra uther*
> *I wait nocht wiell quhiter on fit or hors*
> *Quhilk ay sensyne was callit the Re-corss*

King William took measures to secure the Vale of York against attack from the north-west by creating a strong marcher lordship based on Richmond. The precautions were sensible, for Malcolm Canmore mounted further invasions of Northumbria in 1080 and 1091.[28]

During the first century and a half of its history therefore, Appleby was a small settlement in a 'debatable land' whose possession passed between England, Northumbria, Strathclyde and Scotland while at times it may have been little affected by any of them. It must have been an uncomfortable time, with no security beyond that afforded by local muscles and weapons and little defence against the armies of kings and great lords seeking to exert what often proved transient authority. Wealth must have been near-impossible to accumulate, and would only attract looters. At the time of its rise to a greater prominence Appleby still lay in a debatable land, but one in which both England and Scotland were to make substantial investments.

CHAPTER 2

A New Appleby

KING William the Conqueror was probably too busy consolidating his hold on the heartland of England to worry too much about the remote north-western borderland, although he did 'harry' the rebellious north-east viciously in 1069-1070 and Malcolm Canmore's incursion of 1080 must have been a further irritant. But things were different in the time of his son, King William II (Rufus). In 1091, while the English King was in Normandy, the Scots raided Northumbria once again and King William was stung into bringing a large army northwards in retaliation. War was averted when Edgar the Atheling, Malcolm Canmore's brother in law, acted as peace-maker. Indeed, King Malcolm did homage to William, who promised him all the land he had held in the time of the Conqueror.[44]

A year later, the promise was broken. In 1092 William Rufus "went north to Carlisle with great levies, and restored the town, and built the Castle. He drove out Dolfin who had formerly ruled that district, and garrisoned the castle with his own men. Thereafter he returned southwards, sending very many peasants thither with their wives and livestock, to settle there and to till the soil."[44]

Twenty six years after the Battle of Hastings, therefore, Norman England engulfed the whole Eden Valley, from the Rey Cross on Stainmore to Carlisle. Dolfin, thus summarily ejected, was Malcolm Canmore's cousin as well as the ruler of Cumbria on his behalf. He was the eldest son of Gospatric, Earl of Northumbria, and great-nephew of King Duncan, Macbeth's rival.[29; 32; 33] By ignoring Malcolm Canmore's homage for Cumbria and displacing Dolfin, William Rufus made it clear that the grant to the King of Scotland was ended and that he was going to rule the land directly.[29] In 1093 injury was followed by insult. Malcolm Canmore, not surprisingly, "sent and desired the fulfilment of the treaty which had been promised him."[44] King William summoned him to Gloucester, again with Prince Edgar as escort, but then refused him an audience and repudiated his promises. The two rulers "parted in great enmity, and King Malcolm went back to Scotland."[44] He then gathered an army and harried Northumbria – where he was entrapped and killed, together with Edward his eldest son, by Earl Robert of Northumbria and his steward Morel of Bamburgh.[44] With their death, followed a few days later by that of Queen (later Saint) Margaret, the Norman-English hold on the borderlands tightened.[28]

They consolidated their grip by building castles. Carlisle itself was fortified by William Rufus, who "intended it to be instead of a bulwark against the Scots on those west marches."[53] Other strongholds were built soon afterwards, either by order of the King, or by the nobles to whom he granted land. The record in the Anglo-Saxon Chronicle that "very many peasants" with their families were sent to the district implies a plan to strengthen civilian settlement as well. Presumably these 'peasants' were bondmen attached to the estates of the new feudal lords, and the idea was that they would both provide extra manpower and grow food for the garrisons.

Ivo Taillebois was the first Norman lord to hold the upper Eden Valley. He may well have already held lands around Kendal before 1092, making him a logical candidate for rule over the newly-conquered region next door. His wife, Lucy, was a great heiress in Lincolnshire and some at least of the 'peasants' settled in the north may have come from her lands around Spalding.[54] But Ivo proved short-lived, dying in 1094. Before he died he granted the church of Kirkby Stephen, with land there and at Winton, to St Mary's Abbey at York.[40; 54] Lucy, his widow, was soon married off to Roger fitz Gerold de Roumare, who may have gained some interests in Westmorland at the same time but followed Ivo to the grave in 1098.

At this time neither Westmorland nor Cumberland was a 'shire' or 'barony' in the formal sense, although they may have been managed in a similar way. The whole 'land of Carlisle' seems rather to have been a frontier lordship remitted by the King to the management of a powerful warlord, supported by lesser lords and Royal officials.[54] The lesser lords ruled areas some at least of whose boundaries may have been defined many generations before, and Westmorland, centred on Appleby, may have been one of these.[79]

By 1100 the overlord of the whole land of Carlisle was Ranulf de Briquessart, more commonly known as Ranulf le Meschin (which some

A New Appleby

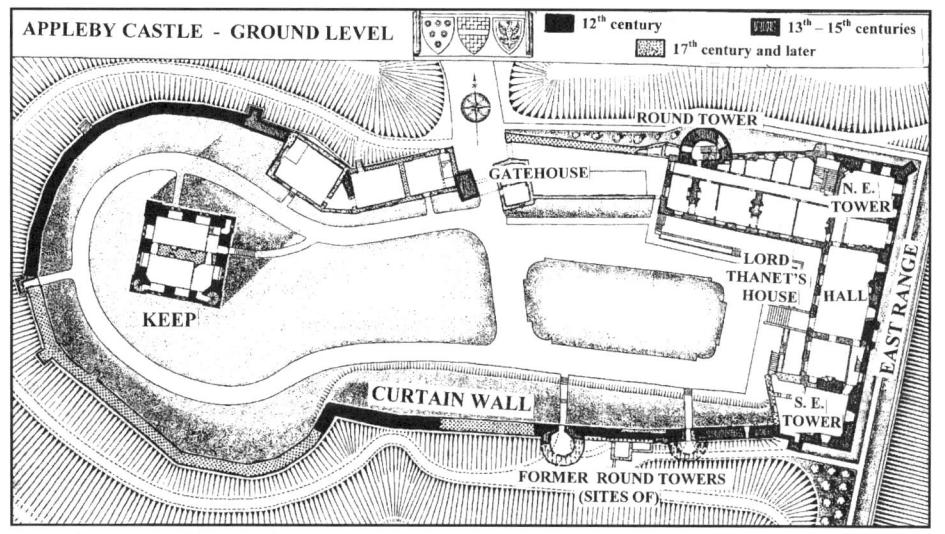

Plan 1 - Appleby Castle: ground level plan. Simplified and reduced from plan in the Report of the Royal Commission on Historical Monuments, © Crown copyright, (reference 9). See also Plan 3, page 164

say means 'the cadet or younger son' and others[20] 'the wretch'). Ranulf married the twice-widowed Lucy and gained authority over her Lincolnshire estates. He was an immensely important figure in the history of both Appleby and Westmorland. He was overlord of the whole Eden Valley for more than twenty years, and it was probably in his time that the original castles of Carlisle, Appleby and Brough were completed.[40] Brougham does not appear to have been fortified until around 1215.[25] Penrith, though it had risen to prominence as a town before the Norman conquest and became a Royal Borough, had an even later and slighter castle which played no significant part in national affairs.

It is very understandable that these castles were set along the main Roman road from Carlisle to Stainmore. Those at Carlisle, Brough, Bowes and the later fortress at Brougham, were placed next to, or within, earlier Roman forts which probably still had substantial stone ramparts. At Brough, the castle actually incorporated some of the earlier defences,[9] and Appleby may have taken in a Roman fortlet or guard-post (it is suggestive that the dimensions of the east end of the Castle bailey more or less match the 50 yards by 40 of Maiden Castle on Stainmore). However the new strongholds at Appleby and Brough were themselves earthworks surmounted by timber, of the kind now referred to as 'motte and bailey.' The motte, or citadel, was a high, conical, earthen mound surrounded by a deep ditch and crowned by a wooden palisade wall. This mound was too small to support many buildings, so it was usual for there to be a larger, lower, outer enclosure (the bailey) surrounded by its own ditch and palisaded rampart. Here the Great Hall, kitchens, stables and other offices of the castle were grouped. The bailey was linked to the motte by a wooden bridge spanning the ditch. The combination of round motte and oblong bailey gave the whole plan something of a 'keyhole' appearance.

Most of the Westmorland motte and bailey castles were later walled in stone, obliterating the original details. However, an unmodified earthwork castle remains at Tebay (immediately north of the slip road at Junction 38 on the M6) and the stone castles of Appleby and Brough retain the 'keyhole' outline of their earliest earthworks (see Plan 1, page 37).[9] At Appleby, the Norman overlord (whether Ivo or Ranulf) chose the summit of the knoll that rises abruptly from the river Eden and dominates Bongate ford. The Norman earthworks are among the most impressive in the country: the main ditch is still nearly ten metres deep in places and the site is strengthened by other ditches and scarps lower down the hillside.[9; 20] It seems clear that the builder intended Appleby to be his centre of power in the upper Eden Valley.

At this time, the settlement called Appleby was still in present-day Bongate. The presence of the hog-back tombstone suggests that there may have been a tenth-century church there,[9] amid houses flanking the track that dipped to the ford. If Ivo Taillebois had brought 'peasants' from Lincolnshire to his new northern lands, this is where he would have settled them. But in the twelfth century many new towns were 'planted' by powerful lords close under the protective (and intimidating) ramparts of their new castles, and Ranulf le Meschin resolved to do this at Appleby. Towns are, in essence, places where the houses are closely packed and agriculture is not the dominant occupation. Many twelfth century new towns like Appleby were also *boroughs* – that is, places where the burgages – the tenements – were free from land taxes and had other rights granted by the Lord of the Manor, in return (of course) for the rents they paid. Ranulf also stood to gain income from tolls paid by non-residents who traded in the market or the town's fairs, and from fines paid to the market courts by people who infringed various rules of commerce. It was a profitable business for the overlord, bringing in much more than he could have obtained from farmland.[55] Elsewhere in

Cumbria the same pattern was followed at Cockermouth and Egremont – the latter created by Ranulf's brother William, Lord of Copeland, between 1130 and 1140.[2; 54]

The site for a new town at Appleby almost chose itself, for north of the castle the river makes a great loop, returning to flow within 250 metres of the western end of the castle knoll (Map 3). The Eden thus provides a degree of protection while the castle dominates the whole, reminding everyone that they lived there by their lord's grace. But there are snags, as Dr W D Simpson pointed out in a careful analysis of the anatomy of the new town.[56; 57] "The first essential for an efficient market is ease of access: in Appleby the market place is hemmed in on three sides by the Eden." Although the main road between Brough and Carlisle was probably diverted in pre-Norman times from the original Roman line half a mile to the east, to pass by 'Old Appleby' in Bongate and along the Sands, the river barred access to the new town. Something had to be done to attract merchants into the market place, and this meant a bridge. "But in the choice of site there emerged a further complication. Room had to be found in the burghal ensemble for parish church and cemetery. On this restricted site these could be placed nowhere else than in the apex of the loop, if church and graveyard were not to compete for valuable frontages on the market street. Hence the remarkable right-angled approach from the bridge to the market place, which is one of the most arresting features in the town plan of Appleby."[57] Another 'arresting feature' which Dr Simpson did not comment on is the width of Boroughgate, 'the town street', which actually broadens slightly as it climbs the hill from the market place to the castle gates. The implication is that Ranulf had high ambitions for his creation, seeing the whole axis as one broad trading area.

We can assume that Appleby's original bridge was built by around 1110, but there is no way of telling whether it was constructed of stone or of timber, possibly with stone piers. From the beginning it may well have had some kind of gate at the town end, with accommodation for officers who regulated the flow of people and goods to the market and collected tolls. Some people have speculated that like the 'Devil's Bridge' at Kirkby Lonsdale it was built by the monks of St. Mary's Abbey in York, known to be associated with both towns,[58] but the Kirkby Lonsdale bridge dates from a much later period.[9]

Ranulf le Meschin (or his agent) would have been responsible for laying out the plan of the new borough and for providing its public buildings – bridge, church and possibly a market hall or court house. St Lawrence's Church belongs to the 'new borough' and it would have been paid for by Ranulf. If St Michael's was a pre-Conquest foundation, its parish was presumably divided to provide the new church with territory. The original St Lawrence's was probably built around 1115 although no masonry of this period survives today. The foundations of the Norman north wall were however reportedly uncovered in 1856, showing that this building was only slightly smaller than the present structure. In 1115 it, and perhaps the Castle Keep and the bridge, would probably have been the only stone buildings in the town. It is ironical (though the irony is surely unconscious) that although most of the site rises well above the river and is immune from flooding, the church, vicarage and three acres of vicar's croft or glebe are sited on the lowest land, most liable to inundation by 'act of God'!

When was 'New Appleby' founded? It must have been before 1121 because in that year Ranulf relinquished his lands in Cumberland and Westmorland to the crown, having succeeded his cousin as Earl of Chester.[40; 54] It is unlikely to have been much before 1110. Some time between those two dates Ranulf granted to the Abbey of St Mary at York "the Church of St. Michael and the Church of St. Lawrence of my castle of Appleby with all things pertaining to them, as Radulphus my chaplain held them, in peace and free from all land service."[48] The Abbot later assigned the churches to the Priory of Wetheral, which had been founded by Ranulf and was a cell of St Mary's, but remained responsible for appointing the vicar, for whose stipend six marks a year were assigned from church revenues (a mark was two thirds of a pound, or 13s - 4d).[59]

Twelfth century Appleby was almost certainly smaller than the mediaeval borough became at the height of its prosperity. Most probably its original boundaries were close to those of what was later termed 'Appleby township' on tithe maps and the earliest editions of the Ordnance Survey.[60] This embraced all the land within the loop of the Eden north-east, north and north-west of the castle, the western boundary running south of the modern Holme Street and west of Doomgate to

Map 3 - The development of 'New Appleby'.
Upper map: the probable layout of the town when first founded in 1110.
Lower map: probable layout of the town at the height of its prosperity in around 1300. North is to the left in these maps.

A New Appleby

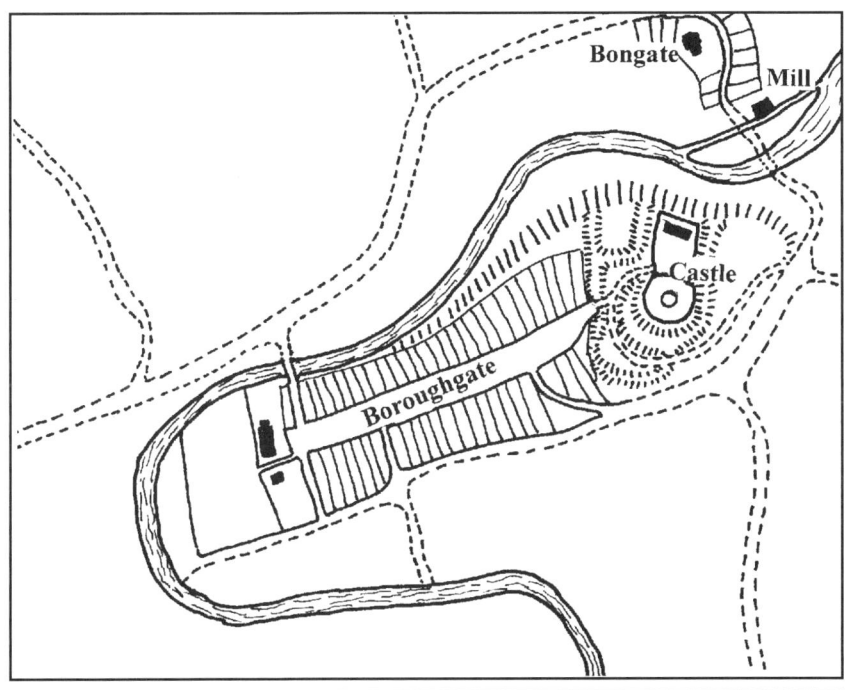

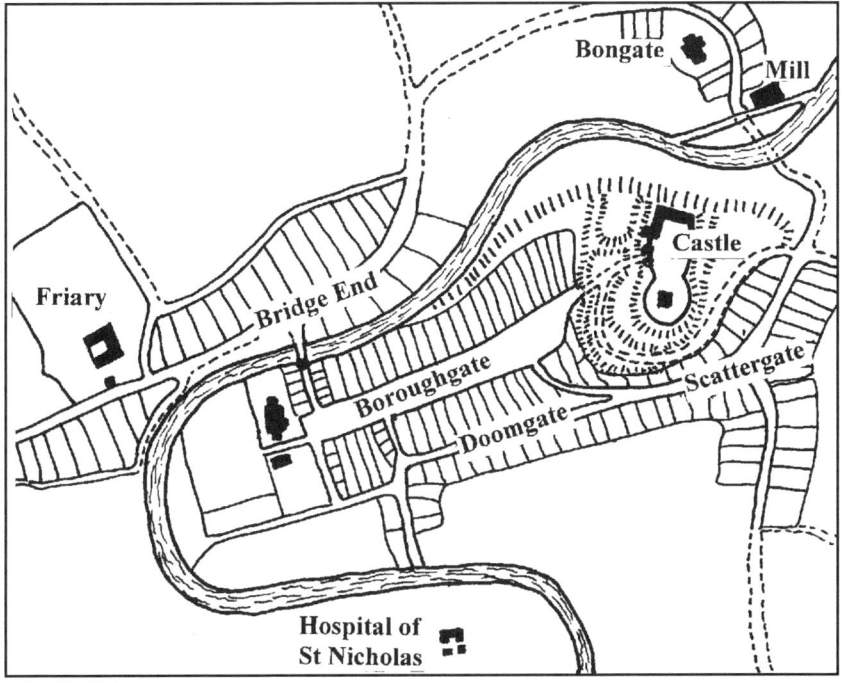

41

the edge of Scattergate. Boroughgate was its axis and focus, and originally this street extended as far as a 'Borough Stone' on the edge of the outer castle bailey. This is still marked on the map made in 1754 to show the burgages whose owners were permitted to vote in Parliamentary elections although by this time the southernmost burgages had been swallowed up by the Castle Park, and the Borough Stone itself was buried under the roadway to the castle (Map 1; Map 3).[61]

The 1754 map suggests that there were some 28 to 30 burgages on each side of the original Boroughgate. Each plot had a frontage some thirteen yards (12m) wide, and those on the east side of the street extended back for around 60 yards (55m): on the west they were a bit longer. This would give an area of around 26 *virgae* per plot (a *virga* was a square pole, or one 160th of an acre), so the plots were a bit over a sixth of an acre which was quite generous for a planned town and would have left room for intensively-cultivated gardens.[55; 62] The occupants of the burgage plots would have borne the cost of their own buildings. If Appleby was like other new towns, they would have been required to construct their houses within a year or face a fine – though Ranulf may have helped by providing free timber, stone or clay from local woods, quarries and pits.[55]

Appleby's site placed another constraint on its plan. In many towns the burgage plots terminated at 'back lanes' which separated the private land from common fields beyond, but in Appleby the burgages on the east of Boroughgate ran to the edge of the bank above the river and there is no trace of a lane behind. On the west, however, the original plots probably ended at back lanes which later became Doomgate and the first part of its continuation, now Chapel Street. Some still extended as far as this in 1754.[61; 63] In most towns, direct access from the main street to the back lane was provided by narrow passageways which ran between plots, and west of Boroughgate these now persist in High and Low Wiend and Shaw Wiend, adjacent to the modern castle wall. Because there was no back lane on the east there was no need for such wiends there, but from the beginning there was one important thoroughfare on that side, Briggate or Bridge Street, leading from the market to the river.

'New Appleby' would have started with a single row of cottages on each side of Boroughgate, one on each burgage plot. The houses would have had timber frames, wattle and daub walls, and thatched roofs. In some new towns the rents were lower if the houses were built gable-end on to the street rather than right across the frontage, because in this way access to the land behind was maintained and it was easier to construct other buildings later.[55] The land in the plots was probably used for storehouses and workshops, and as gardens, poultry-runs and possibly yards to which farm stock could be driven for protection.[62] The boundaries of the borough were tightly drawn and marked by Borough Stones at key points, and this was important since tax regimes, citizens' rights and (at a later date) Parliamentary representation differed on either side of them.[55]

The borough, being built as a trading centre rather than an agricultural settlement, contained no communal fields: the castle estates were doubtless expected to supply food to the market, thereby further aiding le Meschin's profits. Very probably some burghers rented and cultivated strips in fields to the west along what is now Colby Lane or to the south above what became Scattergate and possibly over the river to the east in Bongate. It is suggestive that 'terriers' or inventories of land belonging to St Lawrence's Church list several plots in Scattergate township, including Banks Wood, Banks Garden and Greater Vicar's Banks extending to around 20 acres: these seem to have been west of Doomgate where the modern housing development of Glebe Road and Murton View now stands.[64] The borough does not seem to have had its own corn-mill, presumably relying on the one at Bongate ford. To some extent, therefore, 'Old' and 'New' Appleby were complementary.

If this interpretation is correct, the original 'new Appleby' would have contained about 60 burgages (Map 1; Map 3). This is about the same as in the new towns of Caernarvon, Thame and Totnes, and larger than at Cranborne in Dorset or Harlech.[55] Where did the tenants come from? Ranulf le Meschin may well have allowed or encouraged some villeins to move from Bongate, which remained a farming settlement and housed workers belonging to the castle estate. But he would not have wanted to deplete his labour force too far – and his town needed merchants and craftsmen, not farm labourers. So just as William Rufus had sent 'country people' into the land of Carlisle after 1092, Ranulf probably tried to attract settlers from outside the district to 'New Appleby'. Some may well have come from Lucy's lands in Lincolnshire.

By 1100, what had once been the northern part of Northumbria, north of the Tweed, had become more or less firmly incorporated into Scotland while the land south of the river was definitively English. On the west,

Strathclyde had also been absorbed by Scotland, but Cumbria must have seemed equally firmly English. When the lands of Carlisle were surrendered by Ranulf le Meschin in 1121, they were retained by the crown. In 1122 King Henry I himself visited Carlisle and established a number of local fiefs that later became Baronies.[54] He also appointed officials to oversee the collection of the money due to the crown and its payment to the exchequer. In 1130 Richard fitz Gerard held this position in Appleby.[54] Before King Henry I's death in 1135 the two counties of Cumberland and Westmorland were probably established, and sheriffs appointed for both.[54] Westmorland at this time consisted only of the upper Eden Valley with Appleby as its administrative capital.

There was an ecclesiastical reorganization to parallel the secular one. At the time of King Henry's visit to Carlisle in 1122 the city lay within the Diocese of Glasgow, which Earl David of Scotland (later King David I) had reconstituted in 1107.[54] The first Bishop, Michael, had been a Cumbrian, consecrated by the Archbishop of York and acting as suffragan to him.[54] But in the 1120s John, second Bishop of Glasgow, was reported to be consecrating churches and undertaking other Episcopal functions in the English territories in Cumberland without reference to Archbishop Thurstan. The Pope ordered Bishop John to submit to York, but he remained obdurate, and it is likely that this struggle led directly to the excision of Cumberland and Westmorland from the Diocese of Glasgow in 1133. The new Diocese of Carlisle, which included only Allerdale and the Eden Valley, was created with the Pope's firm support, and the church of the Augustinian Priory King Henry had endowed became its cathedral.[65] As King Henry's brother-in-law and protégé David I was by this time King of Scotland, poor Bishop John was probably squeezed by the combined might of two sovereigns as well as one Pope and one Archbishop!

In the twelfth century there were strong trans-Border ties of kinship and allegiance. King Malcolm III Canmore of Scotland's wife, Margaret (canonised as Saint Margaret in 1250), came of the English (Anglo-Saxon) royal house: she was sister to Edgar the Atheling and great granddaughter of King Ethelred. After she and her husband had died within days of one another their 'half-English' children were exiled for a while, although three of their sons were destined to rule Scotland in succession. Malcolm and Margaret's daughter Edith (Matilda) married King Henry I of England and that king proved a particularly powerful patron to his youngest brother-in-law, David, who was brought up at the English court. David obtained the earldoms of Huntingdon and Northampton by marriage, and at King Henry's insistence, and under his patronage, he was granted land and authority in southern Scotland by 1113.[28] Established there, he remained Henry's client and virtual viceroy, and agent of the 'Normanization' of Scotland. He promoted Anglo-Norman families with names like de Brus (Bruce), Avenel, de Soules and de Morville (all originating in the Cotentin Peninsula in western Normandy). Walter, third son of a steward to the Lords of Dol in Brittany, arrived in Scotland in 1136, served as steward to three Scottish kings, and founded the Stewart family which became great landowners in Ayrshire, Bute and the west Highlands.[28, 66] David I's first land grant when he succeeded his brother Alexander in 1124 was of the marcher lordship of Annandale to Robert de Brus.[28]

After the death of King Henry I in 1135 the succession to the English throne was disputed between his daughter Maud (or Matilda), called 'the Empress' because she was the widow of the Holy Roman Emperor, and his nephew, Stephen of Blois. War soon broke out between these rival claimants, and in this war King David I took the part of his niece Maud – we may guess because he knew that King Henry had wanted her to take the throne. Paradoxically, Stephen's queen, also named Matilda, was another of David's nieces. About Christmas time 1135, as the contemporary chronicle of Richard, Prior of Hexham, tells us, the Scots invaded England with a great force and occupied the towns of Carlisle, Alnwick, Norham, Newcastle, and Wark upon Tweed.[67] In 1136 peace was made between King Stephen and King David, Carlisle "with all belonging to it" being granted to the Scots. In this grant the county of Westmorland (as then constituted) was included and the Border was brought south once again to the Rey Cross on Stainmore. Appleby was back in Scotland!

It stayed that way for twenty years. The war broke out with renewed vigour in 1138 when the King of Scots, "advancing with very great power and ferocity either subdued all the northern parts of England to him, or undertook their de-population by fire and sword."[67] During the summer the Scots penetrated far south of their lands in Westmorland, allegedly wasting the province of Craven and the lands of Furness Abbey. Provoked by these ravages, Earl William of Aumerle and other Yorkshire Barons raised an army which defeated the Scots at the battle of the Standard, fought near Northallerton on 22 August 1138.[67] But though the battle was won by the English, the Scots did well in the peace for in 1139 King Stephen restored to King David and his son and joint-ruler, Prince Henry, all the lands which they had held before. Prince Henry was made Earl of Northumberland, received the honour of Huntingdon (previously held by his father), and acquired a high-ranking English bride.[66]

King David no doubt saw this turn of events as the restoration of Cumbria to the country to which it properly belonged. It made geographical sense, for Carlisle is the natural hub of all the valleys radiating from the Solway – Annandale, Eskdale and Liddesdale on the north as well as the Eden Valley to the south. The land was rich, and by special decree of King Henry I of England the mines of Alston in the South Tyne Valley were attached to Carlisle. A vein of silver had been found there in around 1120, and by 1133 it was said to be bringing £500 a year to the royal coffers.[54] The mines gave King David a cherished source of metal for his new currency.[66] And, despite the criticisms of the English chroniclers, his rule may well have saved the north of England from the anarchy of Stephen's reign – a time "when men said openly that Christ and his saints slept."[44] The Scottish king became a regular visitor to Carlisle. His son, Prince Henry, founded Holm Cultram Abbey, granting it lands in Galloway and Dumfries as well as on the south of the Solway, and linking it to Melrose which was presided over by his half-brother Waltheof (later St Waltheof).[66] It was David I who granted the Barony of Westmorland with its castles of Appleby and Brough to Hugh de Morville, probably in the late 1130s.[25; 66] He also rebuilt the keep of Carlisle Castle, where he died in 1153.

Kings of this period were not to be trusted to keep their promises. David I kept his to his patron and brother-in-law, Henry I of England, but he was less true to his nephew by marriage, King Stephen. Although it was by agreement with the latter that David and his son Prince Henry had ruled Cumbria and Northumberland and held the Honour of Lancaster, this did not stop a new conspiracy in 1149. In that year King David received the Empress Maud's son Henry of Anjou, the future King Henry II of England, at Carlisle, knighted him and plotted with him and the Earl of Chester, Ranulf le Meschin (son of the Ranulf who had previously held Appleby) to overthrow King Stephen.[66] Had this come off, all the country north of the Howgills and the Tees would have been incorporated in

Scotland, while Ranulf of Chester would have got the honour of Lancaster. Henry of Anjou took an oath that if and when he became King of England he would not challenge the Scots' possession of Cumbria and of Northumbria north of the Tees.[66]

Eight years later, secure as King of England and a vigorous warrior aged 24, he broke his promise. King David and his son Prince Henry had both died within six months of one another, and in the summer of 1157 David's fifteen-year-old grandson, Malcolm IV, called the Maiden (he never married, and left no heirs), was ordered by his second cousin the English King to return Carlisle, Cumberland and Westmorland. Six months later Henry II summoned King Malcolm to meet him at Carlisle and made it clear that the Border now stood on the Solway.[33] Appleby was thus restored to England. Despite the change in sovereigns, Hugh de Morville, who was also Lord of Knaresborough, kept Westmorland and entrusted the Castle of Appleby to a constable. But, a little over a decade later, de Morville blotted his copy-book twice over. First, he was one of the four murderers of Archbishop Thomas Becket in 1170 (although this did not cost him his lands). Second, in 1173 he sided with the English Prince Henry, eldest son of Henry II, in a rebellion against the king. This was taken much more seriously, and Westmorland and Knaresborough were declared forfeited to the crown. That edict was not, however, easy to enforce for Prince Henry had formed an alliance with William the Lion, King of Scotland (brother of Malcolm the Maiden), and encouraged him to invade the north of England.

We have an eye-witness account of that campaign, written in Norman French by Jordan Fantosme[68] who was a clerk in the service of the Bishop of Winchester. According to this chronicle, Prince Henry promised William the Lion the restoration of the lands his grandfather, King David, had held:

> *I will give you the land which your ancestor had,*
> *The border land; I know no better under heaven.*
> *You shall have the lordship in Castle and in tower;*
> *I will give you Carlisle that you may be the stronger*
> *All Westmorland, without any gainsaying.*

A simple scan of the dates shows how the possession of these lands had oscillated:

945-1032 (87 years)	Scotland
1032-1058 (26 years)	England
1058-1092 (34 years)	Scotland
1092-1136 (44 years)	England
1136-1157 (21 years)	Scotland
1157-1174 (17 years)	England

England, 87: Scotland 142. Advantage, Scotland. Moreover, most impartial historians of the time would probably have conceded that Cumbria was part of Strathclyde, and the latter a traditional fiefdom of Scotland, even if, at times, the Kings of Scots had done homage for it to the English King. William the Lion had never acquiesced in his brother's forced return of this territory to England in 1157. When he joined 'the young King Henry' in 1174 he was engaging in what he saw as action to recover his legitimate rights. And he tried both ways! He obviously respected Henry II as a redoubtable ruler, and first attempted to obtain a grant of the lands he wanted from him! Only after these negotiations had failed did he join the rebellion and invade the Border counties.[68; 69]

The first Scottish attack was against Northumberland. Later, in the summer of 1174, William the Lion "laid siege to Carlisle, but perceiving that he could not win it in any short time, he left part of his army to keep siege before it, and with the residue marched into the country alongst the river of Eden, taking by force the castles of Brough and Appleby, with divers others."[53]

The Chronicle of Jordan Fantosme goes into richer detail:[68]

(The King of Scotland) went to Appleby, thither he marched.
There were no people in it, therefore he took it quickly.
The King had very soon the Castle of Appleby;
There were no people in it, so it was quite unguarded.
Gospatric, the son of Orm, an old grey headed Englishman,
Was the constable; he soon cried mercy.
The King had nearly forgotten his grief
When he had Appleby, the Castle and the tower.

and a few lines later:

*King William of Scotland has already taken Appleby,
And Roger de Mowbray, who was his friend,
And put therein their Border sergeants.
And they have placed three constables in the Castle.
They have amongst themselves great fun and laughter
They think never to lose them until the day of Judgement.*

It is clear from this account that the Scots took Appleby without difficulty, in contrast to the stubborn resistance they met with later on at Brough. Perhaps the castle was surprised, for Jordan Fantosme records "that Appleby was taken at dawn." But you do not need an extra-sensitive nose to scent duplicity. Hugh de Morville came of one of the Anglo-Norman families David I had promoted in Scotland and had held Westmorland first as David's vassal.[66; 69] Gospatric son of Orm, the constable, was a grandson of Gospatric Earl of Northumbria and his mother Gunilda was a sister of Dolfin, ejected from Carlisle by William Rufus. It seems likely that Gospatric, like de Morville, was a Scotland supporter!

In 1174 the triumphant Scots expected to hold Appleby Castle "until the day of Judgement." Their garrison included sergeants appointed as Wardens of the Marches. William the Lion doubtless hoped that this time he had got the land of Carlisle for good. In fact his triumph was of short duration. His army had a hard time taking Brough, where six knights made a staunch defence of the 'tower' until they were forced to surrender because it was set on fire by the attackers. Having secured Brough, and hence reached what he considered his proper Border at the Rey Cross, the Scottish king turned back to Carlisle, arranged the surrender of its garrison, and went campaigning in Northumberland – where he blundered into an English army in the fog near Alnwick, was captured, humiliated by being led into Northampton with his feet tied beneath his horse, and imprisoned in the Castle of Falaise in Normandy.[28] That was that. The Border counties were quickly re-occupied by Henry II, and (apart from a hiccough in 1216) have remained English ever since. Later in 1174, King William did homage to Henry II "for Scotland and all his other lands." It was a reminder that he was back on his throne by grace of the King of England.[29]

The King dealt firmly with the traitors of Appleby when the affair was over in 1175, although (rather remarkably) nobody was hanged. The town and castle, and the rest of Westmorland with them, were kept in the hands of the crown (this may be why the Chronicler William of Newburgh refers to Appleby as a 'Royal fort').[70] Gospatric son of Orm was fined 500 marks, a vast sum in those days, for his share in the surrender. At the same time, Ralph de Cundal (Kendal?) was fined 40 marks, Odard de Burgham (Lord of the Manor of Brougham) 20 marks "for being with the King's enemies" and Humphrey Malchael (Machel) 15 marks. It cost John de Morville (presumably a relative of the errant Hugh) £20 while Reginald the cook was fined £5 for supplying food to the Scots and William, clerk of Appleby, was fined 10 marks. In all, some 25 persons were fined for being concerned in the surrender of Appleby Castle, and for aiding and abetting the Scots.[48]

There is some dispute as to the state of both Appleby and Brough Castles at the time of William the Lion's occupation in 1174. At Brough there are remains of an early tower of herring-bone masonry, at a slight angle to the existing keep, and parts of the curtain wall are of similar construction, dating them to around 1100.[9] It may well be that the tough defence of Brough was helped by stone walls, although these did not stop the attackers firing the tower. The present keep dates from the last quarter of the twelfth century, and presumably replaced the one burned in the siege.

At Appleby there is more uncertainty. Some historians[56] have argued that all the stonework now visible is later than 1174, and that the Scots captured the original timber and earthwork motte and bailey constructed by Ivo Taillebois and Ranulf le Meschin some 75 years before. If so, most of the present stone keep together with the stone curtain wall which replaced the original wooden palisade around the bailey date from the years immediately following 1174. However the Royal Commission on Historical Monuments[9] dated the lower stages of the keep to around 1170, which might place responsibility for the construction on Hugh de Morville, while Martin Holmes, in his account of the castle, thought that the keep might date back to the time of Ranulf le Meschin and was certainly in existence before the Scots occupation.[20] I favour le Meschin as keep-builder, largely because I cannot see him creating a new town with a stone church and (possibly) a stone bridge, unless his own stronghold, the seat of his authority, also had the dignity of a stone tower. And since he clearly treated Appleby as of greater importance than Brough, surely he would have given it the stronger castle?

Whatever the truth of it, there is no reason to doubt that the castle, borough and the older settlement in Bongate fell undamaged into Scots hands. 'It's an ill bird that fouls its own nest,' and if the Scots were looking to retain the land of Carlisle as their own, they would have wanted to keep it in good order. But once the tide had turned, the retreating army may well have turned to plunder. In 1174 and 1175, the Sheriff of

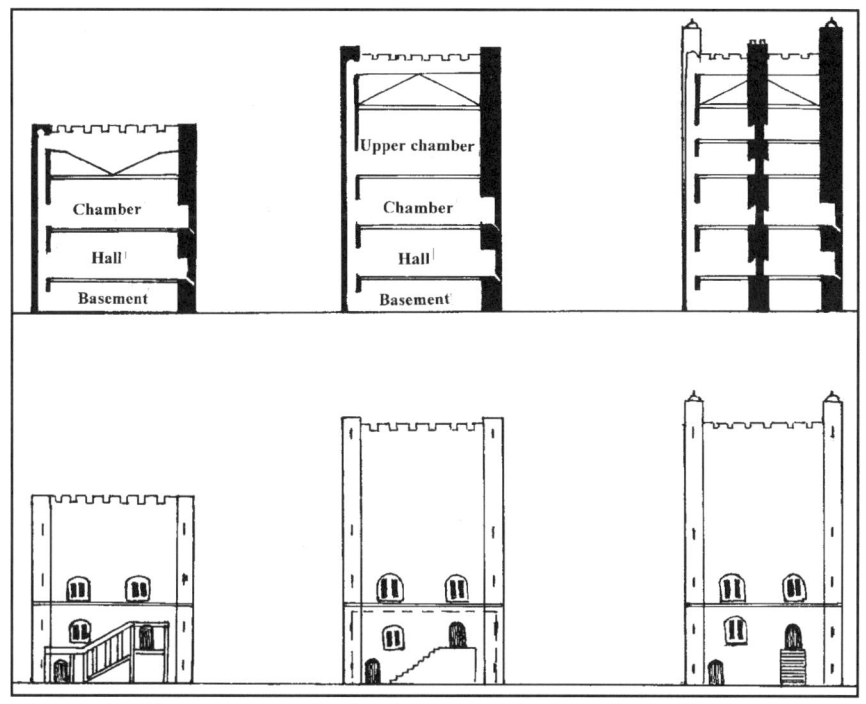

Figure 2 - Three stages in the development of Appleby Castle Keep.
Left: Elevation and section of the original tower, possibly built by Ranulf le Meschin. A spiral staircase would have climbed the tower on the left, and two privies are shown in the wall on the right. There was a water catchment gully on the roof, presumably discharging to a tank below. The covered timber external stair to the main doorway is conjectural.
Centre: The keep as raised in the late 11th century. The upper chamber was lit only by two small windows on the west. The dotted line drawn around the lower third of the tower marks the possible position of a forebuilding protecting the two doors: this would be expected in a tower of this period, but no trace remains at Appleby.
Right: The keep as restored by Lady Anne Clifford. A central cross wall with fireplaces has been inserted in the middle of the tower and the upper chamber divided into upper and lower rooms (both still very poorly lit). The external stair mounting to the main door is a modern replacement.

Cumberland paid no money to the crown "because of the wasting of the county after the war."[71] The revenues of Westmorland also dipped in the period, and in 1175, 1176 and 1177 a total of £45-2s-6d was allowed by the crown for restocking and restoring to cultivation lands that had been devastated.[71] In 1179 the Honour of Westmorland was granted to Ranulf de Glanville, the King's Chief Justice and Sheriff of Yorkshire, who retained it until the accession of Richard I in 1189.[69]

There was a lot of reconstruction in Appleby. The church of St. Lawrence is stated to have been rebuilt by the king's command in 1178, and the lower stage of the present west tower and the base of the east wall of the chancel date from this period – so that the church had clearly attained its present length before 1200.[9] The castle was strengthened at the same time,[9; 72] either by the Royal Sheriff or under Ranulf de Glanville (the statement that the castle was held, and the rebuilding done, by de Glanville's father-in-law, Thibault de Valognes may result from a misinterpretation of the Pipe Rolls[69]). A fourth storey was added to the keep, the bailey was walled around in stone and a great hall, doubtless with adjacent kitchen, stores and chambers, was built along its east side. This new range of buildings had its own gateway, complete with portcullis, although the main access to the bailey probably remained on the north side, attained after a circuit under the walls (Figure 2, Plan 1).[20]

As a result of this work, by soon after 1175 the keep of Appleby Castle was complete. It was a typical 'tower keep' with only one major room on each floor (the present subdivision by a cross wall is the work of Lady Anne Clifford, Countess of Pembroke in 1651-53).[9; 20] At ground level there was a store room which (unusually) had a door to the outside. The principal communal living room or 'hall' was on the first floor, with a large door reached by an external staircase. Although no traces remain, both the ground floor and first floor doors may possibly have been protected by enclosure in a forebuilding. The 'hall' was lit by windows on all sides and had a lavatory (garderobe) in its north-east corner. Two spiral stone staircases climbed to an upper room of identical size, probably designed as the 'great chamber' or private apartment of the Lord of the Castle: it too was lit on all sides and had its private privy. A stone corbel carved with the semblance of a face is still visible high up in this room and would have supported the main cross-beam carrying a V-shaped gully in the original roof: when the fourth stage was added at the end of the twelfth century the corbel became internal to the chamber as

A New Appleby

a new room was added above, capped by a flat roof and parapets.

The period after the reoccupation of Appleby in 1174 saw a profound change in the status of the new borough and its relationship with the castle. When first founded by Ranulf le Meschin, the borough would have been 'his', erected on land he supplied and paying its rents and tolls to him as manorial lord. This arrangement was replicated elsewhere in Cumbria at Cockermouth and at his brother's town of Egremont.[73] The main difference between the borough and Bongate was that the latter remained an integral part of the castle estates, occupied by farm workers and other servants or 'bondmen' rather than free tenants. But, some time around the end of 1179, King Henry II, in consideration of a fee of 40 marks paid by the burghers, granted the borough its first charter, which "confirmed to our burgesses of Appleby to hold all the liberties and free customs which our burgesses of York have."[48; 74; 75]

This grant did not give freedom from tolls: in 1197 the burghers paid an account of 40 marks in tallage[72] and in the period preceding 1200 they were in debt for unpaid tolls of about £15. As was usual in charters given by Henry II, the land was also retained by the king, whose officers would have collected a rent from each burgage. The borough's second charter, granted by King John in 1200 in return for a fee of 100 marks, was of greater importance for not only did it confirm the privileges of Henry II's grant, but it also gave the burghers freedom from "toll, stallage, pontage and lastage" throughout England, except for the city of London, and it "granted to them the town of Appleby to be held in their hand by payment of the due rent to our Sheriff of Westmorland at Appleby" half at Michaelmas and half at Easter.[48; 74; 75]

In those days tolls were the chief sources of municipal revenue, levied by boroughs on people passing through or selling goods. To be exempted from such dues made travelling and trading cheaper and easier and gave the merchants of Appleby the prospect of greater prosperity. The right to hold and raise the fee farm rent was even more valuable. The fee farm was a fixed annual sum replacing the former payments of burgage rent, market tolls and market court fees. It protected the feudal overlord (in this case the crown), from fluctuations in the profits of trade, but at the same time allowed the burghers to keep their profits once they had paid the fee farm.[55] King John's charter made the burghers responsible for tax collecting in their own town, and made them largely independent of the lords of the castle – although this was not to go unchallenged in the turbulent years ahead.

CHAPTER 3

Prosperous Borough

AFTER the grant of King John's Charter in 1200, the borough of Appleby developed separately from the castle and the Barony of Westmorland, although the three remained closely interlinked. The burghers were no longer tenants of the lord of the barony. They elected their own officials and collected their own taxes – although they had to pay the fee farm rent of twenty marks through the Sheriff of Westmorland, and as the lord of the castle held this office, he could not be completely by-passed. Moreover, as the castle was the only stronghold in the neighbourhood and its garrison the main source of military defence, it did make sense for the burghers to keep on good terms with the lord of the barony – something they did not always do!

The newly-chartered borough inherited some officials from earlier times, but soon built up its own administration. William, described as *clericus de Appelbi*, who was fined ten marks for being implicated in the surrender of 1174 was almost certainly an ecclesiastic: there were no 'town clerks' in this period. However the sergeant certainly was a borough official, with responsibility for the custody of suspected criminals, and in 1194 one Waldeve who held this post was fined half a mark for allowing a prisoner named Agnes to escape.[71; 72] His debt was not finally paid off until 1198. After the grant of the fee farm rent in 1200 the burghers elected two bailiffs to collect this tax and pay it to the sheriff in two instalments, at Michaelmas and Easter. These may later have become the provosts, who appear as signatories to an undated deed of Henry III's reign (1215-1272),[48] although two bailiffs with responsibility for arresting wrong-doers were certainly still being elected in the 1290s.[76]

There is one piece of evidence to suggest that the town that received King John's Charter in 1200 was bigger and more prosperous than Ranulf le Meschin's original foundation. It stems from the fact that the fee farm rent was set at 20 marks (£13-6s-8d). If this was paid at the customary rate of about one shilling per burgage,[55] it would imply growth from the original 60-odd burgages to 266. And, since the fee farm remained at 20 marks for the following 180 years, it may imply that the main period of expansion was between 1120 and 1200 and that the town then grew slowly until disaster overtook it in the fourteenth century.

How big was Appleby during the prosperous years of the thirteenth century? The customary way of estimating the population has been to calculate the number of burgages from the fee farm rent and other early records, check the calculated total against maps that show the original town pattern, and then assume that there were five people living in each burgage. Some earlier historians have come up with very large totals for Appleby through such computations. Gibson (in his revision of Camden's *Britannia* in 1722)[77] and Canon W A Mathews in 1892 both assumed that the fee farm rent was paid at a rate of 2d per burgage, giving the immense total of 1,600 burgages, which at five people per burgage would have meant a population of 8,000. "Allowing for the presence of labourers, servants, and the descendants of old villani who had not any borough rights," Canon Mathews computed a total population of 10,000-12,000.[78] This is now accepted as erroneous (among other things it would have made Appleby second only to London among English towns), but there must have been a basis for the calculation. One possibility is that Gibson and Mathews had access to Appleby Castle estate records, which show that the rents paid by burgage tenants in the eighteenth century were indeed around 2d per annum[63] though these are not comparable with the original fee farm charges.

The estimate of 266 burgages in the early thirteenth century would, at five people per burgage, suggests a population of around 1330. Bongate, outside the borough, would no doubt have added a few hundred to the conurbation. This makes sense, for not many planted towns had more than 250 burgages. Appleby was more or less on a financial par with Chipping Sodbury (176 burgages, revenue £12-11s-7d in 1295), Newport in Wales (275 burgages, revenue £13-15s-0d in 1314) and Llantrisant (226 burgages, revenue £12-3s-8d in 1314). Its fee farm was less than that of Richmond (Yorkshire), which paid £29 in 1137-45 but more than that of Liverpool (£10 in 1229) or Clitheroe (£6-13s-4d in 1272-91).[55] It emerges from these comparisons as a significant medium-sized mediaeval town, probably larger than any other in the modern county of

Cumbria except Carlisle.

Success brings success, and if Appleby did expand in the twelfth century, this would be one reason for the king to give it new status by charter. This in turn would have been a spur to further growth through the immigration of merchants looking to share in its prosperity. By the mid-thirteenth century it would have been the principal local market for corn, sheep, cattle, pigs, wool, woollen and linen cloth, leather and leather goods and iron – and presumably also for pottery and ironware.[79] Another reason for the charters was that they made sure that the crown would go on getting the fee farm rent even if – as happened in 1203 – the king assigned the castle and its lands to a new feudal lord.

As the town grew, it would have become more densely packed. There was always a strong conservatism over the boundaries of burgage plots in mediaeval towns. Extension forward was impossible because it would have encroached on the common street while extension backwards was restricted in many places because it would have broken across the back lane and into the common fields, and in Appleby it was impossible because of the limitations of the site.[56; 57] Consequently, new growth took place within the original plots, whose land was becoming too valuable to be left as gardens or poultry-runs. Instead of containing only a single house with its outbuildings, many plots therefore became filled with a series of houses and sheds surrounding a long, narrow courtyard or passage running back from the street. This is the origin of the clusters of buildings about central yards which are still conspicuous on either side of Boroughgate. The lateral corridors off Boroughgate – Bridge Street, Low Wiend, High Wiend and Shaw Wiend – also became lined by rows of dwellings facing onto the streets (Map 3, page 41).

The 1754 burgage map and associated inventory[61] and castle estate books,[63] together with the evidence of place-names, suggest that the growth in the twelfth and thirteenth centuries took 'New Appleby' beyond the confines of the original planned town along Boroughgate. At least 26 burgage plots were built up on the west side of Doomgate, transforming it from a back lane into a substantial street. There were at least ten other burgages on the east side of Doomgate south of Shaw Wiend, though these, like sixteen or so at the top of the original Boroughgate, had by 1754 vanished by incorporation in the Castle Park (though they still entitled their possessors to a Parliamentary vote!). South of the castle, there was clearly a substantial settlement of as many as 40 burgages on both sides of Scattergate, which is recorded as a place-name as early as 1230. It has an insalubrious meaning, being in all probability derived from *scitere,* an open sewer, and *gate,* a street.[43] The open sewer in question was the Doomgate Sike that carried the effluvium from Scattergate to the Eden, and Doomgate may well have started life as '*doemgate*' or 'mucky street.'[43]

The 1754 map also shows some 20 burgages to the east of the bridge, rising from the main road along the Sands to an obvious back lane on the line of the present Garth Heads Road. This may well be the district named as 'Bridge End' in 1518-19.[43] To the north yet more dwellings – on at least ten plots – lined Battlebarrow. Southward, there were others along the sunken lane of Howgate ('hollowgate'). The map records a Borough Stone at the southern end of this group of plots, next to the suggestively-named Drawbriggs Lane. The implication is that the borough had expanded south and east of the original township and that the 1754 map (Map 1 and Map 3)[61] records its extent at the height of its prosperity in 1295, when the holders of the burgage tenements first elected two representatives to Parliament. The map and inventory record 269 burgages in all, a figure that accords well with the estimate from the fee farm rent of 266 burgages in the flourishing days of mediaeval Appleby.

It is not clear whether the boundary of the parish of St Lawrence – always seen as the borough church – ever coincided with that of the borough. What is obvious is that it would have ceased to do so by 1295, if the town grew as I have just suggested. For while the extension of the borough into Scattergate and the southern end of Doomgate lay within the parish (which also included Colby, Burrells, Hoff and Drybeck), the eastward expansion meant that some 50 burgages lay within the parish of St Michael's Bongate. The latter extended east and north of the Eden, including Battlebarrow, Crackenthorpe, Hilton, Murton and Langton.

Two pieces of evidence support the conclusion that the borough never got bigger than this. First, it never outgrew the capacity of the two mediaeval churches of St Lawrence and St Michael. While northern towns lacked the profusion of mediaeval parishes and buildings seen in places like Cambridge, an Appleby of three or four thousand would surely have needed more churches. Second, and perhaps more telling, big and prosperous towns could afford to invest in communal defences, but there is no record that Appleby ever had a town wall, and although it certainly had a gatehouse at the west end of the bridge, this is far more likely to have been a toll-bar than a serious piece of military architecture.

There is, it is true, a puzzling entry in the pipe rolls (exchequer records) for 1195 when ten shillings were allowed for "the repair of the walls" (*muri*) "of Appleby" but this is the sole such reference and the simplest interpretation is that this payment was for the castle, even though castle and borough were normally distinguished in the records of this period.[72] Mention by Thomas Pennant in 1773[80] of 'the town wall' near the Friary on Battlebarrow is probably an error, while the statement that Burrells, several miles to the south, means 'the borough walls' and indicates the former extent of the town is nonsense: the name probably comes from the Old English *byrgels* meaning burial place.[43] It is conceivable that weaker and less durable defences – such as an earth bank and wooden palisade – were thrown up around the loop of the river, with some kind of bank and ditch between the western earthworks of the castle and the marshy junction of Doomgate Sike and the Eden,[56] but no trace of any such work has ever been recorded. Moreover, only Boroughgate could have benefited from such defences, which would have left Doomgate, Scattergate, the Sands and Battlebarrow outside the ring. It seems most likely that, in contrast to bigger cities such as Carlisle, Newcastle upon Tyne, Berwick on Tweed or York, Appleby had to rely on the natural protection of the river and the arms of its people, helped, if their strength allowed it, by the garrison of the castle.

Although King John's Charter of 1200 made the borough independent of the lords of the barony and castle, the latter remained an essential bulwark to the town so what happened at the top of the hill was very important. Ranulf de Glanville had been dispossessed of the castle by King Richard I in 1189 and the king had kept it in his own hands throughout his reign and paid for its upkeep. In 1196 eight shillings were allowed for alterations to the 'house' (*domus*) of Appleby (this may have been the castle hall). In 1198, 40 shillings were spent on the bridge belonging to the castle (presumably a bridge over the moat). Forty shillings were paid again in 1199 on castle repairs, with another 100 shillings later in the same year. In 1200 Richard Pipard, Constable of Appleby, and the Constable of Brough were allowed ten marks for the repair of these castles.[72]

In 1203, three years after his charter to the borough, King John granted "Appleby and Brough and all the appendages of the same" together with the sheriffwick and Barony of Westmorland to Robert de Vieuxpont (also called Vipont or Veteriponte, meaning 'old bridge').[20; 48; 71] He was the nephew of Hugh de Morville, being the son of his sister Maud whose name is commemorated in Mauld's Meaburn, so that he had some claim by descent as well as by his services to the king to succeed to the forfeited estates. More importantly, at a time when King John's hold over the north of England was under threat from the rebellious barons, he was loyal to the monarch. He also had a rival claimant to hold off, in the shape of Alan, Lord of Galloway and Constable of Scotland, who was a descendant of Hugh de Morville's elder brother, Richard. While King John tussled with his barons in the south, it was far from certain that the Scots would not once again take the Eden Valley.[25] King Alexander II, successor to William the Lion, certainly wanted it back and raided into Northumbria in 1215.[28]

It may well have been the renewed Scots threats that led Robert de Vieuxpont to obtain from Gilbert de Burgham half of the Manor of Brougham.[25] Shortly after 1215 he began to build Brougham Castle on the south bank of the River Eamont, close to the Roman crossing of the river and right against the old fort of Brocavum, where three Roman roads met. He was prescient, for in 1216 the Scottish army did force its way down the Eden Valley into Yorkshire, and Alan of Galloway became, for about a year, Lord of Westmorland and Governor of north-west England for King Alexander II.[25] By the end of 1217 the latter had made three more incursions. The new king, Henry III, bought him off by marrying him to his sister, Joan, and restoring him to the Earldom of Huntingdon. By 1237 Scottish royal claims to Cumbria were finally at an end, and the Treaty of York fixed the Border on its present line from the Tweed to the Solway.[28] Thereafter, Scottish incursions into Cumbria would be for plunder rather than territory, and the more damaging in consequence.

Robert de Vieuxpont is depicted by some historians as somewhat of a ruffian "who augmented his fortune by plunder and rapine during the civil wars"[71] and who, at his death in 1228 was indebted to King Henry III for £1,997-11s-6d "besides five great horses" (warhorses capable of carrying a knight in armour) "and five tuns of wine."[71; 81] His building at Brougham may have absorbed most of his money, for it is clear that he spent little on Appleby Castle. After his death the Justiciar[4] Hubert de

---

Note 4 - A Justiciar was the highest officer under the Crown responsible for the administration of justice in a region.

Burgh had custody of the castles until the second de Vieuxpont, John, came of age. This John arranged to have Appleby put in order, advancing the carpenters 22 marks for the work but also demanding pledges that could be called on if they did not do it properly,[20] but he himself died in 1241 leaving his son, the second Robert de Vieuxpont, to endure an even longer minority.[25]

During that minority, the Prior of Carlisle was responsible for the management of the estate and neglected his duty, allowing the castle keep to decay so badly that it cost 22 marks to put it right. An official inquiry revealed that the carpenters had not repaired the roof; the Prior had neither chased them nor called in the guarantees, and "the chamber of the knights" (probably the chamber above the hall in the keep) "which was in need of repair in the said John's time fell down in the time of the Prior and the timber became worthless." Brough and Brougham Castles had been similarly neglected, trees in Whinfell Forest had been cut down and the deer had been poached in the park.[20; 25]

The result was a lot of rebuilding. Martin Holmes suggested[20] that the uppermost stage of the keep may in fact date from this time rather than that of Ranulf de Glanville, although the Royal Commission on Historical Monuments preferred the earlier date.[9] All authorities agree that the curtain wall at the eastern end of the bailey was greatly strengthened in the mid-thirteenth century with the addition of a projecting round tower on the north side and two smaller ones on the south. This pattern of curtain walls with projecting towers was an important thirteenth century development, copied from the Byzantine castles seen by the Crusaders and later used by Edward I in his great fortresses in Wales. The towers allowed archers to cover the walls on either side of them, and made it much more difficult for attackers, including miners seeking to tunnel under the walls, to get close. If the intention was to bring Appleby Castle up to the standard of the King's works in Wales, however, it was never realised. The curtain wall around the keep remained low, weak and devoid of wall towers, making it questionable how much use the three that were built in the eastern section would have been.

The second Robert de Vieuxpont took part in the rebellion of Simon de Montfort against King Henry III. His death before June 1264 has been attributed to wounds received at the Battle of Lewes, fought on 14 May. But records show that he was active in the north between Michaelmas 1263 and May 1264, holding Richmond and Bowes castles for de

Montfort and (with others) briefly taking Carlisle in April 1264, so it is more likely that he received his death-wound in some northern skirmish.[25] Clearly he died a rebel before 1265, and once the king had squashed the revolt the Barony of Westmorland, including the castles of Appleby, Brough and Brougham, was seized. Robert de Vieuxpont's two young daughters, Isabella and Idonea, were placed under guardians by the king, who, in August 1265 "in consideration of the laudable service performed by Roger de Clifford, grants to him the custody of the lands and tenements of Isabella, eldest daughter and co-heir of Robert de Veteriponte, together with the disposal of her in marriage." The younger daughter, Idonea, was placed in the care of Roger de Leyburn.

In both cases the heiresses were married (as was probably intended from the first) to the sons of their guardians, and it was as the husband of Isabella de Vieuxpont that a member of the great family of Clifford first came into possession of Appleby Castle and of the Hereditary High Sheriffwick of the County of Westmorland. While both co-heiresses were alive the barony was partitioned, the Cliffords holding Appleby and Brougham Castles, the manor of Brougham and the shrievalty of Westmorland while the Leyburns got the castles of Brough and Mallerstang (Pendragon) and the manor of Kirkby Stephen.[25] Other manors were divided, and both heiresses got a share in the forests of Whinfell and Mallerstang.[71] Subsequently, when Idonea died in 1333 without descendants, Brough Castle and the lands which had been her portion passed to the heirs of her sister. While the lands were divided between the two heiresses Appleby Castle was neglected. Roger de Clifford seems to have spent time at Brougham and built up the wealth of that manor, while the Leyburns for their part repaired Brough, which had been dilapidated in 1245, and Idonea is thought to have lived there for most of her long life.[71; 82]

Between 1200 and 1314 mediaeval Appleby achieved its greatest prosperity (Map 3). As the borough grew in status it developed new institutions. It was the assize town for the county. It had a charter of confirmation of its rights and liberties from Henry III in 1232, and according to one source, during the reign of this king "there was an exchequer here called Scaccarium de Appleby."[77] This comment may refer to Robert de Vieuxpont's arrangements as sheriff for collecting revenues due to the crown, as did a later reference in an inquisition to Roger de Clifford's 'exchequer of Appleby.' Certainly Appleby never had an exchequer of national importance. The church of St Lawrence also received new endowments at some date between 1246 and 1255. In place of the original six marks stipend from St Mary's Abbey in York, the vicar was in future to have "the whole altarage with all tithes of hay and mills, the mansion house and other houses on the west side of the church with the waste ground thereabout, with 20 acres of land and the whole common of wood and pasturage belonging to the said abbey." The 'waste ground thereabout' may have been the field later known as Broad Close and the 20 acres the Vicar's Banks and Banks Wood and Gardens.[64] Reference is also made to 48 acres in 'the field of Appleby' and 37 acres in the 'field of Hoff' being given to the church – both lying outside the borough, probably as strips in the common fields that fed the borough, castle and adjacent hamlets.[59]

The assizes were held in the castle, which was also the gaol. In 1256 "Roger de Thurkleby, the abbot of Peterborough and the sheriffs of Westmorland held the assize," and one of the cases gives a little vignette of life at the time:

> *William le Lockesmyth broke into a certain shop in Appleby and carried away the goods in the same and fled to the church of Appleby and acknowledged the theft there and renounced the realm for ever before the coroner. His chattels are worth four shillings for which the township answer.*[59; 83]

By 1264 Appleby had a mayor and two provosts, although the two bailiffs originally appointed to gather the fee farm rents seem to have remained and been given responsibility as law-enforcers. The first evidence for the existence of a mayor is in an undated deed of King Henry III's reign conveying a 'messuage' from 'Richard de Appleby, Clerk' to Robert, son of John de Vieuxpont. It is witnessed by William de Goldington, the mayor, and Robert de Goldington and John le Breton, provosts.[48] As this Robert de Vieuxpont died in 1264 Appleby must have had a mayor by that year, and very possibly a year or two earlier.[84]

There is a curious tradition regarding the status of the Mayor of Appleby. By the eighteenth and nineteenth centuries it had become established that by 'immemorial custom' the mayor took precedence over the Judge of Assize, even though the latter is generally treated as the personal deputy of the sovereign.[84] One suggested explanation is that the

Mayor of Appleby had already gained the status of the king's representative in the Royal Borough before the system of assizes and judicial circuits was established by King Henry II in 1176. This might also explain why the mayor still has the right to have a sword – symbolising the king's justice – carried before him as well as a mace, and until recently also sat as a magistrate by virtue of his office.[84] However, it would be strange if Appleby had a mayor as early as 1176 since York, on which the town modelled itself closely, did not elect one until 1217. Certainly there is no mention of a mayor in any document prior to that of around 1264.

A common seal was certainly used by the Corporation of Appleby in the first half of the thirteenth century. This bears on the obverse the three running (*passant guardant*) leopards that were the arms of Henry II and his descendants, displayed on a shield suspended from a seven-branched apple tree. Around the edge is the inscription:

SIGILLVM: COMMVNITATIS: BVRGHII: DE: APPILLBI

terminating with an apple in allusion to the name of the town. The reverse of the seal has a representation of the martyrdom of St. Lawrence, patron saint of the burghal church, and the background includes the royal arms (this time displayed on a rectangular banner) and an apple.[84]

Some historians have suggested that at the time of King John's Charter the borough was also granted the coat of arms it used until recently – three gold lions (or, more correctly, leopards) *passant guardant*, displayed on a red ground but 'differenced' from the royal arms by wearing gold crowns (the heraldic definition is "*gules*, three leopards *passant guardant or*, crowned with ducal coronets of the last").[78] However this is extremely improbable, for in the early thirteenth century arms were generally borne only by the greater nobility. Moreover, even after King Edward III quartered the three leopards with the lilies of France in 1340, as a symbol of his claim to the French throne, the leopards remained the badge of England and no town would be likely to be granted the right to use them, with or without coronets. The mistake probably arose because it was assumed that the coat was the one represented on the borough's original seal. This is wrong: the leopards on the shield and banner incorporated in the seal are not crowned.[71] They are there because a borough with no coat of arms of its own was expected to display those of its feudal overlord, and the borough of Appleby owed its allegiance directly to the crown.[84] It is the apples and apple-tree on the seal that are the device of the borough. The seal may well date from the time of King John's Charter, but it throws no light on how Appleby acquired the arms it used for so long. It seems to have happened in the eighteenth century, and is discussed further in Chapter Seven.

Between 1250 and 1350 the de Goldington family became very prominent in Appleby, as mayors, provosts, merchants and MPs. It has been suggested that they were a junior branch of the de Goldingtons of Bedfordshire, established in Appleby by the Vieuxponts.[76] Working out who was who is hampered by their habit of recycling a very small number of Christian names – especially William, Thomas, John and Robert.

'Master William de Goldington,' the town's first mayor, must have been born in around 1225 because his son, William II, was born in 1250. But Master William was probably not the first of the Appleby clan. The founders of the Chantry Chapel dedicated to the Virgin Mary in St Lawrence's Church are recorded as "Thomas de Goldington and John de Goldington the elder his son and their ancestors." The chantry was already well established when William de Goldington endowed it with a further five and a half marks per annum in 1280, this sum being charged on fifteen tenements in the town.[48] Thomas therefore belonged to a previous generation and may have been the first of the family, coming to Westmorland soon after the grant of the Barony to Robert de Vieuxpont.[76] Master William, 'John the elder' and Robert the provost who witnessed Master William's mayoral signature in around 1264 may all have been Thomas' sons. Robert, whom we had better style Robert I, owned the property next door to the one conveyed to Robert de Vieuxpont in that deed.[48] As for Master William, we know that he had at least three sons: William II, Thomas II and John II, and they all come into the story later.[76]

In the 1270s relations between the burghers of Appleby and the lords of the castle and barony took a turn for the worse. The Vieuxponts had been absentee landlords and were probably well content to see the borough running quietly under the leadership of their protégés the de Goldingtons. This was a time of relative peace on the northern borders, and the growth of the town as a trading settlement was not imperilled by the neglect of the castle. But once Roger de Clifford and Roger de Leyburn came on the scene as husbands of the Vieuxpont heiresses they began to flex their muscles in a fashion that brought trouble with the town of Appleby in 1275.[48] Roger, the lord's chamberlain, was assaulted by several men and very severely wounded, and the court of enquiry that followed noted that "many other men of Appleby were present, whose names are not known."

The trouble stemmed from King John's grants three quarters of a century earlier. The charter of 1200 gave the burghers of Appleby freedom from tolls, and the right to hold the fee farm in their own hands, although they had to pay the money they collected to the sheriff on behalf of the crown. Shortly afterwards, in 1203, "Appleby and Brough, with all belonging to them" had been granted by King John to Robert de Vieuxpont. In 1275, the Vieuxpont heirs were asserting that this grant entitled them to the fealty of the burghers, and gave them control over the activities of the borough. In 1276 the burghers finally issued a writ summoning Roger de Clifford and Isabella his wife, and Roger de Leyburn and Idonea his wife to answer to a long statement of grievances.

The writ demands (among other things):

> *why, since the said burgesses are the tenants of our lord the King, and hold nothing of the aforesaid, the aforesaid do not allow the said burgesses to grind their corn at such mills in their neighbourhood as they may think most convenient, nor to permit them to take stallage in the fairs and markets of the town nor customs of the merchants trafficking there, as they and their ancestors in former times were accustomed to do, and distrain them day by day to compel them to do fealty to the said Roger and Roger for their tenements in the town aforesaid as if they were their homagers of whom they hold not any thing at all nor of any other but our lord the King?*[48; 71]

The defendants admitted that they had done the things of which they were accused, but claimed that this was by right of the grant of 1203. The matter was therefore brought to trial before a jury empanelled from Cumberland, Northumberland and York, and judgement was given for the burghers. The jury found that:

> *Neither Robert de Veteriponte, nor any that succeeded him as heir, ever had seisin of the Borough of Appleby in which the burghers dwell, but that King John gave the said Robert Old Appleby where the bondmen dwell and Brough under Stainmore with all the*

> *appurtenances thereof. And, as for the fealty done to the said Robert and his heirs by the said burghers of Appleby for the said borough, they find that the said burghers never did any such fealty except by two bailiffs chosen by the community of the said borough so as to be responsible for the rent of the said borough as Sheriff in fee and not as lord of the borough. They find, also, that if the said burghers at any time have done any fealty to them, it was by distress and force and not by their will.*[48; 71]

The 'old Appleby where the bondmen' (or villeins) 'dwell' (in Latin *vetus Appilbi ubi villani manent*) mentioned in this judgement was Bongate, 'the bondmen's street,' the original settlement on the east of the Eden. The borough lands had originally been excised from this territory, and although the borough appears to have extended into the parish of St Michael Bongate that did not make the burghers subject to the barony. The distinct separation of the bondmen's and burghers' settlements was deliberate, and common in new towns.[55] There has been a mill beside Bongate ford since the thirteenth century, and it was probably at this castle mill that the Cliffords wanted the burghers to grind their corn.

The jury's verdict was a great victory for the burghers, but they pushed their luck a bit too far. In 1279 the town undertook further litigation in an attempt to secure certain rights (the return of writs and pleas of withernam) on the grounds that the citizens of York had these rights and that Appleby had the same privileges by charter.[48] They failed, it being held that the rights were reserved to the sheriff, and had to pay costs. Not surprisingly these disputes led to a marked coolness in the relations between Roger de Clifford and the citizens. In 1280 there was a further dispute, and a formal enquiry was held at Carlisle. The verdict was that "Sir Roger de Clifford never commanded or prayed any persons not to sell wood, turves or suchlike fuel to the burgesses of Appleby: however the jurors believe that his will was that there should be no such sales... because of the ill will between him and the said burgesses."[48; 71] Clearly, the Cliffords, having lost their bid for a direct take-over, had resorted to the subtler methods of the trade embargo.

Only three years after the verdict of 1280 Roger de Clifford was drowned in the Menai Straits during King Edward I's final campaign to conquer Wales.[85] He was 34. His widow, who remained in the north, continued to carry out the office of High Sheriff of Westmorland. Most of the duties of this post were, however, delegated to an under sheriff, and the two sisters disagreed over the rights of appointing this official. The final compromise was that Isabella de Clifford should nominate the candidates and Idonea de Leyburn approve them.

The friction between castle and borough may have been the reason for an important administrative change, made in a new charter granted by King Edward I in 1286. After rehearsing all the privileges conferred on the borough under the charters of Henry II and John and confirmed by Henry III in 1232, the new text also says that "whereas aforetime our burgesses were customed to pay the fee farm rent of the said town to us by the hand of our sheriff of Westmorland they may pay the said rent by the hands of the bailiffs of the said town in the future into our treasury at the wonted terms."[74; 75] That severed the last formal obligation of the borough to the lords of the castle, and may have been seen by the latter as something of a royal snub! It is unlikely to have made them more tenderly disposed towards their independent neighbours. Indeed, only a year later, in 1287, Isabella de Clifford and Idonea de Leyburn sued William de Goldington II who had by this time become mayor, John de Goldington his brother (John II, presumably a provost) and other burgesses of Appleby for infringing the rights of the sheriffs by holding courts for pleas which should have been heard in the King's Court. They claimed a massive £1,000 in damages, and the town's liberty was seized until the matter was settled.[48; 76]

The de Goldingtons were at the heart of Appleby affairs in the 1280s. They appear in a number of records, from which it is clear that they did not always measure up to the standards we now demand from people in public life. This was a rough-and-tumble age and the family firm had some things in common with the mafia! Its most prominent member in the 1280s was William de Goldington II, described as 'Merchant of Appleby' though his father Master William probably lived until around 1290. William II was born in 1250, he was licensed to trade in 1274, and it was probably not long afterwards that he married Christian le Hastings, daughter of Sir Thomas le Hastings of Crosby Ravensworth. Their eldest son was named John (here styled John de Goldington III), and their second son, born in 1280, was William de Goldington III who also became a prominent Appleby citizen. William II's younger brother Thomas II married another le Hastings daughter, Amice.[76]

In 1286 tragedy and scandal struck the le Hastings-de Goldington family. Nicholas le Hastings, one of Sir Thomas' three sons, was 'slain in a ditch.' The bailiffs of Appleby, Hugh le Granger (himself a prominent merchant) and Peter de la Dring, arrested Robert de Meaburn "at the insistence of William le Hastings and Thomas son of Master William de Goldington" (brother and brother-in-law of the dead man) "and held him in Appleby gaol until he was set free by the King's writ."[76]

Freed by the royal get-out-of-gaol card, Meaburn counter-sued the bailiffs for exceeding their authority and Hugh le Granger and Peter de la Dring were ordered to be imprisoned. Hugh got off by paying a fine of 20 shillings at the pledge of John de Goldington (presumably Provost John II) and Thomas Oversleigh. Things seem to have simmered down for some years but flared up again in 1292 when Thomas le Hastings (the third brother) and his sister Amice (wife of Thomas de Goldington II) petitioned against the alleged murderers. They do not seem to have waited on 'the law's delays' though, for later that same year William le Hastings, Thomas son of Master William de Goldington, John son of Robert de Goldington (this must have been a different John, possibly son of Robert I, provost in 1264, and here referred to as John IV), Hugh le Granger and others were accused of assaulting Robert de Meaburn to avenge Nicholas le Hastings' murder![76] We don't know what they did, but they seem to have stopped short of killing him.

This was only one of a host of shenanigans involving the leading citizens of Appleby in this period. In 1291 Thomas le Breton and Thomas Wynd, bailiffs, were arrested and deprived of their office for setting free Nicholas Oversleigh, a prisoner accused of the murder of his maidservant Beatrice, and John de Karleolo (Carlisle), coroner of the borough, was accused of connivance and of making a false declaration as to the cause of her death. John de Goldington (?IV) and Hugh le Granger were elected bailiffs instead of le Breton and Wynd – and John de Goldington promptly let the miscreants out of gaol "without Hugh le Granger's knowledge or consent" but with the connivance of William de Goldington II the mayor![76]

William de Goldington II was in the middle of fresh rumpuses in 1292. They involved Peter de Appleby, merchant and citizen of York, with whom the borough seems to have had a long-running feud. We do not know much about Peter, but it is tempting to imagine him as a local man who had moved to York and was exploiting the privilege it gave him of freedom from tolls in his old home town! In 1291 he sued William de

Prosperous Borough

Goldington, mayor, and the whole community of Appleby for interfering with his trade in the town to the damage of 200 marks, and they were admonished.[78] In 1292 Peter accused William de Goldington II, John de Carlisle, Hugh le Granger and Thomas (II) son of Master William de Goldington of having in 1287 taken from him two tuns of wine priced at ten marks, five ox hides priced at ten shillings and two stone of wool priced at seven shillings. Compensation of £10 was claimed but the jury found that the defendants had not taken the hides or wool, but only one tun of wine worth four marks: they therefore awarded reduced damages of twenty shillings.[76] Presumably nobody worried much about the mayor and other worthies being found guilty of stealing a barrel of wine – especially from the obnoxious Peter!

This seems to be a separate case from one which led John de Carlisle, the coroner, to be ordered in 1292 to cause Gilbert de Burneside, deputy sheriff of Westmorland, to come before the king and explain why he had failed to return the king's writ of the Statute of Merchants in favour of Peter de Appleby against Sir William de Strickland for a debt of 100s.[76] William de Strickland was another member of the de Goldington circle – in 1293 his son Walter married William de Goldington II's daughter Eleanor (they were divorced in 1298) – so that the denial of justice to Peter may be another part of the feud.

But this was not the only set of murky dealings. In 1292 Maud, widow of John the son of Reginald of Appleby, complained that Thomas le Breton and John, son of Robert de Goldington (John IV), had not paid for cloth they had bought from her. That same year, William de Goldington II and Hugh le Granger were indicted for selling bread and wine at Appleby contrary to the statute of assize and a year later William de Goldington II, his brother Thomas II and Sir Robert l'Engleys were prosecuted for unpaid debt. In 1294 William de Barwise, later MP for the borough, appeared with Peter de la Dring (one of the bailiffs formerly sued for wrongful arrest by Robert de Meaburn) before John le Surreys the mayor to acknowledge a debt of £10 to Henry le Scot of Newcastle upon Tyne: later they were ordered to be imprisoned for non-payment. In 1304 William de Goldington II and his brother Thomas II were sued for trespass by the Master of St Leonard's Hospital in York. In 1307 William de Barwise, who had been MP two years before, was also sued for trespass. Being on the wrong side of the law seemed no disqualification for election as mayor, provost, bailiff or coroner of Appleby in the late thirteenth century – or, indeed, as representative of the borough in Parliament when it began to return two members from 1295 onwards! In fact, of 34 people listed as MPs for Appleby between 1295 and 1326, three had been imprisoned at some time, two had been fined and six more had been at the wrong end of various judgements.[76]

Almost all the earliest mayors of Appleby were de Goldingtons. Master William held office in 1264 and 1265: William II in 1291, 1292 and 1294; William III, second son of William II, in 1322 and 1337; and Robert III (who could have been the younger son of William III) in 1361. As to other families, John le Surreys was mayor for a brief spell in 1292 but non-de Goldington names do not take over until John de Burgdon in 1353, followed (after Robert de Goldington III in 1361) by John de Threlkeld (1373, 1374), William de Hiltonne (1376), Thomas de Warcopp (1377, 1378), Thomas de Corbrigg (1388), Thomas de Malestang (1389), William de Thornburgh (1391, 1397) and John Mauchaile (1398).[74] Assuming that the list is complete, the implication is that the mayors did not hold office for fixed periods.

The list of MPs for the borough commences in November 1295.[48; 76] In this early period Parliaments were summoned at intervals and sat only for short periods, in York and even Northampton and Carlisle as well as London and Westminster, so that membership was an occasional commitment. Appleby's first representatives were Robert de Goldington and John de Carlisle. This Robert may have been Robert II, son of the provost of 1264: he served as MP again in 1315. John de Carlisle, who also represented Appleby in 1298, was the coroner of the borough caught up in the scandal over the release of Nicholas Oversleigh from gaol. Hugh le Granger (one of the bailiffs accused of wrongfully imprisoning Robert de Meaburn), William Green and William Spavys served in 1298 and 1300. William de Goldington II and William de Berwys (Barwise) were members in 1302 and 1305. William de Goldington II also represented the county of Westmorland as a 'shire knight' in 1307, and sat for the last time for the borough in 1315: he died in 1319. It is clear that by the time of his death he had acquired property outside Appleby for in 1309 he and Sir Walter de Strickland were summoned to defend their demesne in the Marches against Scots incursions.[76] Among other members of 'Appleby's First Family,' Cuthbert de Goldington was MP in 1313 (his parentage is unknown), William de Goldington III in 1319 and 1322 and William IV 'son of John' in 1322.[76] This latter William may

The de Goldingtons of Appleby

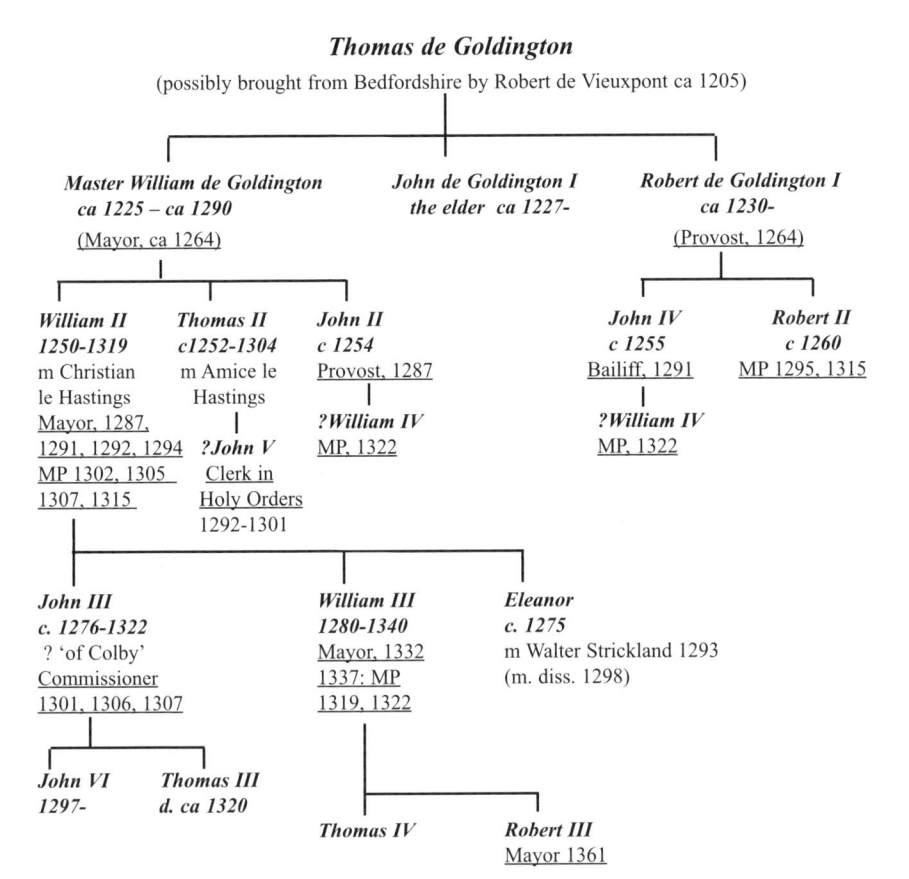

Thomas de Goldington
(possibly brought from Bedfordshire by Robert de Vieuxpont ca 1205)

- **_Master William de Goldington_** ca 1225 – ca 1290 (Mayor, ca 1264)
  - **_William II_** 1250-1319
    m Christian le Hastings
    Mayor, 1287, 1291, 1292, 1294
    MP 1302, 1305 1307, 1315
    - **_John III_** c. 1276-1322
      ? 'of Colby'
      Commissioner 1301, 1306, 1307
      - **_John VI_** 1297-
      - **_Thomas III_** d. ca 1320
    - **_William III_** 1280-1340
      Mayor, 1332 1337: MP 1319, 1322
      - **_Thomas IV_**
      - **_Robert III_** Mayor 1361
    - **_Eleanor_** c. 1275
      m Walter Strickland 1293 (m. diss. 1298)
  - **_Thomas II_** c1252-1304
    m Amice le Hastings
    - **_?John V_** Clerk in Holy Orders 1292-1301
  - **_John II_** c 1254
    Provost, 1287
    - **_?William IV_** MP, 1322
- **_John de Goldington I_** the elder ca 1227-
- **_Robert de Goldington I_** ca 1230- (Provost, 1264)
  - **_John IV_** c 1255
    Bailiff, 1291
    - **_?William IV_** MP, 1322
  - **_Robert II_** c 1260
    MP 1295, 1315

have been the son of John II, the provost of 1287 or John IV, the bailiff of 1291. The list of MPs also includes members of the Barwise, le Breton, de Carlisle, de Corbridge, Franceys (ancestors of the de Cliburns), le Granger, de Harcla, de Lowther, de Penrith and de Warcop families.[76]

I have attempted to compile a family tree, putting all the perplexing de Goldingtons in some sort of order, but a lot of it is guesswork. For example, which John was the 'John de Goldington of Colby' who was Commissioner for Westmorland in 1301, 1306 and 1307? We know that he had at least two sons, John who must have been born in 1297 as he was 25 when he succeeded his father in 1322 and Thomas who died before that year.[76] I have tentatively equated him with John III, son of William II, but this is pure conjecture as is the suggestion that 'John, son of Thomas,' Clerk in Holy Orders in 1292-1301 was the son of Thomas II. And I cannot place Cuthbert, MP in 1313 anywhere! Nor do we know whether the Appleby family was related to Thomas de Goldyngton, King's Clerk and royal surgeon, who was Master of the Hospital of St Nicholas in Carlisle in 1333 (but is described as a 'burgess of Derby').[86] As late as 1450 a house known as Goldington Hall stood in Boroughgate, though by then it belonged to 'William Oerdo junior.'[59] The site is thought to have been at the top of the hill, where what is now Shaw's Wiend swings round and joins Boroughgate. The de Goldington family loom out of the mists of Appleby's past, as a powerful (and probably unscrupulous) tribe of merchants in the most prosperous period of its history. They would repay further research.

Appleby was on the beaten track in the late thirteenth century. In 1292 it was visited by a group of officials enquiring into the burning of Carlisle.[70] Its prosperity led to an almost complete rebuilding of St Lawrence's Church, most of the present fabric dating from the late thirteenth or early fourteenth century.[9] The rebuilding must have included the chantry chapel dedicated to the Virgin Mary that Thomas and John de Goldington had founded and William de Goldington had endowed in 1280. A second chantry, dedicated to St Nicholas, was founded in the same church by Robert de Threlkeld, and endowed with several burgages. St Michael's Church, though an appendage of the castle rather than the borough, was also extended by a south aisle and transept in around 1300.[9]

It is quite possible that the bridge across the Eden was rebuilt in this period. We know that a river crossing must have been an original feature of the new borough, but the record in the Pipe Rolls for 1198 of expenditure of 40 shillings on "repairs to the bridge of the Castle of Appleby" probably did not refer to this structure.[72] In 1382, in contrast, there is a clear reference to 'the stanebrigg' of Appleby,[43] confirming that there was a proper stone bridge by the fourteenth century. It is also mentioned in four wills between 1357 and 1374.[59] We cannot be sure of the date of the bridge drawn by the celebrated artist Thomas Girtin in 1793 (frontispiece, page 8) and surveyed by Joseph Bintley the Westmorland County Surveyor in 1887, but both drawing and survey describe a mediaeval stone structure, with two round, ribbed arches. According to Bintley it was 103 feet long, with steep approaches and an original road width of about thirteen feet (later widened to fifteen feet).[87] The masonry rested on huge oak foundations[58] (as the borough's ceremonial gavel, presented by Mr C R Rivington in 1895, was made out of one of these oak timbers taken from twelve feet below the river bed,[78] in theory it could be used to date the structure, but at the cost of partial destruction of the gavel!) Resemblances to the Devil's Bridge at Kirkby Lonsdale (which received a grant of pontage for repair in 1365) have been pointed out,[58] but the Royal Commission on Historical Monuments considered that "the round form of the arches" of the Devil's Bridge "would seem to indicate that the existing structure was rebuilt not earlier than late in the fifteenth or early in the sixteenth century."[9] If this is valid, the comment would apply equally to Appleby old bridge.

The Appleby bridge differed from the one at Kirkby Lonsdale in having the gatehouse at the western end, incorporating the Chapel and Oratory of St John the Baptist. A plan, drawn when this building had been extended and turned into the county gaol in the seventeenth century,[88] suggests that the ground floor originally consisted of a pair of

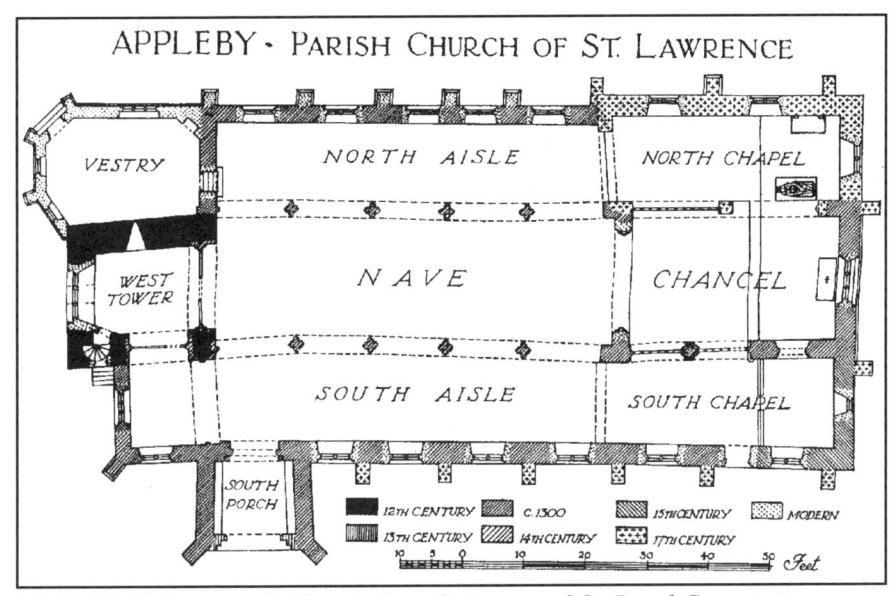

Plan 2 - St Lawrence's Church, from the Report of the Royal Commission on Historical Monuments, © *Crown copyright.*

rooms, one on either side of the roadway. We can speculate that one was used as a kind of 'porter's lodge' by guards regulating the flow of traffic to and from the market, collecting tolls and (perhaps) apprehending people accused of malpractices. The other may well have been the chapel, where wayfarers went to pray for a safe journey home. A spiral staircase gave access to an upper floor, part of which may have been the oratory (perhaps with a lodging for the chantry priest), and another part a strong room for tolls received and possibly also for municipal documents. Over the arch of the gateway there was a Latin inscription:

> *PORTA PATENS ESTO NVLLI CLAVDATVR HONESTO*
> *Gate be open! Closed to no honest man!*

which again suggests a homily for fair trade rather than a defiance of enemies.[48]

Like all well-to-do towns Appleby began to attract religious foundations. The first was the Hospital of St Nicholas, granted to Shap Abbey by John de Vieuxpont in 1235. It was almost certainly located west of the borough across the Eden, on the site now occupied by the Holme Farm (and within St Michael's rather than St Lawrence's parish). Such evidence as we have suggests that it was primarily a grange (or farm) but with a chapel and place for the sick. Confirming the gift in October 1240, the Bishop of Carlisle, William Mauclerk, imposed the condition that the monks should there maintain three lepers for ever.[48; 59] It was still flourishing in 1411, for in that year Abbot Robert of Shap let "to farm to John Milthorpp junior for the term of ten years the Hospital of St Nicholas near Appleby within the vill of Bondgate with all its meadows woods pastures and also two oxgangs of land" at a rental of four marks paid in equal instalments at Pentecost and Michaelmas.[89]

The largest monastic foundation in Appleby was the house of Carmelite Friars (White Friars) known as the Friary of St Mary.[90] This was established in 1281, supposedly by the Lords Vesey, Clifford, and Percy[48] in Battlebarrow, *battel beorg*, 'the fertile hill' in St Michael's parish[43] (Map 4). Religious houses were often built on the edge of towns, or just outside their boundaries, and the location of the Friary in Battlebarrow is a pointer to the built-up area extending to the present Station Road by the 1280s. The Carmelite order, which as the name suggests originated around Mount Carmel,[90] was brought to England by returning Crusaders, and a Lord Vesey and Lord Percy were concerned in the establishment of its first House at Hulne in Northumberland in

1241. It soon became one of the most popular of the orders of Friars. Although Carmelite houses were rarely large or ostentatious, the Friary must have had a church and graveyard, cells for the friars, a kitchen and a gatehouse. We know that it had fishponds, supplied by a stream from a spring called the Lady Well. It also had accommodation for travellers, and in 1300 it provided lodging to no less a person than King Edward I, for he sent "four shillings to the Appleby brothers of Mount Carmel for one day's maintenance" from Brougham on 23 July that year, and gave a similar amount on his return south in the following November.[25; 90] In 1305 John de Crumbewell and his wife Idonea, formerly de Leyburn, endowed it with a plot of land in Battlebarrow.[90]

What would it have been like to visit Appleby in around 1300? Imagine you came from the north, branching off the Roman road from Kirkby Thore below the Gallows Hill with its dark gibbet. As you followed the rutted lane down Battlebarrow, the meadows, paddocks and orchards of the Friary would have spread on your left around its modest church, its cluster of cells and its refectory, kitchen and guest house, all surrounded by a low wall and approached from the road through a simple gatehouse. The gate, church and principal buildings were probably

Figure 3 - Appleby from the Sands. The most picturesque of the old views, showing the bridge and St. Lawrence's Church. Drawn by T. Allom, 1813.

of stone, but the barns and byres would have been of timber and roofed with thatch. Your horse would have been glad to pause and drink at a roadside trough fed from the Lady Well. Opposite, on the west of Battlebarrow, stood the first of the town's houses – timber-framed and thatched and very possibly with a central door giving access on one side to the living room, with sleeping loft above, and on the other to the byre and hayloft. The Battlebarrow tenements were less densely packed than those in the town centre, and some were probably smallholdings, herding their livestock on their little tofts and cultivating strips of land on the lord of the manor's field to the west.

From Battlebarrow you would drop downhill to the Sands, where another row of simple houses and sheds faced the road and the river. Across the Eden you would have seen the Vicar's Croft, with its three acres of gardens, orchard and corn-land, and the town Butts where archery was practised by all the able-bodied young men. Ahead, the narrow stone bridge with its two high, round arches and its gatehouse guarded access to the heart of the borough. The low, thatched roofs of the town would have packed densely beside Briggate and Boroughgate, the tower of St Lawrence's Church and the distant castle keep rising above them much more grandly than they do over today's taller buildings. A fume of peat- and wood-smoke would have hung over all, and the place would have smelled strongly of horse, cow and manure. Pigs (lean, reddish-coloured and hairy, like today's Tamworth) and chickens would have rooted and scratched in piles of rubbish, and the roadside gutters would have borne slops and effluent to the river.

People and animals would have mingled on the streets. Carmelite Friars in their long habits might be pacing down from Battlebarrow to serve in a church chantry or preach in the market. On market days the narrow way over the bridge would have been packed with country and town folk, many in homespun woollen tunics, gathered at the waist, and the grander merchants in woollen doublets and hose, with coloured cloaks over their shoulders and bonnets on their heads. A few might have pushed through the crowds on horseback, and packhorses bearing bales or panniers laden with goods would have jostled for position with horse- and bullock-drawn wooden carts.

Crossing the bridge, you might well have had to give an account of yourself at the gatehouse and pay a toll, and the chantry priest might bid you give thanks for your arrival and offer alms for a safe return. In

Prosperous Borough

Boroughgate, barley, wheat, vegetables (especially cabbages, kale, peas and beans), butter, cheese, eggs, leather, bales of wool, measures of cloth, pots, pans, earthenware and barrels of ale and wine would have been spread for your choice on wooden stalls, the attendants shouting their wares much as they still do in street markets all over the world. You could buy chickens, ducks and geese in season, but turkeys had not yet been discovered. Higher up the hill, the butchers' stalls and shambles would have offered freshly-killed meat, and the smell, blood and offal would have marked where beasts had been slaughtered. Squeals, bellows or bleats might well ring out as another animal was despatched to meet customer demand.

Boroughgate probably had some bigger, stone-built, houses even as early as 1300 and Goldington Hall, up near the castle gate, would have been one of them. The bulk of the houses and sheds, however, would

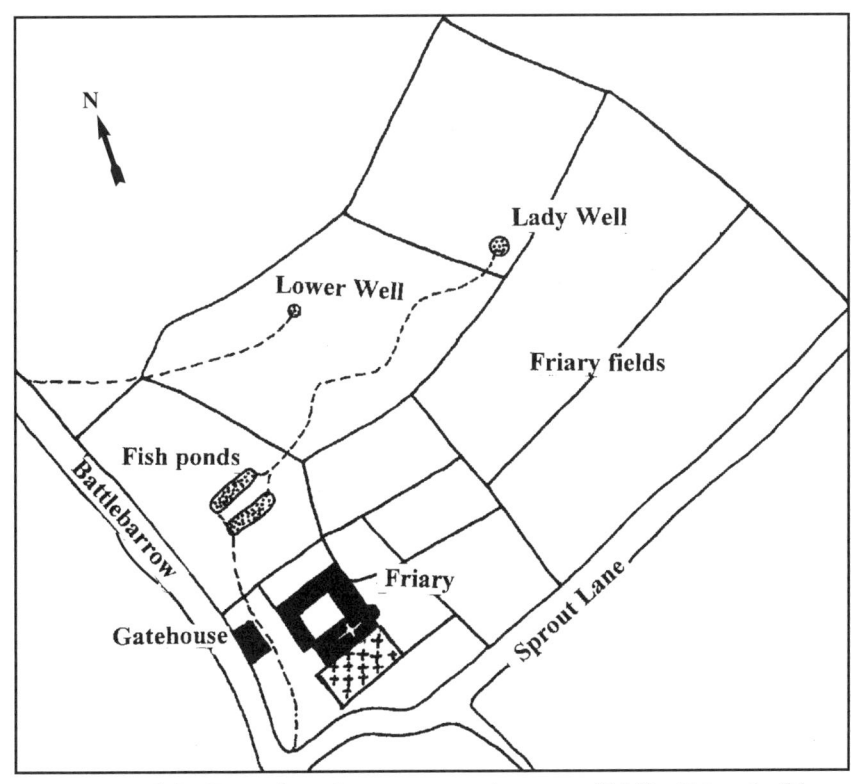

Map 4 - Appleby Friary based on a manuscript map of 1543. Friary buildings and gatehouse conjectural. Redrawn from Thwaytes, reference 90.

have been timber-framed and thatched and packed closely about narrow yards that opened off the main thoroughfare. There would have been numerous taverns where you could get refreshments after your travel. But you could not have had a cup of tea or coffee: the first coffee house in England was not opened until 1652.[91] Nor could you smoke a cigarette: tobacco was 300 years away in the future. Your drinks would have been ale of varying strength (and without hops), red wine from Gascony, or milk. The foods on offer would have been barley or wheat bread with butter, meat, fish or cheese and vegetable concoctions like pease pudding. Cooked dishes would have been highly flavoured with spices or vinegar (covering up the taint of meat that had been stored too long in an age without refrigeration) and many would be highly coloured with dyes like saffron. In the most up-market taverns you might have been served game. If you had a sweet tooth, honey was the best option, for sugar was a rare delicacy before the 1640s.[91]

The castle doors would have been firmly shut to any except grand visitors, but St Lawrence's Church would have been a port of call for most, and you would feel more at home there for the church was roughly the same size and shape as today and the tower would have been familiar, though the porch and nave arcade might not yet have been rebuilt in their present form. Inside, however, the walls would have been plastered and decorated and figures of the Saints, some richly coloured and gilded, would have stood in the niches. The decoration and fittings of the two chantry chapels would have reflected the wealth of their donors – especially the de Goldingtons – and the flame of a lamp would have burned perpetually in the Chantry of the Blessed Virgin Mary.

So, as the fourteenth century opened, we can glimpse Appleby as a vigorous market town, led by powerful merchants who were well able to defend its rights even against the lords of the barony. It had a representation in Parliament equal to that of the county. It had gained two religious foundations, one of them big enough to be used as lodgings by the king. War had not touched it for nearly a century. The future must have looked bright indeed. But the brightness proved the falsest of false dawns.

CHAPTER 4

Decline and Fall

THE thirteenth century was a time of national prosperity. The climate was good, agriculture flourished and the population of England soared to four million or more. In the north, there was peaceful co-existence between England and Scotland, tied together by inter-marriage and by many noblemen who held lands in both countries.[92] This peace was the key to the rise of Appleby as a prosperous borough. In contrast, the fourteenth century was "scarred by a war of attrition... interspersed by periods of uneasy truce."[28] At the heart of the conflict lay the insistence of successive English kings – including Edward I, II and III – that they were sovereigns of the whole island of Great Britain.

In 1286 King Alexander III of Scotland, last of the macMalcolm kings whose lineage traced back through Malcolm Canmore to Kenneth macAlpin, died. He was Edward I's brother-in-law and they had been on friendly terms, but Alexander's death, followed in 1290 by that of his only surviving grandchild, Margaret 'the Maid of Norway', created a power vacuum in Scotland.[28; 93] In 1291 King Edward told his council that he would resolve it by assuming rule over the northern kingdom himself.[93] He was already well on the way to the conquest of Wales, which he completed in 1295, encircling the Principality in a ring of great castles.

He gained his opportunity when he was invited by the Scots, as a respected jurist, to adjudicate between thirteen claimants or 'competitors' for the throne. He agreed to do so – on condition that all the competitors acknowledged him as feudal overlord and ceded him possession of the royal castles in Scotland.[92] In 1292 he awarded the kingdom to John Balliol, Lord of Galloway and descendant of David I, who did, indeed, have the strongest claim. Balliol did homage to Edward and was duly crowned at Scone – and the English king forthwith did his best to make the new King of Scots his puppet.[93] But there were powerful lords in Scotland who grabbed control of the strings. In 1295 Edward called upon Balliol to support England in a war with France which would have taken Scottish aristocrats overseas in Edward's army. There was a 'palace revolution' in which a council of lords pushed Balliol aside and made an alliance with France.[28; 92] In 1296, Carlisle was attacked and Lanercost Priory ten miles to the east was burned.

King Edward was not one to tolerate impertinent subordinates, and he retaliated by taking war across the Border, capturing Berwick on Tweed and thrusting northwards to Edinburgh and Stirling.[93] King John Balliol was seized and despatched to the Tower of London along with the Stone of Scone, King Edward commenting scornfully that "a man does good business when he rids himself of a turd."[28; 93] Rather than set up another puppet, Edward appointed Earl Warenne as Governor of Scotland, under his direct command.[92; 93]

This English take-over was the spur to William Wallace's revolt of 1297 (which sought Balliol's restoration). Victorious at Stirling Bridge, Wallace chased Warenne and his supporters out of Scotland and began raiding into Northumberland and Cumbria. One thrust, late in 1297, may have hit Appleby for the Scots swung south from Carlisle through Inglewood, crossed Stainmore and menaced Durham.[93] Edward I once more thundered northwards and in 1298, true to his nick-name 'hammer of the Scots', thumped Wallace at Falkirk and re-imposed his authority. A ding-dong of punch and counter-punch none the less rattled on until 1305 when Wallace was captured and butchered.[93]

After Wallace's execution an illusory quiet fell over the Borders and the folk of Appleby may well have breathed more easily and got back to business. But early in 1306 Robert Bruce, Earl of Carrick, descendant of King David I and grandson of the other leading 'competitor', began his rise to power. In February of that year Bruce murdered his bitter rival John 'the Red' Comyn and claimed the kingship of Scotland: on 25 March he was enthroned at Scone. But only a few months later he was chased out of his kingdom by Edward I, now aged and ailing, his son Edward of Caernarvon (later Edward II), and their supporters.[92; 93] Among the latter was Robert Clifford of Westmorland, first Lord Clifford, son of Roger and Isabella. With Henry Percy, Clifford led an invasion on the west that occupied Dumfries.[93]

Robert Clifford was a powerful figure in the closing years of Edward I's reign. He had become Lord Warden of the Marches at the age of 23, and subsequently Lord High Admiral of England, Earl Marshal, and one of the four guardians appointed by the king for Edward of Caernarvon.[48; 85] He greatly strengthened Brougham Castle, enlarging the keep, building the adjacent double gatehouse, and adding the so-called Tower of League in the south-west corner of the bailey. With these extensions, Brougham became a more formidable stronghold than Appleby, despite the relative weakness of its site.[25] But neither castle could hold back the tide that was to come.

When King Edward I died on the shores of the Solway in 1307, Robert Bruce's gateway to power re-opened. During 1308 he recovered more and more land, including Robert Clifford's Castle Douglas.[92] By 1309 he had held his first parliament and mounted his first raids into England.[28] Robert Clifford does not seem to have been involved in resistance to these incursions, though he was one of the emissaries sent by Edward II in November 1309 to negotiate an extended Border truce. He remained Warden of the Western March, and in 1310 was granted the castle and lands of Skipton in Craven in exchange for the earlier Clifford holdings in Monmouthshire. In the same year he raised a strong force of eight bannerets, 26 knights and maybe 150 mounted troopers, presumably as a contribution to a royal army that invaded Scotland. One of the knights was Andrew de Harcla: another was Henry de Appleby, who had served Clifford first in 1307.[94; 95]

It was not until 1311 that the Scottish threat to the Marches really boiled over into action. In August King Robert Bruce launched two raids into northern England, both from Solway into Tynedale. They lasted eight and fifteen days respectively.[93] The English court, meanwhile, was absorbed in a power struggle against Piers Gaveston, Earl of Cornwall, King Edward II's hated favourite. Even Border lords like Robert Clifford were busy pursuing Gaveston, neglecting the defence of Cumberland and Westmorland in the process.[92; 93]

Robert of Scotland took advantage of the turmoil among the English nobles and began to loot the northern counties.[92] Unlike the campaigns over a century before, the aim was plunder rather than territory and there was relatively little loss of life, except among those who resisted. The raids were carried out by hobelars – fast moving and lightly armed mounted soldiers – and they usually lasted only a couple of weeks (though as they got bigger and bolder the period stretched to over a month). Money, precious metals, armour, iron and other high-value portable goods were the preferred booty, along with captives who could be ransomed. Cattle were also taken, because they could be driven back into Scotland.⁽⁹²; ⁹³⁾ What could not be carried off was burned, and the timber-framed and thatched houses of this period were bonfires waiting for a light. The code of chivalry in those days did not extend to the common people.

The English, moreover, were offered a choice. They could have a truce if they paid for it! In 1311 Northumberland did pay £2,000 for six months immunity from raids. Durham paid 900 marks for 'protection' between August 1312 and June 1313 while Northumberland paid a second £2,000 in 1313.⁽⁹⁶⁾ This bought safety for the eastern March, but not for the west. In 1312 Robert Bruce actually based himself at Lanercost Priory, raiding as far south as Durham and burning Corbridge and Hexham. By this time Robert Clifford had been replaced as Warden of the Western March by Sir Andrew de Harcla, but this did not stop the rot.⁽⁹⁵⁾ In April 1313 Edward Bruce, King Robert's brother, established himself at Rose Castle, south of Carlisle, and collected cattle and prisoners in Inglewood Forest and the surrounding countryside. Penrith was burned on 17 April and Appleby may have been affected for the Royal manor of Hoff is listed among those that suffered loss.⁽⁹²⁾ This experience, perhaps rubbed in by the Scottish capture of the Isle of Man in 1313, giving Bruce control over the northern part of the Irish Sea, may explain why the Western March raised £1466 in 1313-1314, and gained a brief respite from raids.⁽⁹⁶⁾ It was all carefully planned. As one of Bruce's own poets put it:

> *the King went oft on this manneir*
> *In Ingland for till riche his men*
> *That in riches aboundanit then* ⁽⁹⁷⁾

While these events rolled forward, Robert Clifford was elsewhere. But in 1312, following Piers Gaveston's capture and execution, Clifford was appointed by the barons to seek a reconciliation between them and the king.⁽⁸⁵⁾ By October 1313 this had been achieved – after a fashion – and King Edward at last moved to crush King Robert and put an end to the systematic looting of his northern borders.⁽⁹³⁾ In May 1314, Edward II marched through Northumberland to Edinburgh with a massive army, and Robert Clifford was one of the commanders. On 23 June Clifford and Henry Beaumont led a force of cavalry that sought to relieve the gar-

Decline and Fall

rison of Stirling.⁽⁹³⁾ This assault was blocked by the Earl of Moray, King Robert Bruce's nephew, and on the following morning Clifford was among the thousands slain in the main battle of Bannockburn. When he died, his sons Roger and Robert were both minors.

Bannockburn was not only a disaster for the English army, but effectively put paid to Edward I's dream of making all of Great Britain a Plantagenet empire, although Edward II never conceded this. It was, as the passionately anti-Scots poet John Skelton put it,

> *When Edward of Carnarvon*
> *Lost all that his father won* ⁽⁹⁸⁾

Although Carlisle remained strongly garrisoned by Andrew de Harcla during the Bannockburn campaign, with five esquires, 50 men at arms, 30 hobelars and around 200 archers,⁽⁹⁵⁾ the defeat threw the northern Borders wide-open to incursions, which lasted longer and penetrated even farther south than before. The raids began to follow a pattern, beginning on the richer eastern lands of Durham and Yorkshire, then crossing the Pennines and returning either down the Eden Valley or, on occasion, along the west Cumbrian coastal plain.⁽⁹²⁾ In August 1314 Edward Bruce led a force that thrust south from Berwick on Tweed to Richmond and crossed Stainmore. Somewhere near the Rey Cross he was waylaid by Andrew de Harcla, but the latter seems to have had the worst of it, losing sixteen horses, and the Scots re-grouped, burning Brough, Appleby and Kirkoswald on their way home.⁽⁹²; ⁹⁴; ⁹⁵⁾ The castles of Brough, Appleby and Brougham escaped destruction, but the Westmorland county court could not be held at Appleby Castle because it was surrounded by Scots raiders.⁽²⁵; ⁹²; ⁹⁵; ⁹⁹⁾

For the next three years King Robert kept up the pressure. His political aim was to force the English to recognise his sovereignty in Scotland, and he did so by dominating an ever-widening slice of territory. In 1315 he threatened the fortified towns of Carlisle and Berwick-on-Tweed, while his brother Edward began a systematic campaign to make himself King of Ireland.⁽⁹²⁾ On the western march the Scots "robbed and wasted the countries of Allerdale, Copeland and Westmorland,"⁽⁵³⁾ attacking Penrith and setting siege to Carlisle. The city was staunchly defended by Sir Andrew de Harcla, at the head of a garrison of six knights, about 100 men at arms, 46 hobelars and 326 archers. Indeed, de Harcla not only held out but launched a counter-raid into Scotland where he seized over 100 head of cattle and captured Sir John de Morreve and Sir Robert Bard.[92; 94; 95] But de Harcla was himself captured in another such engagement, and was not ransomed until 1316.

That year began with another truce (while yet more inconsequential peace talks went on), but turmoil as usual resumed at midsummer. Although the English still had the option of paying protection money the records suggest that this system broke down pretty completely on the western march.[96] As raid succeeded raid, the border regions near to Scotland became more and more devastated and less and less productive of booty, which was one reason why the incursions thrust ever deeper into England.[92] In 1316 the Scots penetrated far into Yorkshire, where Richmond was saved by payment of tribute but manors near Barnard Castle and in Wensleydale suffered badly. One group of raiders then crossed into the Eden Valley where they burned Penrith and Carleton, while others stormed through Kendal and Lonsdale and went home along the west Cumbrian coast.[79; 92] There seems to have been some kind of truce in 1317 (cynics might suggest that it made sense for King Robert to allow a breathing space while his intended victims gathered more potential plunder), but in 1318 Berwick on Tweed was taken by treachery, Wark Castle was captured and a massive raid penetrated as far south as Knaresborough and Skipton, crossing the Pennines to Preston and returning via Lancaster.

King Edward II had played no direct part in the Border wars since Bannockburn, but the fall of Berwick stung him into action.[93] In 1319 he led an army to besiege it – and King Robert responded by launching a major diversionary raid under the Earl of Moray and Sir James Douglas which scattered the local levies at Myton near Boroughbridge before turning home through Lancashire and Cumbria.[93] Later that year there was a second and intensely destructive raid into the western march – again led by Moray and Douglas. It took place in November when the barns were full of harvested grain. The Scots by-passed Carlisle and "kept their journey until they came to Brough under Stainmore, destroying all before them, and returned through Westmorland, practising the like mischief there."[53] Once again a truce was negotiated, and it lasted from November 1319 to January 1322,[92; 93] when it broke down with a vengeance.

Throughout most of this period the key figure on the English side was

Decline and Fall

Andrew de Harcla, Warden of the Western March and Keeper of Carlisle. He held his post despite inadequate manpower (appeals for reinforcements fell upon deaf Royal ears).[95] De Harcla is a surprising figure to find in such a key position. He was one of six sons of Sir Michael de Harcla, who held Hartley and Smardale, near Kirkby Stephen, from the Barony of Appleby. Sir Michael represented Westmorland in Parliament in 1301, but was really a minor actor on the regional stage.[76] The family played no significant part in Westmorland history and their castle at Hartley, though on a strong site, does not seem to have been much of a fortress. It is presumed that Sir Andrew achieved fame and power by his skill as a soldier, and some credit him with the first use of mounted archers.[95] He seems to have been a rather autocratic ruler of Carlisle and this may well have made him enemies among the grander aristocracy who almost certainly saw him as an upstart.[92; 94; 95] At the height of his power he also had authority over the Clifford castles of Appleby and Brougham, Roger, second Lord Clifford being only fourteen when his father was killed at Bannockburn, though until 1318 their actual custodian was Roger Clifford's uncle, Bartholomew de Badlesmere, who had at his command a total of 42 men-at-arms and 30 hobelars – scarcely the force to deter powerful incursions, especially when divided between two sites.[85; 94] Andrew de Harcla himself had charge of Pendragon Castle, as tenant of Idonea de Leyburn.[94] His sister married Thomas de Musgrave sometime before 1301, and this may explain why the Hartley estates – after passing briefly through the hands of Sir Hugh de Lowther, Sir Thomas de Rokeby and Ralph Neville of Raby – were granted to the Musgrave family following Sir Andrew's disgrace.[100]

The year 1322 was one of the most turbulent in the whole history of the north of England. There were three massive Scots raids, while the English nobility were engulfed in civil strife. In January the Earl of Moray, James the Steward and Sir James Douglas attacked Durham, seized Darlington and threatened York.[92] There is evidence that they acted in concert with King Edward II's cousin Thomas, Earl of Lancaster, and the Earl of Hereford, who headed a rebellion sparked by enmity to a new group of royal favourites, the Despensers. Roger Clifford and Bartholomew de Badlesmere were both among the rebels.[85] Lancaster's and Moray's armies were however prevented from joining forces by Andrew de Harcla who made a truce with the Scots on the western march and led his men from Carlisle to Boroughbridge. Here on 16 March he defeated the rebel Earls. Hereford was killed, Lancaster and Badlesmere were taken prisoner (and later executed), and Roger Clifford, who was captured with them, only escaped execution because of the severity of his wounds.[85] De Harcla was created Earl of Carlisle as a reward for his services, and granted a number of forfeited Clifford estates including his family manor of Hartley.[95]

A truce was again negotiated, but Edward II began to muster forces for an invasion of Scotland and this led King Robert to launch a pre-emptive strike. In June 1322 a large Scottish army led by the king in person, supported by those seasoned campaigners the Earl of Moray and Sir James Douglas, pillaged the Abbey of Holm Cultram. King Robert then led half the army down the west coast and threatened Furness Abbey (where they were bought off by the Abbot),[79; 93; 95] while Moray and Douglas crossed Shap Fells to Kendal and went south down the Lune Valley. The army re-united at Lancaster, which they looted, and attacked Preston "which town he burnt, as he had done others in the country through which he had passed."[53] On the way back, the Scots devastated the country round Carlisle.[92; 93]

This 'Great Raid' lasted three weeks, but it did not prevent the enraged King Edward II from leading his vast army of 20,000 men up the east coast of Scotland as far as Edinburgh. The English burned Musselburgh and captured the Port of Leith, where they waited to be supplied by sea – to no avail as their fleet had been scattered by storms and Flemish privateers.[92] King Edward had no choice but to retreat again into England, while on the western march Andrew de Harcla's powerful forces at Carlisle were disbanded for want of pay. Back came King Robert, crossing the Solway on 30 September, and thrusting across the Pennines in an attempt to capture the English King. Much of the East Riding of Yorkshire was occupied by the Scots, who spent over a month in England before retreating home.

During this period relations between King Edward and Andrew de Harcla broke down. The latter failed to respond to a royal summons in October 1322 (he was in Lancashire gathering reinforcements and only reached the king after the royal forces had been scattered by Moray and Douglas near Byland in the Vale of York).[93] Laden with loot, the Scots went home in November – and the right royal fury with which King Edward greeted the belated de Harcla may have been one factor leading the latter to negotiate a treaty with King Robert Bruce in January 1323.

However in 1320 King Edward had actually given him authority, together with the Bishop of Carlisle, the Abbot of Holm Cultram, the Prior of St Mary's Priory in Carlisle and others including Michael de Harcla his brother, to seek a lasting peace and in February 1322 the king had again empowered him "to treat of a final peace" with King Robert. So when the two met at Lochmaben in Dumfries on 3 January 1323 de Harcla may well have considered that he was acting under royal warrant.[95] But the agreement went too far for Edward II, for it abandoned all English claims to Scotland. It also went too far for many English nobles, for it recognised King Robert's decree that none should retain the lands they had once held in Scotland.[93] The timing also suggests disharmony, for just when de Harcla was concluding his treaty, his monarch was planning yet another invasion of Scotland.[92] Edward II was outraged by the agreement and ordered Sir Anthony de Lucy to arrest de Harcla for high treason.[95]

De Lucy, who had been Keeper of the Liberty of Hexham (Tynedale) in 1315-16, may well have been one of the northern aristocrats antagonised by de Harcla's arrogant manner. He certainly implemented the king's commands with alacrity, seizing the Earl in his own hall in Carlisle. A few days later de Harcla was degraded of his knighthood and executed after no more than a trumpery trial.[95] The result was to remove the most effective leader of English resistance on the western march.[92; 93] De Lucy gave a full account to the king of the garrisons of Carlisle, Naworth, Egremont, Cockermouth, Appleby, Brougham, Pendragon and Highhead, all of which de Harcla had held, and this shows how lightly the region was defended. All eight strongholds together only had a total of six knights, 64 men at arms, 91 hobelars and between 83 and 92 foot soldiers. The Appleby contingent did not include any knights or foot soldiers at all, but had ten men at arms and 30 hobelars.[94] Nor did de Harcla's disgrace prevent the inevitable: a thirteen-year truce was concluded at Bishopsthorpe in May 1323.[93]

Even then, Edward II continued to manoeuvre to keep his claims to Scotland alive. There were fresh upheavals on the western march, with raiders around Appleby and Kirkby Stephen in July 1327.[92] Matters were apparently settled in October that year, in the Treaty of Edinburgh and Northampton, and by then Edward II had been deposed and his young son proclaimed as Edward III. The treaty was called 'the shameful peace' by the English because it formally acknowledged Scottish independence – in return for which the Scots promised to pay compensation of £20,000 for damage done in northern England and for the loss of English titles to lands in Scotland. This latter concession infuriated 'the disinherited' English magnates, and their anger was later enhanced when they failed to get the money. The treaty also provided for a marriage between King Robert's son David and Joan of the Tower, sister of King Edward III.[92; 93] It was planned for 1338 when both would be fourteen.

The treaty appeared to end fourteen years during which the Scots had come and gone in northern England almost as they pleased. Those years of conflict must have made life impossible for a merchant community like that of Appleby. The town suffered in three ways – first through the direct impact of the looting and burning, second, through the impoverishment of the country around, and third through the near-total disruption of commerce.

Quite apart from the wars, the early fourteenth century was a bad time for farming. The harvests failed in 1315-16, and sheep murrain and cattle plague (possibly rinderpest) followed in 1319-21.[79] Many carts and ploughs were pulled by bullocks in this period, and their loss to disease and Scots raiding must have paralysed agriculture. Warfare and disease drove land out of cultivation and pushed food prices up: in 1316 and 1317 they were twice what they had been in 1310. Expensive food meant poorer diet, weakening people and increasing their susceptibility to sickness.[91]

It is not surprising, therefore, that the fee farm rent for Appleby fell into arrears in this period. On 9 April 1312 "the Treasurer and Barons of Exchequer" had been "ordered to take the town of Appleby into the King's hand and deliver it into the keeping of Alexander de Berewiz" (Barwise), "burgess of the same if they find the farm of the said town has not been paid for two years – as according to the custom of the Exchequer it ought to be taken into the King's hands in default after the lapse of such a time."[76] Alexander de Barwise was a merchant, and probably son of William de Barwise who had been MP for the borough in 1302 and 1305: he himself represented it in 1313.

Whether or not the money was paid in 1312, the town was almost certainly damaged in the raids of 1314 and 1319. These also hit the settlement of Langton to the east, which was recorded in 1326 as "the site of a manor burned by the Scots, worth nothing yearly for want of tenants."[76; 101] In 1317 the dues for the whole county could not be paid because of the damage done by the Scots. The Diocese of Carlisle was valued in 1291 for papal tax ('Peter's pence') at £3,151-5s-7d but in 1318 the value had dropped to a mere £480-19s-0d.[2] The Great Raid of 1322 only aggravated the damage. In 1327 it was recorded that only 66 houses were standing in Appleby, and at least seven plots were vacant.[79] The fee farm due to the crown fell into arrears to the tune of £60 (equivalent to four and a half years' rent), and on 26 September 1327 Robert de Lowther (who had been MP for the borough in 1318) was appointed 'farmer of the town of Appleby'. He still held this appointment in 1329.[76] The borough remained in the hands of the king until 1332 when King Edward III "for a fine" (of five marks) "which the said burgesses have paid us have granted them the said town to hold at a rent even as they themselves or their predecessors burgesses of the said town have had the said town and held it at a rent before the said seizure."[48; 74] In 1332 it was also reported that the Carmelite Friary had lost all its charters and muniments in one of these Scots incursions.[90] As late as 1334 an inquisition described a house in Appleby as having been "burnt by the Scots and not yet rebuilt."

Unlike the borough, Appleby Castle seems to have escaped damage in the turmoil between 1314 and 1328, though its garrison was surely too weak to protect the town below it. Roger, second Lord Clifford, had the barony and castle restored to him after Andrew de Harcla's execution and lived on until about 1327.[85] He never married, although he is remembered as partner in a shadowy romance and his mistress, Julian, with whom he had children, is commemorated in a farm still named Julian Bower within the ancient hunting forest of Whinfell.[71] On his death the estates passed to Robert, his brother, third Lord Clifford, who featured more prominently in the Border action that followed.

In 1332, with their rights restored and their prosperity beginning to return, the citizens of Appleby may well have begun to relax. However, that year brought fresh trouble. The 'shameful peace' had antagonised a number of powerful English lords, 'disinherited' from their Scottish estates. King Robert I Bruce had died in 1329 when his son and heir was only five: the child was consecrated as King David II in 1331.[93] With King Robert's firm grip removed, the disinherited saw their chance. So did Edward Balliol, son of the King John who had been so scornfully deposed by King Edward I. Ignoring the peace, in 1332 a force of the disinherited with Balliol as their figurehead invaded Scotland by sea and won a surprise victory over David II's Guardians at Dupplin Moor near Perth. Among the disinherited was the young Robert Clifford who wanted his lands around Castle Douglas back. Following their victory, Balliol was crowned king at Scone in September.[93]

Edward III had stood aside from this action, though he encouraged it privately despite the fact that the child David II was betrothed to his young sister Joan. But once the disinherited had triumphed at Dupplin Moor he switched to open support for their cause, backed Balliol, and renewed his father's and grandfather's claim to be overlord of Scotland. In 1333 he won a resounding victory over David II's Guardians at Halidon Hill in Northumberland, recovered Berwick on Tweed and seized a broad swathe of southern Scotland. He received the homage of Edward Balliol at York in February 1334.[93] King David Bruce and his betrothed queen went into exile in France. North of the Forth, Balliol ruled what was in essence an English puppet kingdom based on Perth while most of southern Scotland was annexed to England and Lothian was plundered to devastation.[28]

These events would have been welcomed in Appleby, for they must have increased the town's apparent security. Following the restoration of the borough's liberties in 1332, the succession of mayors, which had been broken while Robert de Lowther had been 'Keeper of the Borough', was resumed and William de Goldington III held office in 1337.[74; 76] When the charter rights were restored the fee farm remained at twenty marks, suggesting optimism that the borough would regain its former prosperity. And, indeed, it seems to have soon been back on course, for it paid its share of a 'wealth tax' granted by Parliament to King Edward III in 1332. The border counties had been given two years' grace because of the wars but they paid up in 1334. The tax was assessed at one tenth of the value of the 'movable chattels' of all laymen living in boroughs throughout the kingdom (those living outside boroughs paid a fifteenth).[55; 102] Town-dwellers whose property was worth less than six shillings (and country-dwellers worth less than ten shillings) were let off. The assessment was the first attempt to fix a quota that fairly reflected personal wealth in every town and village.[55] In Appleby, the only borough in Westmorland, 52 men were assessed as liable to the tax, with movable goods worth a total of £30-4s-6d: at a tenth this meant a tax of 60 shillings.[102] The richest person was William Russel, whose goods

The Story of Appleby in Westmorland

Photograph 1 - Appleby Castle from the air, showing the 'keyhole' shape of the original motte and bailey. Photograph by Aerofilms Ltd. from Martin Holmes, reference 20.

Photograph 2 - Appleby Castle Keep.

Photograph 3 - The 'Great Picture', central part of the Appleby triptych commissioned by Lady Anne Clifford in 1646. It shows (left to right) Lady Anne's brothers, Sir Robert Clifford and Francis Lord Clifford, her mother Lady Margaret Russell, Countess of Cumberland and her father, George Clifford, Earl of Cumberland. On the walls behind are pictures of her aunts. The two pictures opposite make up the left and right panels. The pictures are reproduced by kind permission of Abbot Hall Art Gallery, Kendal.

The Story of Appleby in Westmorland

Photographs 4 and 5 - The side panels of the Appleby triptych. Left: Lady Anne Clifford, aged fifteen, with her tutor and governess on the paintings behind. Right: Lady Anne, aged 56 with her two husbands - Richard Sackville, Earl of Dorset, and Philip Herbert, Earl of Pembroke and Montgomery - on the paintings behind her.

Photograph 6 - The monument to Lady Anne Clifford in St. Lawrence's Church. Photographs Peter Koronka.

Photograph 7 - St Lawrence's Church.

The Story of Appleby in Westmorland

Photograph 8 - Lord Thanet's mansion, photograph by the author

Photograph 9 - The courtyard, Hospital of St. Anne.

Photograph 10 - The Cloisters as rebuilt in 1811.

Photograph 11 - The organ in St. Lawrence's Church which is believed to be the oldest working organ in the country. Photographs Peter Koronka.

The Story of Appleby in Westmorland

Photograph 12 - The old Grammar School buildings in Low Wiend, with the extension built in 1826 on the left. From E. Hinchcliffe, reference 101.

Photograph 13 - The doorway from the old school, incorporated into the new building.

Photograph 14 - the new Appleby Grammar School, built in 1887.

The Story of Appleby in Westmorland

Photograph 15 - Bongate Mill and Victoria Bridge over the River Eden, seen from the castle in around 1945.

Photograph 16 - Appleby new bridge, built in 1888. Fragments of the inscription from the gatehouse of the old bridge are set in the the end wall of the house on the right.

were worth 35 shillings, rather than a de Goldington – maybe their family fortunes were on the wane by then, despite William III's mayoralty in 1337 and Robert III's in 1361.

The assessment allows us to judge the relative wealth of different communities in the 1330s. Maurice Beresford[55] did this by bringing them all to the common base of one fifteenth of the tax assessment – which is what non-boroughs paid. On that basis, Appleby would have paid 40 shillings – the same as Liverpool and Boroughbridge, but behind Clitheroe (47s), Leeds (73s), Richmond (100s), Egremont (150s) and Carlisle (180s).[55] York was assessed at 2,160 shillings, Newcastle upon Tyne at 1,780, while London was out of sight in the financial stratosphere, with an assessment of 14,667 shillings. Quite clearly, while Appleby was not a failure – there are 28 'planned towns' below it in the list – it was not doing that well either.[55]

Indeed, the tax levied in Appleby was less than that gathered in Kirkby Stephen (67 shillings) and Kendal (48 shillings). However, in the former settlement (which included Wharton, Mallerstang, Winton and Hartley) only nineteen people had 'chattels' worth over ten shillings, making them liable to the tax.[102] In Kendal, also not yet a borough, eighteen people were worth over ten shillings and were hence caught in the tax net.[102] Interestingly, Bongate parish yielded 35 shillings, and Thomas Orre, whose chattels were worth 75 shillings, came higher up the 'rich list' than anyone in the borough.[102] Maybe he was a well to do castle employee.

The implication is that in 1334 Appleby Borough contained a fairly large number of moderately well-off people but nobody of special wealth. The 52 people with goods worth over six shillings were probably almost all heads of households, living in around a fifth of the town's burgages. This would fit with a town impoverished by the wars but struggling back onto its feet. The renewed continuity of representation in Parliament and of mayors, likewise speaks of a community riding out the storm.

There was enough money about to support further gifts to the town's churches. In around 1330 a new chantry was founded in St Michael's Church by Sir William l'Engleys (English), chief forester of Inglewood and a representative of Westmorland in Parliament between 1319 and 1338.[101] He caused it to be dedicated to the Virgin Mary. In 1331 Robert de Threlkeld added to his gifts to the Chantry of St Nicholas in St Lawrence's Church by endowing it with land in Appleby that brought in

£3-4s-7d per annum. The land included a plot named Pear Tree Garth, at the junction of what are now Chapel Street and Low Wiend and another larger plot later called School House Close that is now part of the King George V playing field. It is more than likely that the same priest served both St Nicholas' Chantry and that of St Mary, endowed earlier by the de Goldingtons, and lived in a mansion house included in the de Goldington's endowments. This priest (who may have been a Friar) probably had charge of a school for the children of the burghers, and it was from these chantry foundations that Appleby Grammar School had its beginnings.[101; 103]

Yet another chantry existed in the castle, and a dispute over it arose in 1359, culminating in a verdict given at York against William Colyn, Vicar of St Lawrence's, Appleby, who had endeavoured to throw the charges of service upon the Priory of Wetheral. It would seem therefore, that although the borough had been separated in secular matters, the vicar of St Lawrence still had the duty of performing service in the castle, a duty which perhaps dated back to the original grant of both the Appleby churches by Ranulf le Meschin to the Abbey of St Mary at York, of which Wetheral Priory was a cell. This duty was also neglected by a later vicar of St Lawrence, Thomas de Branby, who in 1406 was excommunicated for his offence.

Appleby bridge, with the chapel and oratory of St John the Baptist in the gatehouse, received bequests in four wills proved between 1357 and 1374. Of these, John de Morland left 25 shillings, John de Burgdon 40 shillings, and Thomas de Anandale 13s-4d (divided among eight bridges).[59] The Carmelite Friary also prospered. In 1335 the friars were given a new charter from King Edward III which referred to "their manse and area with the Oratory, and other buildings as enclosed by walls and dykes".[90] (Map 4). The Diocesan records of Carlisle name 24 Carmelite friars of Appleby who were ordained variously as acolytes, sub-deacons, deacons and priests between 1294 and 1354. Legacies to the Carmelite friars of Appleby were made in 26 wills between 1343 and 1457,[90] often in conjunction with the Dominican ('black') and Franciscan ('grey') Friars of Carlisle and the Augustinian Eremites ('hermit friars') of Penrith.[104] In 1381-82 Roger, fifth Lord Clifford, also gave land to the Hospital of St Nicholas.[105]

Robert Clifford entertained King Edward Balliol at Appleby, Brougham, Brough and Pendragon in 1333 or 1334, and had his father's

Decline and Fall

lands in Douglasdale restored to him, thereby earning the hostility of the Bruce faction.[25; 106] It was while Balliol was at Brougham that a famous hunt took place in Whinfell Forest where a mighty red stag was pursued by a celebrated hound named Hercules. The stag cleared the boundary fence in its last desperate leap but fell dead on the other side, while the hound fell dead within the forest. The incident was recorded in rhyme:

Hercules killed hart-a-grease;
And hart-a-grease killed Hercules.

The stag's antlers were fixed to a nearby oak, thereafter known as the Hart's Horn Tree, and they became embedded in its swelling bark. Writing in 1658 Lady Anne Clifford recorded that the tree still stood although the horns had been broken off, and it was still there in 1687-8 according to Thomas Denton's *Perambulation of Cumberland*.[107] In 1773 Thomas Pennant could not find the tree, though he recounts the story and illustrates another ancient oak.[80]

Meanwhile, north of the devastated Border, the Scottish pendulum was swinging back again. King Edward III was preoccupied with his campaigns to recover his ancestral lands in France and without his powerful hands on the strings his puppet, Balliol, dangled in increasing insecurity. Scottish raids into Cumberland and Northumberland resumed in 1337 and by 1340 much of the kingdom had been recovered for David Bruce, who returned to Scotland in 1341.[93] There were further raids in 1342[108] and in 1345 there was a massive incursion into northern England. An army of 30,000 men, led by King David II Bruce and Sir William Douglas, burned Penrith and harried the country round – though they were seen off by a smaller force under a militant Bishop of Carlisle.[109]

Neither this incursion nor an even bigger one in 1346 seems to have affected Appleby, and the 1346 adventure culminated in a Scottish defeat at Neville's Cross, near Durham, in which King David was wounded and captured. Edward Balliol made one last effort to recover his kingdom, seizing a wide swathe of the Borders but failing to regain the heartland of Scotland.[93] Tortuous negotiations and a ransom of 100,000 marks, to be paid in ten annual instalments, eventually led to David II's release in 1357. Edward Balliol, his claims finally abandoned, was pensioned off to live out his life in rustic retirement in Yorkshire.[108] By 1384 the Scots had regained almost all the land occupied by the English in the 1330s, and the whole sorry-go-round was starting up again.[28]

The Cliffords continued to be caught up in these mid-fourteenth century troubles. Robert, fourth lord, succeeded his father in 1344 but enjoyed the barony for only eighteen months before being killed in France. His brother, Roger, fifth lord, was involved in the Border warfare of 1345-1346 and was a signatory to a further truce with the Scots in 1369, two years before the death of King David Bruce.[85] Back home, he seems to have had problems with his estates for in 1357 he complained that men were poaching his deer on Milburn Fell, which was one of the two baronial hunting 'forests' in the Westmorland Pennines.[79; 110] In 1377 he brought a suit against Adam de Corry who had been his bailiff for Appleby, Brough and Brougham, demanding that he account for the time he was bailiff and the moneys he had received.[59] In 1378 William de Tunstall was challenged to return £40 which he owed, and to render a reasonable account of the time when he was a receiver of money for Clifford. Adam de Corry was in the firing line again in 1379 when he was accused of forcibly breaking into Roger de Clifford's parks at Appleby, Brough and Murton and his free chases of Brough, Kirkby Stephen, Nateby and Orton and taking away deer, cattle, corn and herbage to the value of £10. De Corry seems to have got away with it by pleading that he was under the king's protection.[59] Maybe he had been taking advantage of Lord Clifford as an absentee landlord.

The warfare in the mid-fourteenth century may have passed Appleby by, but like the rest of the country it was hit by the greatest disaster of the century – the Black Death.[2; 42; 109] This was the most devastating epidemic ever recorded in Western Europe. We are still not quite sure what the disease was, but the evidence points to a new and especially virulent mutant strain of plague. It took three forms. The commonest was the bubonic variety, characterised by painful putrid swellings and transmitted by the bites of rat fleas. Alongside it, and also flea-borne, was a devastatingly lethal septicaemic variety. But a third and also lethal variant was pneumonic, spread directly from person to person by coughing. It produced a high fever and killed its victims within two days.[42]

The plague probably reached southern England by ship from Calais in around June 1348, and was spread as people travelled from community to community.[42] It reached Durham in July 1349 and probably got to the Appleby area around the same time. We have no statistics for deaths in Appleby, but in England as a whole it has been estimated that about a third of the national population, which was around 4.2 million in 1300, died within two years.[42] The death rate was higher among the clergy, 45

Decline and Fall

per cent of whom died, presumably because they tended to the sick and dying, and the poor also suffered disproportionately: in contrast there were hardly any deaths in the royal family. In 1349-50 the plague reached Scotland, again killing around a third of the people.[111] In a second wave of pestilence in 1361-62, 36 per cent of the clergy in Westmorland died and while lay mortality was somewhat less, a quarter of the people probably perished.[109] There were further waves of infection in 1368-9, 1371, 1375, 1390 and 1405, but the virulence of the disease seems to have declined steadily.[42]

On top of these disasters, the climate got colder with the onset of the 'little ice age'. Land that had been cultivated when the population was at its four-million peak reverted to pasture and 'waste' when numbers fell to only around two million. In northern England there was a shift from crop-raising to pastoralism, especially sheep rearing. The whole momentum of town-founding slowed and halted, probably because there were enough urban centres for the shrunken population and diminished economy. For rural market towns like Appleby, whose prosperity depended on trade in farm produce, the cumulative impact of war, climate change and pestilence must have been devastating.

Given these disasters, it is not surprising that quite a few planned towns declined and some settlements were abandoned altogether.[55] Between 1060 and 1370, 172 new towns had been founded in England, and of these twelve proved abortive and fourteen decayed. In Wales, plagued like Cumbria by war, seventeen out of 84 were unsuccessful and a further seventeen decayed. In Cumbria the boroughs of Newton Arlosh, Kirkoswald, Greystoke and Pooley Bridge failed: Church Brough was redeemed only by the success of nearby Market Brough and only Carlisle, Cockermouth, Penrith, Keswick, Egremont, Appleby, Kendal, Ulverston and Dalton in Furness succeeded.[79] But many places far away from conflict fared even worse. In Elizabeth I's reign the Cornish borough of Boscastle was described as "the meanest and poorest that can bear the name of town, for it consisteth of two or three houses," while Newtown in the Isle of Wight had about fourteen surviving cottages set amid decayed streets flanked by over 40 vacant burgage plots. Some towns were marked only by churches, standing amid grassy mounds.[55]

Appleby was certainly in trouble by the latter years of the fourteenth century. On 22 June 1380 there was a grant "to the mayor and burgesses of Appleby, in compassion of their impoverishment by pestilence, by removals, and by the wars with Scotland of a moiety of the profit pertaining to the King from forfeitures incurred by merchants and others carrying their goods from thence to Kirkby Stephen, Overton (Orton), Crosby Ravenswarth, Bamton, Shappe and Morland."[81] This may have been in response to a complaint that merchants were taking goods along the western road from Penrith by Eamont Bridge to Shap, and selling them there "on Sundays, in churchyards and elsewhere" thereby circumventing the formal markets.[25] In 1382 the exchequer made a further grant of pontage on merchandise crossing the River Eden and Coupland Beck between Kirkby Stephen and Sowerby Bridge in order to pay for repairs to Appleby bridge (another grant for repair was to follow in 1418).

The mention of removals suggests that Appleby had become unattractive to merchants, probably because trade was too poor to off-set the risk of Scottish raids. Although there was, in theory, a fourteen-year truce that should have lasted until 1384, Border troubles were breaking out again by 1377, and Appleby's pessimists would have had their fears confirmed in 1380 when Carlisle was attacked (unsuccessfully) and Penrith fair was looted. This last event back-fired on the looters for in addition to their booty, the Scots took another dose of the plague home with them.[111] These events obviously alerted those responsible for the defence of the northern borders. Although Appleby, as the county town and seat of the assizes, was important to the Cliffords, Brougham was by this time their strongest fortress and it was further extended by the fifth lord (his is the inscription 'This made Roger' originally placed above the great hall and now over the outer gatehouse).[25] In 1383 an order was sent to the sheriffs of Cumberland and Westmorland directing them:

> *To take stone cutters, masons and other labourers for the repair of certain castles and fortlets of Roger de Clifford, Knight, in the said county near the march of Scotland, which are useful as a refuge for the King's subjects.* [25]

It is not certain what work was done at Appleby, and the remodelling of the eastern range which Dr W D Simpson assigned to this period is almost certainly the work of Thomas, eighth Lord Clifford in 1454.[9] It is most likely that the repairs of 1383 were purely to strengthen the

Decline and Fall

tower, curtain and defences against the mounting probability of attack.

The work was done none too soon. In 1384 Annandale – England's sole remaining territory north of the Solway – was taken by the Scots.[93] King Richard II sent his uncle, John of Gaunt, on a retaliatory raid into the Lothians and in 1385 the king himself led an English army 14,000 strong as far as Edinburgh.[93] The Scots responded by raiding the western march, attacking Carlisle, spreading fire down the Eden Valley and wasting the country around Cockermouth in the west and Hexham in the east.[93] It may have been in this campaign that an army of Scots under the Earl of Douglas fought a battle near the bridge at Hoff at the place formerly known as Douglas Ing where bones and weapons have been dug up.[48; 109] Carlisle and its hinterland suffered again in 1387,[71] and in August 1388 a large force under Robert, Earl of Fife (brother of King Robert II the first Scottish Stewart king) attacked Carlisle and raided deep into Cumberland and Westmorland.[25; 93; 108] Although Carlisle held out and the Scots withdrew, on 18 August another Scottish force led by the Earl of Douglas gained a narrow victory over Sir Henry Percy ('Hotspur') at Otterburn in Northumberland.[93; 108]

Many histories of Westmorland have stated that it was after Otterburn that the Scots mounted an immensely destructive raid across the county, sweeping from Bampton and Shap through Crosby Ravensworth and Maulds Meaburn to Drybeck, Appleby and Brough. Later inquisitions give St Stephen's Day – 26 December – as the date for the sack of Appleby. Despite its strengthening, Brougham Castle seems to have fallen and was recorded in 1403, with its manor, as "totally waste after destruction by the Scots."[25] Appleby Castle was also recorded as 'ruinous' in 1391. It is an article of faith among local historians that the destruction was so complete that the town never recovered, and that the greater part still lay in ruins over a century later.[48; 71; 75] But there are oddities about this tale. One is the date – mid-winter is a strange time to be raiding, for there would have been far fewer cattle to lift than in August and the miry tracks would have been much harder to travel on. Another is the lack of chronicled reference to the incursion – whereas the Earl of Fife's summer raid is well recorded. It seems likely that the later inquisitions got it wrong, and that Appleby and the rest of the upper Eden Valley were actually devastated in August 1388, before rather than after Otterburn. But a recent detailed account of the Border wars[93] not only agrees that Appleby was torched by Fife in August, but states that

Cumbria was raided again "immediately after the turn of the year." It is possible that the borough was hit twice in six months, which would account for the tales of devastation to follow.

Be that as it may, there seems no reason to doubt that something nasty happened to Appleby in 1388, though in the next chapter some questions are raised about just how bad it was. It has been suggested that the town was the more vulnerable because Roger, fifth Lord Clifford, was unable to help defend it: he was away at sea on a naval expedition against France and Castile until October 1388 and was then in the last year of his life, dying at Skipton in July 1389. His son and heir, Thomas, who had been Master of the Horse to Richard II, had been banished from court at that same time.[85] There are signs that by this period the Cliffords were making Skipton their chief place, treating the northern castles as outposts.[25] But the garrison of Appleby would have had limited capacity to help the borough anyway, even had the traditional coolness between town and castle been set aside by mutual need. Ironically, the raids of 1388 were among the last such events on the Borders, for in 1402 a Scottish army was massively defeated at Homildon Hill near Wooler and extensive raids into the north of England ceased.[28; 93]

The real lesson from the events between 1312 and 1388 is that the upper Eden Valley was no place for a successful trading community. Appleby prospered when England had a strong government that was at peace with its northern neighbour: it was repeatedly looted and burned when the English crown weakened. The problems might have been averted had the Kings of England abandoned their claims to overlordship over Scotland and sought a lasting and equal peace, but this did not really happen until the Union of Crowns in 1603. As it was, the Border wars, coupled with repeated outbreaks of plague among the people and murrain among the cattle, and aggravated by a cooling climate, undermined such success as Appleby had achieved. It would almost certainly have been no different had the Border remained at the Rey Cross on Stainmore as it was in 1150, for Appleby would then have been the last Scottish Borough on the marches of England. Geography and history were against the town, and it never fulfilled the potential briefly glimpsed in the thirteenth century.

CHAPTER 5

Depressed Area

THERE are no contemporary descriptions of the state of Appleby in January 1389. The extent of the town's devastation can only be guessed from oblique references and from reports written years afterwards. But Northumberland, Cumberland and Westmorland all got a remission of tax arrears in 1389, presumably because of their impoverishment by the war.[112] An inquisition *post mortem* on Thomas, sixth Lord Clifford, in 1391, recorded Appleby Castle as 'ruinous' while one on Maud, widow of the fifth Lord Clifford, in 1403, emphasised the destruction of Brougham, though in both cases the damage may have been exaggerated.[25] Clearly, something was badly wrong.

The Clifford family, too, was in partial eclipse. In 1396-97, only two years before his overthrow by his cousin Henry of Bolingbroke, King Richard II granted the Honour of Penrith to Ralph Neville of Raby, made him Earl and Sheriff of Westmorland and granted him a tax called cornage - which, like the shrievalty had been in the possession of the Cliffords since the time of King John. Was the king trying to set Neville up as a rival power to the Cliffords in Westmorland?

There was certainly antagonism between the two families in the years to come, but the appointment may have been made out of necessity. The Cliffords were short-lived, six out of the ten lords between 1282 and 1523 being killed in battle leaving young heirs. Four of them inherited when less than ten years of age, and three more when under sixteen.[85] John, seventh Lord Clifford, was only three when his father was killed in 1391, and hence only eight in 1396 when Ralph Neville – himself a seasoned warrior – was made Earl of Westmorland. The Clifford Barony and estates were not affected by the appointment, and after examining the records, the king restored the grant of cornage which the Vieuxponts and Cliffords had enjoyed since 1203.[25]

Clearly the royal eye was sharply on Westmorland in the 1390s, and it must surely have flickered over the Royal Charters to Appleby, and considered the status of the town. If it was too impoverished to pay its fee farm rent, surely the crown must have known about it. But all that we have is silence. Unlike the situation after Bruce's raids in 1314-1322 there is no record of the appointment of a 'Keeper of the Borough', as should have happened if the fee farm payments fell two years into arrears. The implication is that either the fee farm was being paid despite the destruction, or that it was waived and the records of the waiver have been lost. This, however, is highly improbable because any such waiver would surely have been common knowledge and referred to when the state of Appleby was assessed in 1515 and thereafter. It may be significant that the sequence of Royal Charters for Appleby is broken between 1332 (Edward III) and 1528 (Henry VIII).[74] But in 1415 the borough paid the second lay subsidy (wealth tax) of £3-0s-5d to King Henry V, apparently without difficulty.[59] This was designed to yield the same sum as in 1322 and so cannot be used as a means of measuring relative affluence, but it is hard to see how it could have been levied had the place been a sea of rubble and ash. I conclude therefore that, somehow or other, the fee farm rent went on being paid.

This squares with the fact that, again unlike 1312-1327, there was no obvious break in the sequence of mayors. Thomas de Corbrygg (Corbridge) held office in 1388, Thomas de Malestang in 1389, William de Thornburgh (Thornborrow) in 1391 and again in 1397, 1406 and 1407, and John Mauchaile (Machell) in 1398, 1410 and 1427. The families of Wharton, Warcopp (variously Warcop and Warchope), Hilton and Machell dominate the remainder of the fifteenth century.[74] Once again, the mayors seem to have held office for irregular periods.

There were prosperous people around. Although the de Goldingtons had gone, there was a prominent family with the strange name of Oerdo, of whom John, senior, flourished in 1390. In 1450 Robert Oerdo was a churchwarden, Thomas Oerdo was chantry priest and William Oerdo 'junior' owned Goldington Hall (could it have come through marriage with a Goldington heiress)? Presumably there was a John 'junior' and a William 'senior' but we have no record of when they lived or what they did. And business went on. In 1390 Richard Pathnell, Chaplain of the Chantries of St Nicholas and St Mary in St Lawrence's Church, "with the consent of the Mayor, Bailiffs and commonalty of the said vill" granted to John Oerdo senior for the term of 200 years "all the burgages of the Chantry of St Nicholas lying in Boroughgate between Ralph Penny's tenement on the one side and that of John Morill on the other... with a certain chamber belonging to the Chantry of St Mary within the stone house in front of the said tenements" the rent being fixed at four shillings, paid half at Pentecost and half on the feast of St Martin in winter.[59]

The implication is that there were rentable, and therefore habitable, tenements and at least one stone house in Boroughgate only two years after the sack. Richard Pathnell was still chantry priest in 1397, and probably also acted as schoolmaster.[103] There was also enough money to pay for a good deal of rebuilding at St Lawrence's Church in the early part of the fifteenth century. The nave was re-roofed, the present clerestory added, the upper part of the tower re-built and the south chapel possibly extended eastwards.[9]

A number of property transactions are recorded in mid-century. In 1450 John Day and William Hanson, described as "keepers of the Lamp of the Blessed Virgin Mary in the Church of St Lawrence of Appleby", with the consent of four 'kirkmaisters' (churchwardens) and the parishioners, granted a 60-year lease of a burgage on the north side of Boroughgate "between the burgage of William Oerdo junior called Goldyngton Hall on the south side and the burgage of Lord de Clifford called le Wynehouse on the north answering yearly to the Lamp aforesaid at the terms of Pentecost and St Martin in winter 20 pence by equal portions."[59] If there were 'keepers of the lamp' it is likely that there was a guild or fraternity of the lamp among whom John Day and William Hanson were prominent.[113] In the same year Sir Thomas Oerdo, chaplain of the two chantries, let four acres of land for 40 years to Thomas Hanson, mercer, for an annual rent of 2s-8d and a burgage in Battlebarrow to John Helton for 20d a year.[59] In 1493 John Hartley released a burgage in the west of the borough "between the Prior of Wetheral's burgage on the south and the burgage of the Lamp of the Blessed Mary on the north."[59] These records give a clear impression of 'business as usual'.

Some records do mention repairs. In 1445 John Marshall was priest of the two chantries (presumably he was Thomas Oerdo's predecessor) and in that year "Robert Warcop, Mayor, and the burgesses of Appleby" granted to him "a certain ruinated Chapel upon the west end of the stone bridge of St. Lawrence in Appleby, to hold the same to him and his successors and repair it at his own expense; also to repair a certain chamber or oratory over the said Chapel." This grant was made subject to a yearly rent of 2d "if demanded."⁽⁴⁸⁾ The chapel was that of St. John the Baptist in the gatehouse at the west end of the bridge, and it is significant that this important building was in disrepair in 1445, though it may have been cobbled up enough to serve for the collection of tolls.

By 1452/53 John Marshall had been appointed vicar of St Michael's, Bongate, and sold to Thomas, eighth Lord Clifford "a burgage on the west side of the street called Kirkgate, extending in length to a certain narrow street called School House Gate."⁽¹⁰¹; ¹⁰³⁾ Kirkgate, as a place name, is now lost but was probably the lane leading from the Market Place past the Vicarage to the 'Vicar's Close' or glebe (the site of today's cricket ground), while School House Gate is now the Low Wiend. It has been suggested⁽¹⁰¹⁾ that this burgage was Pear Tree Garth, part of the original de Threlkeld endowment, but that, surely, would have been granted to the church in perpetuity and would not have been Marshall's to dispose of?

In the late fifteenth century, the dependence of the school on the chantry foundation led to a dispute between the corporation and the vicar of St. Lawrence over the appointment of the schoolmaster.⁽¹⁰³⁾ The vicar claimed this right because the schoolmaster was also the chantry priest, paid from the chantry endowments. But in 1478 it was the mayor and burgesses that granted to Thomas Whinfell, Chaplain, "the chantry of the blessed Virgin Mary, which Thomas de Goldington and John his son and their ancestors had founded in the Church of St. Lawrence, together with the chantry of St. Nicholas in the same Church, and also the chantry founded by Sir William English in the Church of St. Michael, binding him to keep yearly a sufficient grammar School, in the said borough... taking from the scholars of the School aforesaid the customary fees and payments according to the ancient custom of the School itself."⁽⁴⁸; ¹⁰¹⁾ 'Grammar' in this period meant Latin, which was taught as a conversational language as well as through the great classical authors, whose style served as a model for literary composition. Greek may also have been taught.⁽¹⁰¹⁾ It is however very strange that the mayor and burgesses assumed jurisdiction over the chantry in St Michael's church which lay outside the borough.

Appleby Friary also seems to have recovered. In 1446 it was given the right to cut timber from Whinfell forest, and it received various bequests.⁽⁹⁰⁾ In 1501 Thomas Langton, formerly Provost of Queen's College, Oxford, Bishop successively of St David's, Salisbury and

Depressed Area

Winchester and Archbishop-elect of Canterbury at the time of his death from plague, left the friars twenty marks (£13-6s-8d) to pray for him.[114] Langton had been born in Appleby and is said to have been educated by the Carmelites, although other authorities suggest he was more likely to have been taught in the 'grammar school':[101] both interpretations converge if a friar was the chantry priest, as is hinted at by reference to the 'Friar's Mansion House of the Chantry of the Blessed Virgin Mary' in some early documents.[103]

Records for the castle also suggest a smooth recovery from 1390 to 1460, though the period was one of bitter contention between the Cliffords and the Nevilles, now Earls of Westmorland.[25] Although the building was recorded as 'ruinous' in 1391 this did not stop Elizabeth, widow of the sixth Lord Clifford, staying there in the following year.[25] At some date before 1422 a great gatehouse was built on the north side, presumably during the tenure of John, seventh Lord Clifford.[56] This structure, once a major feature of the castle, has now disappeared except for a massive fragment on the west side of the modern entrance, but it was complete in the time of Lady Anne, Countess of Pembroke, who described it as "that strong and fine artificial gatehouse all arched with stone and decorated with the arms of the Veteripontes, Cliffords, and Percies." John, Lord Clifford, Knight of the Garter and a great jouster, had married Elizabeth Percy, the only daughter of the celebrated Sir Henry Percy, called Hotspur, and that is why the arms of the Percys were displayed on the gate.[48; 57]

Further major rebuilding was done in mid-century under Thomas, eighth Lord Clifford, who succeeded his father at the age of five when the latter was killed in 1422 at the siege of Meaux in France – the same siege at which King Henry V caught the dysentery that ended his life.[85] In 1454 this Lord Clifford oversaw an extensive re-construction of the eastern range of the castle; so extensive indeed as to cause his descendant Lady Anne to say that he had "built the chiefest part of the Castle towards the east, as the hall, the chapel and the great chamber were then fallen into great decay." He appears to have re-modelled the eastern range of the castle as a 'hall house' of the then-customary type with "a central Hall having at its lower end the kitchen and offices, and at its upper end the Chapel and the great Chamber."[56] The original Norman gate in the east front, with its portcullis, was incorporated, standing at the end of the screens passage that ran across the building between kitchen and hall.

The Story of Appleby in Westmorland

Square towers, probably more prominent then than they are now, were built at either end of the eastern range, as was common at the time (compare the near-contemporary Lumley Castle near Durham, or Bolton Castle in Wensleydale), and Dr W D Simpson suggested that the architect might have been the great Durham master mason, John Lewyn. The masonry of this reconstruction is still conspicuous in the upper parts of the eastern range.[9; 57]

Reading the documents from the period between 1388 and 1460 therefore, we get an impression of continuity in Appleby's life, and even of reasonable prosperity. There is no record of failure to pay the fee farm rent or of the consequent forfeiture of the liberties of the borough. The Border was relatively quiet, though there were some Scottish incursions in 1414-15, in one of which Penrith was burned[25] and others in 1436 and 1456 which did not affect Westmorland. The Cliffords were somewhat overshadowed by the Nevilles and the Percys, now dominant among the Border lords, but again this probably had little impact on the borough. Between 1450 and 1550 there was renewed expansion in much of Cumbria: agriculture must have been booming for there is considerable evidence of a subdivision of land holdings to create new farms.[79] This new wave of prosperity should have washed over Appleby because the town was a major market for farm produce.

Yet the records we have from between 1492 and 1550 could be referring to a quite different town! In 1492 an order from King Henry VII to the Sheriff of Westmorland[75] refers directly to Appleby, stating that the King:

> *being credibly enformed that the said town hath been by the Scots destroyed, wasted, and burned, whereby the people of the cuntry thereaboute have lost their resorte and commyng to the said town - which town without we of our especial grace put to the inhabitants of the same our hands of pitie and mercie is like to fall to the utterest myre and decaye. We charge you that ye in such place as ye think mooste expedient and according within the said countie do make proclamation that our plaisir is that the said inhabitants have and enjoy the said faires and marketts to be holden upon the Monday or the Saturday onys in the week as it shall be thought moost best for the wele of the cuntrey.*

Henry VII had the reputation for being a cautious ruler, distinctly

Depressed Area

'near' with money, and a confirmation of the weekly market in a town that already had freedom from tolls does not seem especially generous. A formal inquisition of 1515[71; 74] proposed more substantial relief. It recites both cause and remedy, stating that:

> *the said borough or town of Appleby was greatly diminished and fallen into ruin, and that the burgesses of the same are so very poor that they cannot satisfy or reply to the King for the said fee farm.*
>
> *And, further, the said jurors do say that the aforesaid town has been set on fire and burnt by the Scots in the year of Our Lord 1388, and never from the same time until now rebuilt, but the greatest part of the same town as yet lies in ruins. But that the burgesses can pay and bear an annual fee farm rent of 26s. and 8d. and no more.*

A *quietus* reducing the rent accordingly is said to have been granted in 1516 and confirmed in 1534 and 1556.[75] A further inquisition was "held at Appleby on 28 September in the third and fourth year of the reigns of Philip and Mary" (1557-58).[74] Four commissioners, Thomas Blenkinsopp, Thomas Sandford, Christopher Salkeld and Thomas Fallowfield, with a panel of jurors then said on oath that:

> *the town or vill of Appleby aforesaid throughout the time aforesaid is sorely abused ruinous or destroyed in so much that the burgesses and inhabitants of the same whether they dwell there or not or have holdings there liable to payment of the fee farm rent of the aforesaid town are so very poor that they have not the power or ability to satisfy our lord the King and our lady the Queen with respect to the rent of twenty marks as they were wont aforetime and practised. And because the town or vill aforesaid was burnt and set on fire by the Scots on the day of ... the feast of St Stephen, martyr, in the year of our Lord one thousand three hundred and eighty eight and never from that time even to the day on which this inquisition was taken has been rebuilt or repaired and because the greater part of the said town on the day of taking of this inquisition was devastated in ruin and decay but*

> *little repaired without buildings and because the burgesses and inhabitants of said town or vill cannot collect among themselves to pay and sustain to our lord the King and our lady the Queen but by small instalments the sum due for the fee farm rent of the town or vill aforesaid but (the amount they can pay) is twenty six shillings and eight pence and no more.*

This would appear to be a repetition of the 1515 inquisition, leading to the same conclusions. The document gives the date of the sack of 1388 as 26 December, St Stephen's day, probably erroneously, but its most telling statement is that the greater part of the town was "but little repaired and without buildings" 150 years later. The picture of abandoned burgage sites, yielding no revenue, conflicts with the various records of transactions between 1390 and 1450 but it does partly match the 1754 map, which shows around 70 plots without buildings, mostly along Doomgate, on the Sands, on the Colby lane out of Scattergate and at the top of Boroughgate.[61]

How do we interpret this apparently contradictory evidence? I suggest that, first, we need to accept that there was enough money in Appleby between 1388 and 1460 to allow the rebuilding of the heartland of the town, around Boroughgate, including the church and bridge gate. Second, I suggest that the fee farm rent did continue to be paid. Yet I also conclude that the town contracted, abandoning the burgages at the castle end of Boroughgate, on the Sands, along most of Doomgate and in Colby Lane. But how was the fee farm paid if the number of occupied burgages fell dramatically?

There is a clue in the reference in several deeds to burgages being owned by 'Lord de Clifford'. After King John's Charter, the burghers held their tenements directly from the crown: they were "tenants of our Lord the King" as they stated in their writ of 1276. But probably, as the wars and 'removals' of the fourteenth century created vacant tenements, the Cliffords and other leading local families bought them up. It may have been at this time that the Cliffords came by the land at the top of Boroughgate which they incorporated in the Castle Park. Other tenements had been granted to the church as endowments for the chantries and the lamp. The purchasers would have become the primary tenants, answerable for the fee farm rent to the crown, and no doubt recouping the cost from their sub-tenants where they could. They would also have become the electors to Parliament, for voting rights went with the burgages. I suggest that this may be why the fee farm did not fall into arrears after 1388 – for the sack must have provided a great opportunity to the local grandees to acquire vacant plots, and they could well afford their share of a 20-mark tax.

I guess that in around 1380, just before the resumption of major Border warfare but after being weakened by plague and removals, Appleby had around 150 occupied burgages and a population of around 750. In 1390 – as in 1322 – there might have been around 60 burgages that had largely escaped destruction, and another 40 that were in some measure rebuilt. That would fit with a population collapse to around 500 in 1400. If local agriculture enjoyed something of a boom between 1450 and 1550[79] we might expect market profits to rise, aiding reconstruction and a population recovery to around the 1380 total of 750.

This, however, would not explain the plaintive pleas of extreme poverty in 1515, 1533 and 1557-58. While there was trouble with Scotland in the 1450s and a lot of bickering between Percys and Nevilles as a kind of side-show in the Wars of the Roses,[93] there is no record of new destruction at Appleby, and the inquisitions anyway refer specifically to 1388 as the year of disaster. If the fee farm rent was paid in the fifteenth century, there was surely no case for reducing it to ten per cent of its original level at a time when the district should have been getting wealthier after many years of better farming.[79] That does not make sense.

There is a further oddity. In 1617 when King James I and VI visited Brougham, there were reported to be arrears of £159 in the fee farm rent for Appleby which the attorney to "Henry Clifford, Earl of Cumberland, formerly sheriff of the County of Westmorland" was trying to get written off.[74] Which 'Henry Clifford'? In 1617 the reigning Clifford and king's host was Francis, the fourth Earl, who was hereditary sheriff of the county. The reference is clearly to past history, and must relate to either Henry, first Earl or Henry his son, second Earl, who together held the title between 1525 and 1570. But what were the arrears to do with the Earl of Cumberland, when under the Charter of Edward I, confirmed by subsequent monarchs, the sheriff was no longer responsible for collecting Appleby's fee farm rent? Could it have been a personal debt relating to the burgages the Cliffords then held? One possibility is that the fee farm rent did fall into arrears during the mid-fifteenth century when the Cliffords became embroiled in the conflict between York and Lancaster that we know as the Wars of the Roses. The family, like the Percys of Northumberland, were staunch Lancastrians standing by the weak and at times mentally incapacitated King Henry VI, while most of the Nevilles were Yorkists.[48; 85] Thomas, eighth Lord Clifford, was killed in the first battle of St Albans in 1455, where he commanded the vanguard of the greatly outnumbered Lancastrian forces. He was not yet 40, and his son John who became the ninth Lord was only twenty.[85] John Clifford soon proved himself an outstanding commander, but he had a passionate hatred for Yorkists and was to win a dark reputation for cruelty and the nick-name 'the Butcher'.

In the north, King James II of Scotland also detested the Duke of York and in 1456 he denounced the Anglo-Scottish truce and raided into Northumberland in support of the Lancastrian cause.[93; 108] It was probably because of this intervention that no assizes were held in Appleby in 1457 and 1458 "because of the rebellion and insurrection of the Scots."[25] Lancaster seemed to be in the ascendant when, on 30 December 1460, the Duke of York was killed in the battle of Wakefield. John, Lord Clifford, was prominent in that battle and captured York's son, the fifteen-year-old Earl of Rutland, stabbing him, shouting "by God's blood, thy father slew mine and so will I do thee!"[108] In this act "the lord Clifford was accounted a tyrant, and no gentleman." These dark deeds, and Clifford's own death a year later in the big and bloody battle of Towton which shattered the strength of the northern lords and established King Edward IV on the throne, are dramatised at some length by Shakespeare in *Henry VI*, Part III. Even so, Towton did not mark the end of warfare in the north: Lancastrian refugees and loyalists, with Scots aid, fought on in Northumbria until 1464 although again without impact on the upper Eden Valley.[93]

After John Clifford's death his peerage was forfeited and all his estates confiscated by King Edward, who had not forgiven the murder of his father and brother.[85] The Earl of Northumberland, Lord Dacre, Roger Wharton of Westmorland and a host of other northern lords lost their lands and titles in the same way.[93] Appleby, Brough, Pendragon and Brougham Castles and the Sheriffwick of Westmorland were granted to Sir William and Sir John Parr of Kendal.[25; 115] But the Yorkist enmity did not end with John Clifford's death. His two young sons were believed by their mother to be in desperate peril. She successfully smuggled the younger boy out of England, and entrusted Henry, the elder, to the care of a sheep farmer on the family's Yorkshire estates – where he grew up ignorant of his status. Later, after his mother's remarriage to Sir Lancelot Threlkeld, he was moved to an even more remote Border farm.[85]

If the Cliffords had been paying Appleby's fee farm rent, the town's poverty would have been exposed during their forfeiture, which overlapped with the next upsurge of Border conflict in the early 1480s. But one might expect restoration of the status quo after the Battle of Bosworth in 1485 when Henry Clifford, 'the Shepherd Lord', recovered his estates. Although then illiterate, he later became an able administrator and took a keen interest in his land.[85] As Wordsworth wrote:[116]

> *Love had he found in huts, where poor men lie,*
> *His daily teachers had been woods and rills*
> *The silence that is in the starry sky,*
> *The sleep that is among the lonely hills.*
>
> *In him the savage virtues of his race,*
> *Revenge, and all ferocious thoughts, were dead.*
> *Nor did he change, but kept in lofty place*
> *The wisdom which adversity had bred.*

In 1485 the Clifford castles came back to their hereditary owners, and Wordsworth would have us believe that there was a great feast at Brougham to celebrate!

> *How glad is Skipton at this hour,*
> *Though lonely, a deserted tower;*
> *Knight, squire, and yeoman, page and groom:*
> *We have them all at the feast of Brougham.*
>
> *How glad Pendragon - though the sleep*
> *Of years be on her! - She shall reap*
> *A taste of that great pleasure, viewing*
> *As in a dream, her own renewing.*
>
> *Rejoiced is Brough, right glad I deem*

> *Beside her little, humble stream;*
> *And she that keepeth watch and ward*
> *Her statelier Eden's course to guard,*
> *They both are happy at this hour.*
> *Though both is but an empty tower.*

Henry, tenth Lord Clifford, lived most of his life in the country and his favourite home was Barden Tower in Wharfedale, which he built for himself. Part of the tower was fitted as an observatory, for despite his lack of early education he became a studious man, deeply interested in astronomy, astrology and chemistry.[85] But no great lord could escape the conflicts of his generation, and in 1513, when aged nearly 60, he became one of the chief commanders at Flodden – leading his levies from Westmorland and Yorkshire.

Five years after the restoration of the Shepherd Lord, in 1490, Henry Smyth succeeded Thomas Whinfell as Appleby's chantry priest and schoolmaster. Being appointed to the chantries by the vicar, he refused to seek confirmation of the appointment from the corporation. Many years of argument culminated, in 1514, in open assault, when Hugh Machell of Crackenthorpe Hall was ordered to pay Smyth 40s a year for life as reparation for having beaten him. He only had to pay for two years because Smyth then died – whether as a delayed consequence of Machell's thuggery we cannot tell.

It was Henry Smyth who recovered the burgage called Pear Tree Garth from Henry, Lord Clifford, although by lease rather than a reversal of the sale of 1452.[103] This lease also refers to a Schoolhouse in the same neighbourhood and this was probably situated in School House Close. The school seems to have sprawled over a steadily widening cluster of sites stretching from the lane to the west of St Lawrence's Church along the Low Wiend and into the adjacent part of Broad Close, occupied by a variety of buildings, dwellings and gardens[101] (Map 5).

In 1516 Henry Smyth was succeeded by Leonard Langhorne, who was appointed by Richard Garnett, Vicar of St. Lawrence, to teach school for a stipend of seven marks and to officiate as chantry priest. The vicar, however, kept the title to the lands, granting Langhorne only "the use of the orchard, and the fruits thereof, with hay to feed an horse." A clause in the agreement provided that if "the tenements or rents... by the wars of the Scots or other misfortune be wasted or dilapidated, then Leonard

Langhorne shall be excused from teaching or officiating." Two years later – and probably after a further round of squabbling – Langhorne's appointment was confirmed by the corporation, he being granted all the chantries and agreeing to "teach one grammar school in the borough aforesaid."

Langhorne's agreement reminds us that the threat from the north was still taken seriously. The citizens of Appleby could not know that the battle of Flodden, fought only three years before, was to mark the end of major Border wars. On that field, James IV had fallen with the chief nobility of Scotland about him, and Skelton, in another bitterly anti-Scots diatribe, addressed the dead king:[117]

> *At Brankston Moor and Flodden hills*
> *Our English bows, our English bills*
> *Against you gave so sharp a shower*
> *That of Scotland you lost the flower.*
>
> *Your wealth, your joy, your sport, your play,*
> *Your bragging boast, your royal array,*
> *Your beard so brim as boar at bay,*
> *Your seven sisters that gun so gay,*
> *All have ye lost and cast away.*
> *Thus fortune has turned you, I dare well say,*
> *Now from a King to a clot of clay.*

The 'seven sisters' were seven great cannons from Edinburgh Castle, and three of them were captured by Henry, tenth Lord Clifford, and carried off to ornament his Castle at Skipton.[85] Ten years later, in 1523, the Shepherd Lord died at the respectable age (for the period) of 69.

The sixteenth century saw one of England's greatest social transformations – the Reformation. It was, of course, part of a broader swell of change in Europe, sparked by fundamental criticisms of church doctrines and observances by Luther, Calvin and others. In England it was intensified by King Henry VIII's repudiation of the authority of Rome in the Act of Supremacy of 1534. One consequence was that money which had formerly flowed to Rome was diverted to the English crown or church. Furthermore, since as much as one third of the land in England belonged to religious houses, it was obvious that their dissolution would bring immense wealth to the Treasury! Thomas Cromwell, the King's Vicar

General, sent commissioners to value church property throughout the realm.[118] In 1536 the Carmelite Friary of St Mary at Appleby was one of the smaller monasteries listed for dissolution.

The changes in religious allegiance and observance, the dissolution of the religious houses, the plundering of church estates, the arrogance of the King's Council, the new taxes and (in Cumbria) hostility to domineering landlords, combined to spark revolt. First in Lincolnshire, and then in Yorkshire, Westmorland and Cumberland, there was a broad-based popular uprising that came to be called the Pilgrimage of Grace.[118; 119; 120] Although it had a secular dimension, religious traditions and opposition to the loss of the monasteries lay at its heart as its marching song, probably written by a Cistercian monk of Sawley Abbey, made clear. That called on Christ to:

> *Us commons guide*
> *Which pilgrims be,*
> *Through God's grace,*
> *For to purchase*
> *Old wealth and peace*
> *Of the spirituality.*

The rock the Pilgrimage eventually split on was the naïve belief that the king bore no responsibility for the evils from which the nation was suffering. Thomas Cromwell was seen as the villain of the piece, and the oath the pilgrims took bound them "to expulse all villain blood and evil councillors against the commonwealth from his Grace and his Privy Council."[118] Perhaps the most remarkable feature of the Pilgrimage was that it was a popular revolt, led by ordinary people: very few of the nobility and gentry sided with it from the beginning and some of those that did come to lead it were persuaded, cajoled or even threatened into doing so!

The chief leader of the Pilgrimage was Robert Aske from near Richmond in Yorkshire. He was a cousin of Henry, Lord Clifford and also a relative of the Earl of Northumberland. In Westmorland, the rising was sparked by the failure of the curate of Kirkby Stephen to proclaim the Feast of St Luke on 18 October 1536 (the observance of Saints' days as holidays was barred by the new rules, it being decreed that all patronal festivals in the spring, summer and autumn would be merged in a single All Saints' day). Nicholas Musgrave of Kirkby Stephen (probably actually of Hartley), Robert Pullen of Ormside, Christopher Blenkinsop of Brough and Robert Hilton of Burton Hall, Warcop, were the first local leaders of the Pilgrimage,[120] and they mustered with Robert Thompson, the Vicar of Brough, at Sandford Moor. As elsewhere, the commoners tried to attach local gentry to their cause, and the Westmorland caucus sought to win over Sir Thomas Wharton who, after initial talks, prudently made himself scarce.[118; 120]

Musgrave and Pullen, with their followers, marched from Kirkby Stephen to Penrith, which became the centre for action in Westmorland and Cumberland. On Thursday 19 October 1536, before they got there, the town appointed four captains under aliases: Anthony Hutton[5] was Charity; John Beck, Faith; Thomas Burbeck (or Birkbeck), Pity and Gilbert Whelpdale 'Captain Poverty'. Whelpdale was brother in law to Robert Thompson of Brough, who was named as Poverty's Chaplain and swore the commons in using an oath devised by Anthony Hutton.[120] Other captains were chosen from Caldbeck, Greystoke and Inglewood and other local clergy were pressurised into association (they were told that if they refused they would "lose their goods and lives and their heads to be set in the most famous places in all the country").[120] It was at Penrith, too, that that the four captains, with swords drawn, followed the Vicar of Brough into the church. Swords were then put up and the vicar said mass.[119] A few days later, and after ineffectual efforts to win the commons of Carlisle to the cause, the rebels rallied at Moota Hill near Cockermouth, where they recruited several local gentry including Sir John Lamplugh and Thomas Dalston and were joined by the abbot of the rich Abbey of Holm Cultram.[118; 120]

Appleby does not feature in the campaigns that followed, although we know that there were Appleby men among the Pilgrims. Perhaps one reason the town was quiet was that Henry, eleventh Lord Clifford and first Earl of Cumberland, who was certainly one of the targets of the revolt, was at Skipton where he was soon besieged by Pilgrims from Richmond and Craven, possibly augmented by some of the men from Westmorland. There were probably several reasons why Clifford was a target: he was a close friend of the king, he was blamed for weak defence of the western march against the Scots and he had a bad reputation as a hard and avaricious landlord.[118; 120]

Note 5 - Hutton was soon replaced by Robert Mounsey because Hutton was a gentleman and the commons wanted none of that rank among the leaders.[120]

The closeness to the king was a consequence of birth and upbringing. Born in 1493, Harry Clifford was the elder son of the Shepherd Lord and his wife Anne St John, who was a first cousin of King Henry VII (her father was half-brother to the Lady Margaret Beaufort, the king's mother). Probably because of this kinship, young Harry Clifford was brought up around the court and was a boyhood friend of the king's children. He was a wild young man, and his quiet father had disapproved of his violent life, bad company and ostentatious dress.[85] But his friend King Henry VIII created him Earl of Cumberland in 1525, at the same time making him Warden of the West Marches and Governor of Carlisle. He stood by the king during the crisis over the royal divorce from Catherine of Aragon and in 1534 he became Governor of Carlisle Castle for life and Lord President of the Council of the North. None the less, summing up the character of those who stood by him in 1536, Henry VIII described Clifford as "of good power, without discretion or conduct." It may have been these weaknesses, together with his deficiencies in defending Cumbria, that led the king to replace him as Warden of the West March by Sir Thomas Wharton (made Lord Wharton), when the troubles were over.[120]

Henry Cumberland defended Skipton successfully against the Pilgrims, and by one of those sad conflicts of loyalty common in civil strife, a right-hand man in the defence was Christopher Aske, Robert Aske's brother.[118] Afterwards, Clifford was rewarded for his loyalty to the king by the grant of the lands of Bolton Abbey in Wharfedale.[85; 120] Meanwhile, the main thrust of the Cumberland and Westmorland rebels was against Carlisle. Here the defence was headed by Henry, Lord Clifford, Cumberland's son. The siege was inconclusive and in the midst of it came news of a truce agreed at Doncaster between Robert Aske and the Duke of Norfolk, the king's commander. Norfolk agreed to accompany two representatives of the pilgrims to court, where a series of broadly-based articles would be presented to the king. Under these, the liberties of the church would be upheld, the old laws would be maintained, the 'subverters of the law of God' (Cromwell, Cranmer and others) would be corrected, a general pardon would be granted to the rebels, and the king would suspend action on those monasteries that had not yet been dissolved pending consideration of the matter by parliament.[118; 120] This was enough to persuade the Yorkshire rebels to disperse, and when the news reached Carlisle the Cumbrians did the same.

But the truce was no more than a half-time interval in a grudge-match. Neither side trusted the other. The king had wanted the rebellion put down by force and was angry with Norfolk for giving ground. When the representatives came before him he rebutted their complaints and prevaricated over their request for a parliament, though he did agree to pardon all except the leaders of the revolt. The representatives – and Norfolk – were sent back to agree new terms, and this happened at a further meeting at Doncaster in December 1536.[120] This confirmed the free pardon, the parliament to consider the pilgrims' grievances, and a halt to action on the monasteries until that parliament had been held. Robert Aske and the other leaders were won over and dissolved the Pilgrimage, and Aske himself went to court at Christmas-time and was graciously received by the king.[118; 120]

The king, however, was a duplicitous schemer with every intention of reneging on Norfolk's treaty.[120] Aske, too, doubted the good faith of the royal commanders and set up beacons to summon his forces again if things went wrong. In Yorkshire the agreements began to fall apart early in 1537 when Sir Francis Bigod of Malton and John Hallam of Watton started a new revolt. Bills nailed to church doors in Yorkshire called on the people to rise and renew the Pilgrimage. In Westmorland, Sir Thomas Clifford, Harry Cumberland's bastard son, rode to Kirkby Stephen on 6 January to arrest Nicholas Musgrave and his ally, Thomas Tebay – who promptly took sanctuary in the tower of the parish church. The Duke of Norfolk was sent northwards post-haste early in February with orders to deal mercilessly with the rebels, whose pardons were annulled. In Lincolnshire the king's men arrested 140 local ringleaders. Sir Thomas Clifford returned to Kirkby Stephen on 12 February to try once more to seize Musgrave and Tebay – and Clifford brought as retainers a gang of notorious Border reivers. Once more, Musgrave and Tebay took sanctuary in the church – and the reivers went cattle-raiding in Hartley and Winton. While they were away, the common people of Kirkby Stephen seized the Duke of Norfolk's Sergeant-at-Arms and several other Clifford companions, and although these were rescued the citizens chased the whole band out of town in disarray.[118; 120]

Inspired by Robert Thompson of Brough, and led by Musgrave and Tebay, the commons of Westmorland had another go at taking Carlisle. Some 6,000 men from Kirkby Stephen, Appleby, Penrith and Cockermouth mustered outside the city, where they were taken in the rear by 500 men led by Sir Christopher Dacre and scattered by Sir Thomas Clifford's forces, who burst out of the city. Several hundred people were killed and many prisoners taken.[2; 71; 120] A few days later the Duke of Norfolk arrived with 4,000 troops, and although in private letters he made it clear that he had some sympathy with the Cumbrian rebels, recognising that their dissatisfaction had been caused by harsh landlords, he followed the royal command to "cause such dreadful execution upon a good number of the inhabitants... as shall be a fearful warning."[120] Seventy four prisoners were chosen for execution, and Norfolk had them hanged in the places where they lived, to make the message sharper. Fifty three of the victims came from Westmorland, and they included Thomas Tebay although Nicholas Musgrave escaped. Three of those executed came from the parish of Appleby St Lawrence and six from St Michael's (some of whom may have been friars).[90] Christopher Blenkinsop of Brough was also hanged, though the most famous of the Brough Pilgrims, Robert Thompson, died in the Tower in 1537.[120] Ten men were put to death in Mallerstang, where Clifford and Wharton property had been damaged by the mob. Many of the victims were hanged in chains, the bodies being left to rot in their bonds: it was their womenfolk that eventually had the courage to cut down the grisly remnants and give them Christian burial. Henry VIII is said to have been incensed at this news, but although Norfolk, following orders, did arrest and question some of the women he appears to have had the humanity to ignore the order for their punishment.[120]

Sir Thomas Wharton was one of those who gained the king's favour after the Pilgrimage. He was made Warden of the Western March and first Lord Wharton. In 1542 he won a resounding victory over an invading Scottish army at Solway Moss, following it up by extending English lordship once more over a large area of Dumfries and Annandale.[93] One of his minor rewards was the little Hospital of St Nicholas at Appleby, valued in a 1536 inventory of Shap Abbey at £4-0s-0d per annum and let to Thomas Clifford. It was granted to Wharton in 1544 but he does not seem to have taken much care of the buildings. A brief survey made in 1599 records "the dwellinghouse clean destroyed. The Chapel, heretofore a lazar house, now made the dwelling house. An orchard much destroyed. Two closes of arable land adjoining to the house – 8 acres. St Nicholas Holme now ploughed – 20 acres. The middle holme, some meadows some arable – 3 acres."[59; 105; 121] The Wharton family sold a forty year lease of the property to Israel Fielding of Startforth in Yorkshire in 1614.[48]

The site and buildings of the Carmelite Friary, together with those of Hale Grange near Kirkby Thore and the manor of Hardendale, were sold on 6 November 1543 for £255-3s-0d to Christopher Crackenthorpe of Newbiggin.[48; 90] A plan shows a series of small meadows, orchards and enclosures totalling 21 acres, and some of the houses in Battlebarrow are said to have been built out of the ruins (Map 4).[48; 90] By 1773 Thomas Pennant could only find "a ruin adjacent to the town wall" which he thought might possibly be the remains of the Friary,[80] and in 1936 the Royal Commission on Historical Monuments recorded only the name of the site, and a portion of a fourteenth century window head built into a barn.[9] A geophysical survey in 1988 suggested some buried structures near the corner of Station Road and Battlebarrow, where the 1543 plan locates the Friary and cemetery. One of the fishponds remains as a pond in a garden, and the Lady Well (a spring) continues to feed a trough set behind a new housing estate.[90]

The mid-sixteenth century saw the emergence of a new kind of scholar – the antiquarian. Two early members of the breed took an interest in Appleby. The first, also Appleby's first visitor to embody his impressions in a travel book, was John Leland. His *Itinerary* gives a fascinating picture of the state of England during Henry VIII's reign. But of Appleby he had little to say, describing it as "the Shire town, but now... but a poor village, having a ruinous castle wherein the prisoners be kept."[122] The town fared rather better in William Camden's *Britannia* - the first national geographical encyclopaedia – which appeared in 1586. Camden, Clarenceux King of Arms, was a friend and correspondent of Reginald Bainbrigg, schoolmaster of Appleby and a fellow-antiquarian, who gave him a lot of the information.

"The town," wrote Camden,[77] "is seated in a pleasant field, and almost encompassed with the river Eden. But it is so slenderly peopled, and the buildings are so mean, that if antiquity did not make it the chief town of the County, and if the assizes were not held in the Castle, which is the public gaol for malefactors, it would be very little above a village. For all its beauty consists in one broad street which runs from north to south with an easy ascent, at the head of which is the Castle, almost surrounded with the river. At the lower end is the Church, and a School built by Robert Langton and Miles Spencer, Doctors of Law. The worthy master hereof, Reginald Bainbrigg, a very learned person, courteously translated for me several inscriptions which he has removed, some into his own garden." Camden also noted that Appleby was one of the best corn markets in the region.

The suppression of the chantries, first under an Act of Parliament in 1545/6 and then under a further measure in 1548, had a profound impact in Appleby because it altered the arrangements for the town school. In 1533/34 when Edward Gibson was appointed to succeed Leonard Langhorne as chantry priest and schoolmaster, it had been recorded "that the Chantry or Grammar School in the town of Appleby is worth yearly in the mansion house and one close 8s, and in the rents of diverse burgages, £4-3s-3d."[101; 103] By this time Langhorne was Vicar of St Lawrence, and in 1535 the gross church income was recorded as £10-16s-8d.[59] It was recognised by the crown under both Henry VIII and Edward VI that new arrangements had to be made for the schools when the religious role of chantries was ended, and these were entrusted to commissions.[101] At Appleby, the position was investigated by the Westmorland County Commissioners, headed by Sir Thomas Wharton.

They reported in 1548 that "there is a stipendiary used to celebrate mass and other divine service in the parish church there, and to keep a free grammar School. Edward Gybson, incumbent and school master there hath a clear yearly revenue of the same for his salary £5-19s-10d." The lands and tenements were valued, and 47 burgages were recorded as paying rents used for the school (this implies that nearly a fifth of the properties in Appleby had become chantry endowments). A new commission was made responsible for ensuring "the continuance of grammar schools in every county of England and Wales for the education and bringing up of youth in virtue, learning and godliness." In 1549 those commissioners issued a warrant providing that the grammar school in Appleby should continue and that Edward Gibson should retain his post and salary.[101] But the revenues of the former chantries had been granted to William Warde and Richard Venables, and the payment of Gibson's salary fell to the Exchequer which seems to have operated in a dilatory and bureaucratic manner not unfamiliar today! Schoolmasters at Brough and Kendal as well as Gibson at Appleby complained vigorously, but it was not until May 1557 in the reign of Philip and Mary that an Exchequer Decree authorised payment of arrears to Gibson and made a grant of £5-10s-8d out of the rectory of Crosby Ravensworth for the continuation of the school.[101; 103] This salary was below both the national average and local parallels, for the schoolmaster of Brough received £7-8s-10d, that of Kendal, £10-0s-0d and that of Sedbergh £10-17s-0d.[101]

There are some puzzling records relating to the chantry and school lands in this period. In 1534 Edward Gibson, called 'chantry priest and schoolmaster of Appleby' had rented 'a close called Schoolhouse Close' to Leonard Langhorne for 6s 8d yearly as a hay meadow. Presumably this lease fell in when the chantry endowments were granted to Warde and Venables, and it may be that they sold them on to a certain Alan Bellingham, for in 1552 he in turn let Schoolhouse Close together with a burgage on the west side of the Vicarage, an orchard and garden to Bartholomew Gibson of Appleby, tanner, for 35 years at a rent of twenty shillings yearly.[59] Somehow the school lands must have been re-assembled in the following years, for by the end of the century all these properties formed part of its estate[101] (Map 5).

This was a period when local benefactors stepped in and augmented whatever provision the crown made. Kirkby Stephen Grammar School was founded by Thomas, Lord Wharton, in 1565, and other new foundations appeared at Penrith, Hawkshead and St Bees.[101] Appleby's first benefactor was Dr Robert Langton, Archdeacon of Dorset, who bequeathed £200 to the Queen's College, Oxford, "to purchase land and make a School in Appleby, where I was born." Dr Langton was a nephew of Bishop Thomas Langton, Archbishop-elect of Canterbury, who had left money to the Friary in 1501. Robert Langton's bequest, however, was never handed over to the college, but was retained by his executor, Dr. Miles Spencer, perhaps because the future of the school appeared precarious in the 1550s.[101] Under his own will, in 1569, Dr Spencer passed the £200, plus a further £100 of his own, to Queen's College, on condition that it paid a salary of £8 per annum to the schoolmaster of Appleby and gave preference to boys born at Brough and educated at Appleby as scholars of the college.

This Queen's College declined to do. Instead the Provost and Fellows came to an agreement with Spencer's executors who handed over £60 to the college and transferred the remaining £240 to Rainold Hartley of Appleby and Thomas Warwick, vicar of Morland, to be used for the benefit of Appleby School. The college secured the right to nominate future schoolmasters: if they failed to do so within three months of being informed by the mayor and burgesses of Appleby of a vacancy, the latter were to fill the place.[101]

It is clear that Robert Langton's money was not used to pay for the original 'Little School' in School House Close, but the building none the less became known as 'Langton's little School' and he and Miles Spencer were regarded as founders of the new 'Free Grammar School.' Although all traces of the buildings in Broad Close have disappeared, and an eye of faith is needed to interpret faint hummocks in the King George V Memorial Playing Field as their foundations, the inscription

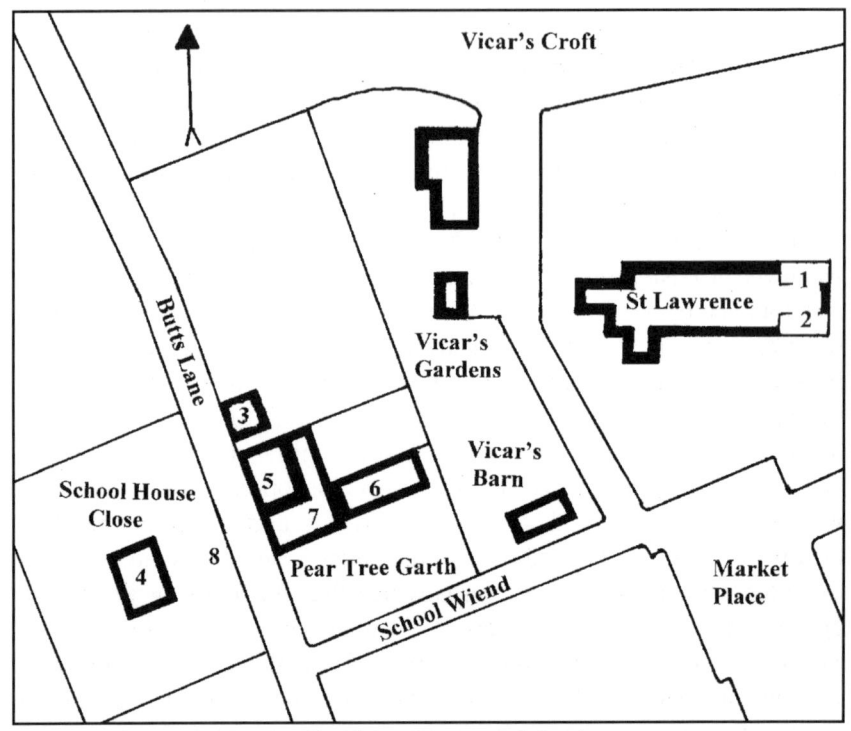

Map 5 - The original site of Appleby Grammar School.
1: Chantry of St Nicholas (1334)
2: Chantry of the Virgin Mary (1286)
3: Mansion House of the Chantry Priest (1535)
4: The original Schoolhouse (1490)
5: Bainbrigg's School (1607)
6: Schoolmaster's House (1671)
7: Extension built in 1826
8: Present location of Bainbrigg's carved stones.
Re-drawn from Hinchcliffe (reference 101)

commemorating their benefaction, carved under the orders of Reginald Bainbrigg, headmaster between around 1578 and 1613, is still set in the wall between Broad Close and Chapel Street[101] (Map 5).

Edward Gibson was schoolmaster until at least 1557, still existing on the meagre salary of £5-10s-8d. After him, the post seems to have been discharged by the Vicar of St Lawrence's Church, Hugh Sewell, and then, from 1573 onwards by a very unusual man, John Boste, born in Dufton, probably educated at Appleby Grammar School and subsequently graduate and Fellow of the Queen's College, Oxford. Boste is recorded as schoolmaster of Appleby in 1573-74, and his signature appears in a book in the old school library. He returned to his Fellowship at Oxford in 1579 but was ejected a year later for being absent without leave, heresy, and quitting the ministry of the Anglican Church. He had in fact gone to France and entered a Catholic seminary, and when he came back to England it was as an itinerant Catholic priest, actively preaching 'the old religion.' He was so energetic in this service in Cumberland, Westmorland, Northumberland, Durham and the Borders that he became the most wanted recusant priest in the country. Sadly, he was betrayed by another Appleby pupil, Henry Ewbank, Vicar of Washington in County Durham, whose election as a Fellow of Queen's Boste had witnessed. John Boste was tortured to extract a confession and hanged, drawn and quartered for high treason on 23 July 1594: in 1970 he was canonised by Pope Paul VI as one of the forty English and Welsh martyrs. As Edgar Hinchcliffe put it: "the headmaster at the time the School received its Elizabethan Charter is therefore now correctly styled John Boste, Saint and Martyr."[101] He is Appleby's only recognised Saint.

Rainold Hartley was a man of stature and influence, for he was steward to George Clifford, third Earl of Cumberland, the father of the Lady Anne. In or around 1573 he persuaded the mayor and corporation of Appleby to apply to Queen Elizabeth for a Royal Charter. Their petition was granted on 22 March 1573/74, a few months after John Boste's appointment. The school was re-established as "The Free Grammar School of Queen Elizabeth in the Town of Appelbie in the county of Westmorland, of the foundatiuon of the burgesses of the Town of Appelbie, for the establishment of education and the instruction of boys and youths in grammar for ever." There was to be one Master or Teacher, one Under-master or Usher, and ten Governors among whom Rainold Hartley was named: the seal granted to the school is of a hart (or stag) on a green ley (field) in allusion to his name. The names of Robert Langton and Miles Spencer also appear on the seal.[101]

Rainold Hartley took steps to augment the master's salary. He had the £240 bequeathed by Langton and Spencer at his disposal, added £60 of his own, and in 1576 bought for £300 the rent charge on the estate of Newton Garth in County Durham. This brought in £20 a year, lifting the salary to £25-10s-8d. On John Boste's return to Oxford, the beneficiary was Reginald Bainbrigg of Hilton. He came of a family of minor gentry: his grandfather was a cousin of Robert Langton and his uncle, Christopher Bainbrigg had been Provost of Queen's College Oxford and then Cardinal Archbishop of York. Both Archbishop Bainbrigg and his nephew were former pupils of Appleby School, as were other members of what was clearly a very distinguished local family.[101]

Reginald Bainbrigg was a fine Latin scholar, fluent in Greek and with a working knowledge of Hebrew. He was a close friend of Rainold Hartley and one of the first antiquaries to visit Hadrian's Wall, making two tours, in 1599 and 1601 and recording his observations in detailed notes. He has been described as 'the ablest of all northern antiquaries' of his generation.[123] He sent copies of inscriptions to William Camden, author of *Britannia*,[124] and made a collection of inscribed stones, some being Roman originals, others copies and yet others his own composition. Some remain to this day, set (in a sadly weathered condition) in the wall between Chapel Street and Broad Close, near to the site of the new school built during his mastership, but a few were moved to the site of the present grammar school when it was built in 1887. He also built up a remarkable library of 295 volumes, including many medical works: 158 survive.[101; 123]

The governors of Appleby Grammar School seem to have been remarkably dilatory about rebuilding its fabric, but during Bainbrigg's tenure things did begin to happen. Around 1600 various plots of land were consolidated, among them Pear Tree Garth, bought back from the Earl of Cumberland in 1603. Bainbrigg then proceeded to plan and begin to build a new school, part of which was completed in 1606 so that he could allocate the original chantry priest's house to the under-master (Map 5). Another part of the building had an inscription dated 1607. It seems likely that Bainbrigg handed over the school at about this time, and his will is dated 1606 though there is evidence he lived on until around 1612.[101] By his will he left everything to the school, including his library which he instructed was not to be sold or split up, in the hope that others would add to it by their own bequests of books.

By the second half of the sixteenth century Appleby seems to have settled down to a steady and uneventful life of reasonable prosperity. According to a diocesan survey the parish of St Lawrence had 147 households, and Bongate 90 in 1563.[125; 126] Not all of these will have been in the borough itself because St Lawrence's parish included Colby, Burrells, Hoff and Drybeck and St Michael's spread to Crackenthorpe, Hilton and Murton, but if we credit it with 80 per cent of St Lawrence's total and ten per cent of Bongate's that would come to 127 households or 633 people. Penrith, with 140 households, was about the same size, while Kirkby Stephen had 300 but was a large parish including several substantial villages. Sixteenth-century Appleby seems to have been a balanced community with all the essential functions associated with church, school, corporation and market, and at least the danger of Scots invasion had been reduced even if it had not yet been abolished.

There is no record of the town's involvement in the 'Rising of the North' in 1569, when the Earls of Northumberland and Westmorland led a rebellion against Queen Elizabeth, seeking to rescue Mary, Queen of Scots, and re-establish the Roman Catholic faith. Yet the Clifford of the day – Henry, second Earl of Cumberland, who succeeded his father in 1542 and had made one of the grandest marriages in the land, to Eleanor Brandon, Queen Elizabeth's first cousin – had been a staunch supporter of Mary Tudor. He had previously supported the claims of Mary, Queen of Scots to the English throne. When the Rising of the North took place, however, he was in command of the garrison of Carlisle and stood firmly by Queen Elizabeth. He went further, damaging his own property by ordering all the roofs to be pulled off Appleby Castle leaving 'not one chamber habitable.' The demolition may have been self-seeking, as a demonstration of loyalty, or designed to deny the rebels a useful stronghold which he lacked forces to defend.[20] It was 80 years before the damage was repaired.

Appleby may have escaped the Rising, but it suffered new blows in 1587-88 and again in 1597-98 when there were renewed outbreaks of plague.[126] Once again, bad harvests in 1586, 1587, and in four successive years from 1594 to 1597 must have made matters worse. In the four bad years of the 1590s food prices rose by 30, 36, 83 and 65 per cent above the norm and this will have made people weak and more prone to illness. The 1587-88 plague does not seem to have hit Appleby as hard as Kendal, Kirkby Lonsdale and Brough, but in 1598 deaths began in the early summer, and by 25 March 1599 no less than 128 persons had died in St Lawrence's parish.[71; 126] In the Deanery of Penrith, which included most of the upper Eden Valley, the total of deaths was 2,260 while 2,500 died in Kendal.[59] To reduce the risk of infection, Appleby market was closed and trading transferred to a site in the open country at Gilshaughlin, near Cliburn, about half way between Appleby and Penrith.

The great years of the House of Clifford – at least if high titles and glamorous adventures equate to greatness – came in the late sixteenth century, although the grandees concerned do not seem to have had much to do with Appleby. The second Earl of Cumberland died at Skipton in January 1570.[85] His daughter by Eleanor Brandon, Margaret, Countess of Derby, was a possible claimant to the throne for those who doubted the legitimacy of Queen Elizabeth.[85] But his elder son by his second marriage was to become a celebrity!

That son, George, the third Earl, was only eleven when he succeeded to the title and the immense estates that went with it. His guardian, the Earl of Bedford, saw to his education at two Cambridge Colleges, Peterhouse and Trinity, where he displayed a flair for geography and mathematics. He was married at eighteen to Bedford's daughter, Margaret Russell, and soon became a great figure at the Elizabethan court. His daughter, Lady Anne Clifford[6], wrote of his devotion to sports including horse-racing, bowling, shooting and hunting. He also wrote poetry, and was especially skilled in the tilt-yard: his magnificent gold-inlaid tilting armour remained at Appleby Castle until 1923, when it was sold to the Metropolitan Museum of Art in New York.[127] But he was most famous as a sea-captain. He commanded the *Elizabeth Bonaventure* in action against the Spanish Armada in 1588, and brought the news of the victory to Queen Elizabeth, who gave him her jewelled glove to wear in his hat and made him Queen's Champion. When he first tilted as Champion he styled himself 'the Knight of Pendragon Castle,'[85] and a paste-board replica of that castle was built in the tilt-yard in

---

Note 6 - Lady Anne Clifford was sequentially Countess of Dorset, Countess Dowager of Dorset, Countess of Pembroke and Montgomery and Countess Dowager of Pembroke, Dorset and Montgomery. She herself used the title 'Countess of Pembroke' in her Appleby years. Here, unless the context demands otherwise, she is referred to as 'Lady Anne' as in the most authoritative recent biography by Dr R T Spence.[129]

Whitehall: his letter of address to the Queen spoke of Uther, Arthur, Excalibur and the Knights among the marvels associated with the place.[128] Between 1586 and 1596 Cumberland also fitted out nine expeditions to the West Indies and the South Seas. Although they brought him great renown, more money went into them than came back in booty, leaving him heavily in debt. But his impact on Appleby came through his daughter, Anne, probably the most distinctive personality in the town's long history.

CHAPTER 6

Appleby's Great Lady

LIKE many of his predecessors, George, third Earl of Cumberland, had little to do with the Borough of Appleby even though the castle was the focal point of his Westmorland Barony. Although born at Brougham and made Warden of the West Marches and Captain of Carlisle in 1603, he spent little time in the north. When he was not voyaging overseas, his life revolved around the court. As an absentee landlord, his influence in Westmorland was indirect, while the families of Musgrave, Wharton and Lowther, who also held large estates but lived locally, became increasingly powerful.[130]

George Cumberland and his wife Margaret, born Russell, daughter of the second Earl of Bedford, had three children but their two sons both died in infancy. Their daughter and only surviving child, Anne Clifford, was born at Skipton Castle in January 1590, and she was destined to leave a greater mark on Appleby than any of her forbears.[127; 129] However this lay far ahead when the baby Lady Anne was removed from Skipton at the age of six weeks, to be brought up by her mother in the court where she was, as she wrote "much beloved by that Renowned Queen Elizabeth." After the Queen's death in March 1603, Lady Anne's father was one of the peers who went to meet the new King, James I and VI, at Theobalds, north of London. The Countess of Cumberland and her daughter accompanied him, and Lady Anne commented disapprovingly that "we all saw a great change between the fashion of the Court as it is now and that in the Queen's time, for we were all lousy by sitting in the chamber of Sir Thomas Erskine" (who had succeeded Sir Walter Raleigh as Captain of the Guard).[131]

The Cumberlands' marriage was unhappy and they lived apart for long periods. Countess Margaret, brought up very much a Puritan, was upset by her husband's wastefulness and his long-standing affair with 'a lady of quality,' but the Earl took a real interest in his daughter's up-bringing and education.[129] In 1605 both parents were much concerned for her future – and especially her marriage. George Cumberland had made his will, leaving his estates to his male heirs – his brother Francis and the latter's son Henry – rather than to his daughter, who would only inherit them if the male line failed. This made a grand marriage for Lady Anne imperative. But her father and mother were united in insisting that she would not be forced to marry against her will, and she had not made a choice by October 1605 when Cumberland suddenly fell ill and died. The Yorkshire estates then passed to the new earl, Lady Anne's uncle.[127; 129]

Much has been made of the supposed wickedness of Lady Anne's disinheritance. In fact, as Dr R T Spence has pointed out,[129] it was probably a clever move on George Cumberland's part, for it landed his brother, the new earl, with his massive debts. The Dowager Countess retained the Westmorland estates for her lifetime, and these included Appleby, Brougham, Brough and Pendragon Castles with lands that should provide a decent income (though she had trouble getting the money out of the tenants).[129] All the castles were in a mess, Appleby having been dismantled during the Rising of the North, Brough burned by accident following the Christmas feast in 1521, and Pendragon also burned accidentally in 1541.[132] Only Brougham seems to have been fit to live in, although Appleby continued as county gaol and in 1608 the assizes were held there.[59] In 1607 Lady Anne and her mother made a tour of these northern possessions because her mother expected to retire there once Lady Anne was married.

Meanwhile, Francis Clifford, the fourth Earl, established links with the county that gave him his title, becoming Lord Lieutenant of Cumberland in 1607 (a post he held until 1641). And for a short while Lady Anne's life seemed to be unrolling as her father had wished. Well-educated by a tutor, Samuel Daniel, who was himself a poet, historian and writer, she had become a woman of strong character and lively imagination. According to the great Dr John Donne, she could hold her own in conversation on any topic from slea-silk to predestination.[129] She had strong principles, an iron will, and obstinacy worthy of the proverbial mule! Lady Anne herself wrote that she had a "strong and copious memory... sound judgement, and discerning spirit, and so much of a strong imagination... that many times even my dreams and apprehensions beforehand proved to be true." She was short of stature (like Queen Victoria, scarcely five feet tall), slender, round-faced, with long dark hair and black eyes "the form and aspect of them quick and lively."[130; 131]

Those quick and lively eyes, linked to a lively disposition and high social standing helped her towards the kind of marriage her father would have wanted. In February 1609 Lady Anne married Richard Sackville, who two days afterwards became Earl of Dorset and lord of Knole in Kent. Like his wife, he was only nineteen and he was popular, affectionate, talented, skilled in the tilt-yard – and a notorious spendthrift. As Edward Hyde, Earl of Clarendon put it: "his excess of expenditure in all the ways to which money could be applied was such that he so entirely consumed almost the whole of the great fortune descended to him that when he was forced to leave the title to his younger brother he left in a manner nothing to support him."[131] But his wife saw his good side, writing that he was "in his own nature of a just mind, of a sweet disposition and very valiant in his own person."[131]

Although the marriage started happily, the young couple fell out over Lady Anne's attachment to her northern inheritance. The Countess Dowager, who had carried out her plan of removal to Brougham, questioned the legality of her husband's will. An entail granted by King Edward II to Robert Clifford centuries before had stipulated that the estates and the Barony of Clifford should descend to the direct heir regardless of gender,[131] and this had led in 1606 to a petition to the Earl Marshal to rule that the Baronies of Clifford, Westmorland and Vescy had passed to Lady Anne on her father's death.[129] Many years later this claim prevailed, but this did not prevent her cousin Henry, son of the new earl, being called to Parliament during his father's lifetime as Lord Clifford on the false assumption that the barony had passed with the earldom.[85; 129] Countess Margaret's researches were the starting point for the Great Books of Record detailing the history of the Clifford family whose compilation was to continue under Lady Anne's direction right up to 1670.[129]

Lord Dorset on the other hand had no interest in these wild northern lands, scattered with ancient and ruinous towers. But he did see his wife's possible claims on the northern estates as a saleable asset which would help his finances by getting money out of the Cumberlands.[127; 129] Legal wrangling came to a head in 1616. A court proposed that Lady Anne's interests in Westmorland and the Skipton estates be sold to her uncle. Dorset was to get, on her behalf, £20,000 if she concurred and £17,000 if she refused. He, Lady Anne's cousin Francis Russell (later Earl of Bedford), and even George Abbott, the Archbishop of Canterbury, all urged her to sign away her rights to her northern lands. She refused, insisting on discussing the proposals with her mother, and on 21 February she left for the north with her husband, in two coaches, each drawn by four horses.[127] However, Lord Dorset wanted to go to the races at Lichfield and turned aside on 26 February. Lady Anne and her servants reached Brougham on 6 March and on the 20th she and her mother sent word to London of their rejection of the proposed agreement.[127]

Dorset was furious and demanded that his coach and horses, but not his wife, should return to London forthwith. Wisely, after a show of compliance, she insisted on accompanying the entourage southwards. She parted with her mother on 2 April 1616 on the road half a mile east of Brougham, where the Countess' Pillar still stands to commemorate their farewell. In London and Knole, the Dorsets continued to bicker over land and money, but remained friendly in other ways. Dorset, who had sent their only child, Margaret, born in 1614, away when the quarrel was at its height, arranged to have her returned. But the couple quarrelled again later in April, Dorset removing to London and to a round of cock-fights, plays, races and bowling-alleys while his wife stayed at Knole "having many times a sorrowful and heavy heart, and being condemned by most folks because I would not consent to the Agreement, so as I may truly say, I am like an Owl in the Desert."[131] Then came news from Brougham that Margaret, Dowager Countess of Cumberland, had died on 16 May.

This altered things. The Westmorland estates had been Lady Anne's mother's for life, but her Clifford uncle and cousin could now be expected to claim them, and this swung Lord Dorset round, for once they were in occupation it would reduce the potential value of Lady Anne's interests. The new amity was sealed by an agreement under which Lady Anne agreed to convey her Westmorland inheritance to Lord Dorset "if Lady Anne had no descendants surviving her."[127] This helped with Dorset's creditors while protecting the interests of baby Margaret. United by this turn of fate, the couple sent word to Brougham that Lord Dorset was taking possession of the estate by right of his wife. Both factions sent agents to secure the various castles and at Appleby in June there was a report of "violent conduct by the Earl of Cumberland's servants and people in breaking up the windows and doors of Appleby Castle and by strong hand putting out the servants of the Earl of Dorset."[59] Dorset's people, on the other hand, held Brougham where Countess Margaret lay unburied.

The Story of Appleby in Westmorland

Figure 4. The Countess' Pillar, Brougham, where Lady Anne parted with her mother, Margaret, Countess of Cumberland for the last time. Drawn by Moses Griffith in 1773. From Pennant's Tour from Downing to Alston Moor.[80]

The agreements with her husband signed, Lady Anne could go north to see to her mother's funeral, and she reached Brougham in early July. Countess Margaret had left the choice of her burial place to her daughter, who wanted it to be in the borough church of St Lawrence in Appleby. On 11 July she was told that this was impossible, but this may simply have been a reminder that the lady of the castle could not command the borough, for once her representative issued a polite request the objections melted away.[127] Margaret Countess of Cumberland was duly buried in front of the high altar, and a magnificent alabaster tomb was commissioned. It is almost certainly by Maximilian Colte, who carved Queen Elizabeth's effigy in Westminster Abbey, and it is indeed of royal quality. Margaret Cumberland sleeps on a base of black marble and alabaster set about with the coats of arms of her ancestors and bearing inscriptions recording her virtues: 'faith, love, mercy, noble constancy.' It was moved in 1884 and now stands in the north chapel, next to Lady Anne's own tomb.

The row between Dorsets and Cumberlands, which was constrained while Countess Margaret lay unburied, soon boiled over. On 29 July Lady Anne sent her people into the park at Brougham to make hay, "where they were interrupted by my Uncle Cumberland's people, two of my uncle's people were hurt by Mr Kidd - the one in the leg, the other in the foot."[131] Complaints were made to the judges at Carlisle, who issued a warrant for the arrest of all Lady Anne's haymakers. She intervened and the combatants were released, and in August an order bearing the King's signature arrived from London. It instructed that since the Earl of Cumberland's people were in possession of Appleby, and the Countess of Dorset's of Brougham, both were to hold what they had until further orders.

Lord Dorset arrived on 22 August, Lady Anne meeting him at Appleby 'Town's End' (perhaps the top of Battlebarrow) and riding with him and Lord William Howard back to Brougham in their coach. But five days later Henry Clifford arrived at Appleby and soon afterwards there was a brawl in Penrith when "there passed some ill words between Matthew, one of the [Cumberland] Keepers, and William Durin whereupon they fell to blows and Grosvenor, Grey Dick, Thos. Todd and Edwards drawing their swords made a great uproar in the town and 3 or 4 were hurt & the men [who] went to ring the [church] bell fell from a ladder and was sore hurt."[131]

Things were clearly building to some kind of climax, and despite an effort at reconciliation in September, on 19 November Lady Anne, still at Brougham, heard that her husband, now back in London, had challenged Lord Clifford to a joust.[129] King James I stepped in, asked Dorset to bring Lady Anne to London, and announced that he would himself sort the quarrel out.[131] And so he tried to do on 18 January 1617, when he asked both Dorset and his wife to leave the whole matter to him - and

Lady Anne told him straight that, "I would never part with Westmorland upon any Conditions whatsoever."[131] Having confronted the king, she went to talk to the queen, who was evidently sympathetic and warned her "not to trust my matters absolutely to the King lest he should deceive me" – scarcely a ringing commendation of the honour of husband and Sovereign![131] Two days later she again defied the king, who "grew into a great chuff." King James, like Cumberland and Dorset, had had enough of Lady Anne's obstinacy by this time, and she was shut out of the negotiations which ended in the King's Award on 14 March. This assigned the estates to the Cumberlands, but Lord Dorset was to receive £17,000 over two years and a further £3,000 if Lady Anne confirmed her acceptance of the judgement (which she never did).[129] If Lady Anne were to survive her husband and start fresh lawsuits she would not only have to pay the money back but would lose all her other rights under her father's will. When the ruling finally arrived, sealed with the royal seal, she could only bow grudgingly to the inevitable.

The award must have seemed like defeat for Lady Anne, but it hurt the Cumberlands quite hard, too. On top of their responsibility for Earl George's debts, they had to find another £17,000 for the Dorsets. The Westmorland estates probably brought in a net income of around £800, and Craven £1,000 a year (these figures are estimates, based on records for 1669, and may be too high), so it would have taken a decade to recoup the payment, and the award must have imposed other costs such as lawyer's fees. Indeed as it turned out the award brought the Cumberlands close to the financial ruin that Earl George had feared his daughter would face if he had left the estates and debts to her![129]

From 1617 until 1649 Lady Anne never visited Westmorland. Her mother's tomb was commissioned by her, but she did not see it for over 30 years. Her uncle Cumberland entertained King James I at Brougham in 1617 at a cost of around £1,200.[25] He did get excused the alleged debt of £159 arising from arrears of money due from the Sheriff of Westmorland for the fee farm of Appleby, but this did little to off-set the crippling cost of entertaining royalty! Nor can he have been delighted when, at the royal business session, his tenants presented a petition against their landlord's exactions![25] His son Henry (as Lord Clifford) served as an MP for Westmorland in 1614 and in 1621-22, and was a member of the Council of the North in 1619. He was joint Lord Lieutenant of Westmorland with his father between 1636 and 1639.[85]

Figure 5 - Margaret, Countess of Cumberland's tomb. Drawn by Moses Griffith in 1773. From Pennant's Tour from Downing to Alston Moor.[80]

Meanwhile, in the south, the Dorsets lived amicably (on the whole), enjoyed grand occasions at court, and had a second daughter, Isabella, who lived and three sons, who died. In 1624 Dorset himself died, in London, while Lady Anne lay sick at Knole. He had frittered away great wealth, selling land to support his extravagance. But he left Lady Anne well provided for, with town and country houses and the revenue for life of large estates – which meant that there was next to nothing for his brother Edward, the new Earl.[129]

In 1628 Lady Anne lodged a formal claim to the succession to the Clifford estates should her uncle and cousin die without male heirs: this did not breach King James' Award but secured the interests of her children. She may well have been prompted to this action because of the approaching marriage of her elder daughter, Margaret Sackville, to John, Lord Tufton: this happened in June 1629, a week before Margaret's fifteenth birthday.[127; 129] Her husband became Earl of Thanet two years later. Margaret Tufton was to have twelve children, the first in 1631 when she was only sixteen – and extraordinarily for the period, eleven of them survived to adulthood.[127; 129]

In June 1630 Lady Anne herself remarried at the age of 40, becoming the second wife of Philip Herbert, Earl of Pembroke and Montgomery, Lord Chamberlain to King Charles I "he being then one of the greatest subjects in the land."[131] She had known him for twenty years: ever since he had been a handsome young man, skilled in arms, a sportsman and a patron of the arts (he and his elder brother had shared the dedication of Shakespeare's First Folio). With him she had two sons, born prematurely, who died soon after birth.

Lady Anne herself wrote that "this second marriage of mine was wonderfully brought to pass by the Providence of God for the crossing and disappointing the envy, malice and sinister practices of my enemies."[131] Clearly she was seeking security, for she was on bad terms with both her cousin Henry Clifford and her brother in law, the new Earl of Dorset (who must have looked jealously at her immense jointure lands). Pembroke was not only an old friend but still reasonably good-looking, rich and wielding great power at court.[127; 129] According to his wife (writing after his death) he was "of a very quick apprehension, a sharp understanding, very crafty withal and of a discerning spirit but extremely choleric by nature."[131] George Sedgwick, who worked for him and later became Lady Anne's secretary, put it differently. "He was very temperate in eating and drinking," he wrote, "but much given to women, which caused a separation between him and his virtuous lady Anne[7]."[48]

The marriage seems none the less to have gone smoothly for several years. It gave Lady Anne the very highest social status. She became mistress of the great house of Wilton where she and Pembroke received King Charles I and Queen Henrietta Maria almost every year.[129] Here she saw at first hand the remodelling of the house and garden by Isaac de Caus, pupil of Inigo Jones. However, she clung tenaciously to her northern interests. "Being still mindful to vindicate my right and interest in the lands of my inheritance in Westmorland and Craven..." she executed another legal claim in 1632.[131] But in December 1634, on the eve of the Royal Christmas celebrations, she and Pembroke had a monumental row. The cause is unclear: it may have been, as Sedgwick says, over his womanising, but it may also have had something to do with the betrothal of Lady Anne's daughter Isabella, whom Pembroke wanted for one of his

---

Note 7 - Sedgwick's manuscript account of his life and service to both Pembroke and Lady Anne is quoted extensively by Nicolson and Burn (ref. 48).

sons while Lady Anne was determined to allow her freedom of choice. It may also be relevant that Lady Anne was 44, that her last two children had been born prematurely, and that she may well have been experiencing menopausal stresses. Whatever the reason, Lady Anne walked out on Pembroke, moving from their Whitehall house to his fine mansion of Baynard's Castle near Blackfriars.[129]

They kept up the appearances, but scarcely lived together after that and Lady Anne's grand position at court was forfeited. Pembroke behaved generously, settling manors in Kent on her for life and renouncing any interests he might have in the Westmorland property in favour of Isabella, on whom he settled £5,000 out of his estates in Craven. He also included Lady Anne in the great Pembroke family portrait that Van Dyck painted in 1636, which still hangs at Wilton. In it Philip Herbert towers imperiously among his handsome sons and daughters, while his wife sits beside him disconsolately, with arms folded, looking as if she wished she was somewhere else.[129]

After the separation Lady Anne still spent some time at Wilton, where she became friendly with her husband's distant relative George Herbert the poet, and also at Baynard's Castle, but her favourite home was the Herbert country house at Ramsbury in Wiltshire. She again registered her interest in her northern inheritance in 1637, and this must have seemed a bit nearer fruition in January 1641 when her uncle Francis died at Skipton Castle at the great age of 82. His son Henry, who succeeded as fifth Earl of Cumberland, was by then the sole Lord Lieutenant of Westmorland and had no male heir.[127; 129]

The 1637 claim was Lady Anne's last before the Civil War broke out in 1642. Its outbreak brought the Pembrokes closer together although they differed in their loyalties.[129] Lady Anne remained a staunch Royalist while Pembroke, though a former favourite of King James I and a close friend of Charles I, took the side of the Parliament. It is said that he broke with the king over the betrayal and execution of Thomas Wentworth, Earl of Strafford.[128] Henry, Earl of Cumberland, became the Royalist Commander in Chief in Yorkshire and the north.[85] He garrisoned Skipton Castle for the king, and also put a Royalist garrison under Sir Philip Musgrave into Appleby, where one of the two powder magazines in Westmorland was located (the other was at Kendal).[133] But the first Civil War was something of a non-event in Cumberland and Westmorland, despite professions of loyalty to the king. Sir Philip

Musgrave's authority was undermined by other local gentry like Sir John Lowther of Lowther, who seemed more concerned to safeguard their estates than to support their king by sending local forces outside the two counties.[133]

In 1643 the fifth Earl of Cumberland died at York at the age of 51. Relations between the cousins had thawed by then, partly, no doubt, because Lady Anne's inheritance appeared inevitable, and she had been godmother to Henry Cumberland's granddaughter earlier in 1643. Now, after 38 years the whole Westmorland estate reverted to her at last, while the lands around Skipton became Pembroke's – and she was far away in Baynard's Castle where she and her unmarried daughter Isabella had been installed for safety.[129]

Cumbria had remained impoverished during the period of Lady Anne's exclusion. The cloth industry was in decline, and the whole area had had a disastrous harvest in 1622.[126] Death rates rose to three or four times the norm, and another outbreak of plague had followed in 1623-24. In the 1630s the two counties of Cumberland and Westmorland had experienced difficulty in raising the money needed by the king for the navy. Appleby was rated at only £5 for 'ship money' and Kendal at £15 "for that latter (Appleby) is most miserably poor and Kendal is not rich."[112] As late as 1657, a Parliamentary assessment valued the two counties at £92 and £63 respectively, whereas Norfolk was valued at £3,106 and Devon at £2,574.[134] However, life in Appleby seems to have been ticking over steadily enough. The succession of mayors continued. The Moot Hall, which was probably built around 1596, was in use as a meeting place by 1614 when the earliest surviving council minute books were compiled.[135] A public bakehouse with stone walls and a thatched roof was built by the mayor and corporation in High Wiend in 1615 at a cost of £11-11s-5d.[136] The town had a charter from King Charles I in 1628, but this merely recited the provisions in earlier documents.[75] The fee farm rent remained at two marks following James I's award of 1618. The school continued to flourish, passing from Reginald Bainbrigg to William Pickering, perhaps in 1613[101] and continuing to send a stream of able scholars to the Queen's College, Oxford.

The advent of the Civil War and the garrisoning of the castle for the king must have jarred old memories, but battle did not come near the town. Lady Anne could not come near it either because war raged across the Midlands, confining her to the relative safety of Baynards Castle. It was while living there that she commissioned the famous 'Great Picture' of her family from an Anglo-Dutch painter, possibly Jan van Belcamp. Two copies were made, one for Appleby and one for Skipton, but only the former survives.[8] It is in the form of a triptych, and stands nine feet high, spreading eighteen feet when opened out. It is clear that the painter was under strict orders about what he was to paint. The central panel – the true 'great picture' – portrays Lady Anne's parents and young brothers, with, on the walls behind them, smaller portraits of her aunts of Derby, Wharton, Warwick and Bath. The side panels depict Lady Anne herself in youth and middle age, backed by portraits of her tutor and governess on the left and two husbands on the right. Books, family coats of arms and tables of descent ornament the backgrounds and margins of the pictures. It is, perhaps, more a work of curiosity than of art, but it is clearly a resounding assertion of family pride and dignity![129]

From London, Lady Anne set about establishing her suzeraignty over her northern estates – and ran into trouble with some of her tenants, especially in Kirkby Stephen and Stainmore, who claimed various rebates and exemptions.[127] One problem may have been that she was an unknown quantity, absent from the district for nearly 30 years. But there was clearly continuing resentment over the system of fines or 'gressums' which had been one of the grievances behind the Pilgrimage of Grace in Cumberland and Westmorland.[119] These were charged when a new tenancy began – and since all tenancies changed on the death of a landlord, fines of 7d or 8d were levied again then. They would have fallen due in 1641 when Lady Anne's uncle, the fourth Earl, died and some of these were still being gathered in 1649, though of course they belonged to Lady Anne's cousin Elizabeth and her husband the Earl of Cork as heirs of Henry, the fifth Earl. Two years later, in 1643, another set became due when the fifth Earl followed his father – and these would have been Lady Anne's.

Collecting double fines in the midst of civil strife must have been deeply unpopular, but we know enough about Lady Anne to be sure that she would have been a stickler for her rights. We also know that there was a political dimension to her tenants' resistance. She was a noted Royalist: Kirkby Stephen and Stainmore people were equally strongly

---

Note 8 - It is now at the Abbot Hall Gallery in Kendal, but the centre panel is too vast to be exhibited, although the side panels have been displayed. It is hoped that it will be possible to exhibit the entire triptych at a future date.

Parliamentarian. Captain Robert Atkinson, tenant of Blue Grass Farm in Mallerstang, was Parliamentary Governor of Appleby Castle and he and those like him were certainly not going to pay willingly to an absentee Royalist landlord! But Lady Anne demanded her dues. Lawsuits were to follow.

Meanwhile the first Civil War was brought to an effective end in 1646, when Oxford surrendered to the Parliamentary forces. The Appleby garrison had capitulated soon after the battle of Marston Moor in April 1644, and that of Skipton, led by Colonel Sir John Mallory, had followed in December 1645. It was the last in the north of England to surrender, and as a tribute to their gallantry the soldiers had been allowed to march out bearing their weapons and banners. The land fell quiet and the Earl of Pembroke had time to visit Skipton and press his and his wife's interests in the Craven estates, from which he needed to raise the £5,000 promised as his step-daughter's marriage portion.[129] He still wanted Isabella Sackville for one of his sons, but she was unwilling, Lady Anne refused to press her, and in 1647 she married a staunch Royalist, James Compton, Earl of Northampton.

Pembroke must have been irritated, but he had other things to worry about. In 1647 he took his old friend Charles I into his custody at Newcastle and conveyed him to imprisonment, first at Holmby House in Northamptonshire and then at Hampton Court. From here, Charles made his way to Carisbrooke Castle in the Isle of Wight (of which Pembroke had been Governor in 1643, and may still have been). This was a signal for the outbreak of the second Civil War in 1648, and this did affect Appleby. A Scots army invaded the north of England in support of the king. Sir Marmaduke Lumley, with men from Kendal, drove Captain Atkinson's Parliamentary garrison out of Appleby Castle. As Winston Churchill put it, "King, Lords and Commons, landlords and merchants, the City and the countryside, bishops and presbyters, the Scottish army, the Welsh people and the English fleet all now turned against the New Model Army. The Army beat the lot."[137]

Cromwell and the Army defeated the Scots in October 1648, and the Royalists at Appleby surrendered to a force led by Lieutenant-General Ashton. It was reported that Ashton's prisoners included Sir Philip Musgrave, Sir Thomas Tilsey, Sir Robert Strickland, Sir William Hudleston, Sir Thomas Dacre and Sir William Blackstone, together with fifteen colonels, nine lieutenant colonels, six majors, 46 captains, seventeen lieutenants, ten cornets, three ensigns, five pieces of cannon, 1,200 horse, 1,000 stand of arms, and all their ammunition and baggage.[59] This extraordinary muster is explained by most of them having been members of a Royalist army which had been blockading Cockermouth and had retreated to Appleby on the approach of Ashton's forces.[48] There were surely far too many to fit into a far larger castle than Appleby, and one may guess that many were quartered in the town.

Unlike most captured Royalist strongholds, Appleby Castle was not 'slighted' (dismantled) by the Parliamentary forces. The keep was not of much use, having stood roofless since 1569, but the protection of the castle seems to have been deliberate, and the result of an order sent in November 1648 to the commander of the Parliamentary forces there "to take care that no harm is done to the castle or the goods therein, and that no spoil be made upon the country when they march out of it."[59] This favourable treatment may have been a result of the Earl of Pembroke's Parliamentarian allegiance. Three months later the king's head fell in Whitehall, on Lady Anne's 59th birthday.[127] Six months after that, on 11 July 1649, having taken leave of Pembroke and her daughters, she left London for the north. She never returned. Her northern estates soon felt the impact of her energy and commitment.

On 18 July Lady Anne reached Skipton "finding most of the old Castle pulled down because it had been held for the King in the Civil War." Indeed it was in such a bad state that she had to lodge in the Long Gallery, from which she paid a visit to Barden Tower, which was also ruinous.[127; 131] On 8 August she reached Appleby Castle "the most ancient seat of my inheritance." Some of it must have been habitable for she remained there until the following February. Using it as a base, she visited Brougham and Pendragon. She was at Appleby in January 1650 when she got the news of her second husband's death, which brought her the undisputed ownership of Skipton Castle and its lands. These were, however, diminished because her cousin, Earl Henry's daughter, Elizabeth Countess of Cork, was in occupation of the Barden Tower and Bolton Abbey estates, conferred on them under King James' Award.[129]

Lady Anne determined to get Barden Tower and its lands back, relying on the fact that the Corks were in trouble with the Parliament and facing heavy fines because the earl had been an active Royalist. Far from showing sympathy with kinsfolk who shared her own political convictions, Lady Anne exploited their difficulties. She occupied Barden

Tower without opposition, and pursued her unfortunate cousins resolutely in the courts with the aim of recovering all the estates that had once belonged to her father. When she met the Corks, courtesy prevailed: when they were apart she did everything she could to dispossess them. Saddened, Cork wrote after one encounter that she appeared to prefer "controversy even with her nearest kinswoman before peace."[129] The dispute rumbled on until 1667 when Cork had become Earl of Burlington and won the final legal tussle over a property in Skipton.[129]

Although these events were far away from Appleby they are important because of the light they cast on Lady Anne's character. It is clear that she was *not* the 'lady bountiful' that some have made her out to be. However generous she might be to those she chose to favour, she was unyielding, litigious and even vindictive when crossed. Even towards the end of her life, when 'the old woman' wanted something she usually got it. In 1649 she got most of what she wanted in Westmorland and Yorkshire, and with her widow's jointures in the south she was very rich.[129] Almost at once she seems to have decided to restore the castles of her ancestors, starting with some work to create comfortable lodgings at Skipton. According to George Sedgwick, some neighbours and friends tried to dissuade her alleging that "as fast as she built it up, Oliver Cromwell would order it pulled down." She replied, "let him destroy my castles if he will, as often as he levels them I will rebuild them, so long as he leaves me a shilling in my pocket."[131] "This being reported to Oliver," wrote Sedgwick, "'Nay, says he, let her build what she will, she shall have no hindrance from me.'"[127]

There was a political problem about starting work at Appleby – the Civil War flared up yet again. In 1650 King Charles II was installed as King of Scotland. In the spring of 1651 a large Scottish army gathered on the Border, to be defeated by Cromwell at Dunbar. The north of England became full of soldiers. As Lady Anne put it "this summer Major General Thomas Harrison came hither with his forces, for then the wars were hot in Scotland. So as then many places of Westmorland and especially my Castle of Appleby was full of soldiers which lay here a great part of the summer. But I thank God I received no harm or damage by them nor by the King and his army who that August came into England and within six or seven miles of Appleby Castle."[131]

"The King and his army" – Charles II and his Scottish troops – marched in August 1651 from Carlisle along the old Roman road through

Brougham to the Lune gorge and Lancaster. High on the moors above Crosby Ravensworth, at a little pool called Black Dub, source of the River Lyvennet, there is a monument that records that the King 'regaled his army' and drank the waters as they marched south. Cromwell and Harrison let them go, allowing the royal army's supply lines to become impossibly extended and then almost annihilating it at Worcester. At Appleby, General Harrison and Lady Anne argued with one another. It would be marvellous to roll back 350 years and eavesdrop on the debate between the little, upright, black-gowned lady and the staunch Puritan soldier and regicide. She made no secret of her Royalist convictions and cannot have been gentle with a man who had condemned her king to death and escorted him to his execution. He, for his part, distrusted her motives and tried to "dispute her out of her Loyalty." Charles II's defeat probably eased things for her, and two years later Cromwell assumed supreme power: she could get on with her building work without hindrance.[127]

The restoration of Appleby Castle had actually begun before the advent of Charles II's army. As a preliminary step, the prisoners had to be got out of the keep, which had served for centuries as the county gaol. In 1651 Lady Anne is recorded as having "erected a gaol in the Borough and removed the prisoners thereto."[59] The new gaol was in fact the old gatehouse at the west end of the bridge, with its guardroom, chapel and oratory, extended by adding a substantial room on the ground floor, south of the original chapel, with a similar extra room above.[88] Judging from the complaints about the building that soon followed, the work was not up to Lady Anne's usual standards.

On 21 April 1651 Lady Anne helped to lay the foundation stone of a new central wall in the keep, called by her Caesar's Tower.[131] This crosswall, which divided each floor into two rooms of nearly equal size, was an architectural necessity since it allowed the new floor joists and roof beams to be less massive, and more readily inserted, than if they had to span the entire structure.[9; 20] Moreover, the new wall included fireplaces and flues, allowing for more effective heating: comfort was also improved by glazing the windows and by inserting hooks from which wall hangings could be suspended. To make the whole structure more useful, a floor was added at the top of the tower, which became a self-contained building suited to the accommodation of Judges of Assize and their servants, or other guests.[20] The four angle turrets of the keep were also added in the restoration of 1651-53. In 1653 Lady Anne completed her work in the castle by building a new block of stables in the outer bailey, near the roadway into the top of Boroughgate, and a little 'bee house' or private oratory on the foundations of an old guard tower in the castle grounds.[129]

In April 1651 she also began a quite different building in Appleby – the Hospital or Almshouses of St Anne at the upper end of Boroughgate. The land – an acre in all comprising four former burgages "abutting on the water of Eden on the east and the street called Boroughgate upon the west" – was bought on 30 December 1650 from George Bainbrigg.[63] The alms houses were finished in 1653 when they were endowed for the maintenance of "a Mother, a Reader, and twelve Sisters for ever." The endowment came partly from lands in the manor of Brougham and partly from the farm and former Grange and Hospital of St. Nicholas, which had been suppressed in 1539, and which she bought for £900.[59; 121] At the start of 1653, "I now put into it twelve good women (eleven of them being widows and the twelfth an injured maid) and a Mother, a deceased Minister's widow."[131] The mother was in fact the widow of Gilbert Nelson, former schoolmaster of Sedbergh, who had been a good friend to Lady Anne's secretary George Sedgwick: Lady Anne took Mrs Nelson's daughter into her own service.[127; 129]

Lady Anne's third work in Appleby borough was the restoration of St Lawrence's Church. This began in 1655 while the benefactress was in residence at the castle. She wrote that she caused "a great part of Appleby Church to be taken down (it being very ruinous and in danger of falling of itself) and I so caused a Bank (vault) to be made in the north east corner of the Church for myself to be buried in (if it pleaseth God). And the repairing of the said Church cost me about some six or seven hundred pounds, being finished the year following."[131] The work in the north east corner entirely replaced the former Chantry of St Nicholas and all the roofs were renewed. According to a Mr Hill, "the south Choir was likewise rebuilt, and a chantry behind the pulpit which projected towards the town called Warcop's Choir pulled down. In taking down the walls of this Chantry several alabaster and plaster images curiously gilded were discovered, several of which Mr Machell had seen when a boy at Colby Hall."[48] Probably they had been concealed from image-breaking Reformation vandals. An inscription on one of the rafters in the south aisle still records that "Ann Conntesse of Pembroke in Ano 1655 repaired all this building."[138]

As a fourth benefaction, in 1656 Lady Anne established the Temple Sowerby Trust which she endowed with an estate in that parish which she had bought in 1653. It brought in £7 a year and the trustees (who included the Mayor of Appleby) were instructed to use the money for the repair of the Countess of Cumberland's tomb, the Moot Hall, the bridge and the Grammar School House.[87; 101; 129] Finally, in 1658 she attended to St Michael's Church, recording that "I did cause Bongate Church, near Appleby, to be pulled down and new built up again at my own charge."[131] Possibly this last restoration was a Royalist rescue operation, for in 1657 a Commonwealth survey had described the parish church of St Michael as "an appendage of the said Corporation, situate less than a quarter of a mile from St Lawrence" and proposed an amalgamation of the two – a piece of 'rationalisation' that had to wait for more than 300 years.[59]

It was not new for the lords of Appleby Castle to pay for work in the town, but Lady Anne's efforts were on a completely different scale and broke with tradition. She seems to have treated the town almost as her fiefdom – and got away with it, probably because she spent money on public works on a scale unmatched by any of her predecessors, and perhaps also because she was clearly committed to the community of which she was a part. She probably also owned quite a lot of property in the town, thanks to Clifford acquisitions down the years and especially since the sack of 1388.

It was almost certainly through her ownership of burgages which conferred Parliamentary voting rights that she gained the control she seems to have exercised over the election of the borough's two MPs. In 1660 she recorded that in the elections for the Convention Parliament two of her cousins – Sir Thomas Wharton and Sir John Lowther – were chosen as Knights of the Shire for Westmorland while Sir Henry Cholmley and Christopher Clapham were returned for Appleby "for the most part by my means."[129] In 1661 she nominated John Lowther (son of Sir John) and John Dalston (a prominent Royalist) as representatives of the borough. The corporation provided the requisite nod of approval. On Lowther's death she insisted on nominating her grandson, Thomas Tufton, even though the town (and most of the gentry) preferred Joseph Williamson, private secretary to the Earl of Arlington who was Secretary of State.[129] Resignedly, the rejected candidate's brother reported that they had "left no stone unturned with the old woman… but to no purpose for she is resolved wholly to stand for her grandchildren."[129] Ninety three years later her great grandson would battle out another election with the chief Lowther of the day.

Lady Anne's works extended far beyond Appleby. Brougham, Brough and Pendragon Castles and Barden Tower were restored at a total cost of £40,000. The churches or chapels at Barden, Brougham, Ninekirks, Skipton and Mallerstang were all refurbished or rebuilt. An almshouse her mother had commenced at Beamsley in Yorkshire was finished.[127] What is somewhat surprising is the form of her reconstructions. Lady Anne was familiar with great and spacious houses like Knole, Hardwick and Wilton, and she had watched Isaac de Caus rebuild the latter. Even in Cumbria, well-lit great houses in modern style had been built at Levens and Sizergh. She could easily have remodelled her northern castles in a fashion that blended tradition, beauty and comfort. Why did she, instead, produce structures that clung to the mediaeval form even if they did have the benefit of extra fireplaces and glazed windows? There was no good military reason, for the Civil Wars had demonstrated that mediaeval castles were of little use against modern artillery. The most likely explanation is that she harked back to her youth, when the 'chivalric revival' was at its height – with her father, George Cumberland, at its pinnacle, tilting as the Knight of Pendragon Castle beneath the cardboard replica in Whitehall. That was a period when others, too, were building in mock-mediaeval mode, as Lord Charles Cavendish was doing at Bolsover.[128] Lady Anne had not been happy at Knole or Wilton – isolated at the former 'like an Owl in the Desert' while her husband gambled and disported himself in London. It is not surprising that she harked back to the days of her happy and well-connected youth, when she had been close to the queen and to the king's cousin, Lady Arbella Stewart, and sought to create her own chivalric revival.[128]

This interpretation makes sense when we consider the Great Picture and the Great Books.[127; 131] The former is not an outstanding work of art – it does not compare (for example) with Van Dyck's portrait of the Herbert family at Wilton. It is a dynastic statement, in old-fashioned mode. Likewise, the Great Books are dossiers of dynasty – records of the genealogy and deeds of the Clifford ancestors. They, the picture and the castles are all of a piece and they are summed up in the inscription from the Book of the Prophet Isaiah (Chapter 58, verse 12) that Lady Anne had affixed to most of her works of restoration:

And they that shall be of thee shall build the old waste places: thou shalt raise up the foundations of many generations, and thou shalt be called, The repairer of the breach, The restorer of paths to dwell in.

Lady Anne was very much the Grand Lady. Like her ancestor the Shepherd Lord, she moved in stately progress from castle to castle. Against the economic norm of the day, she spent money in the north that had come from her widow's jointures in the south. Her works brought a lot of local benefit because she gave direct or indirect employment to so many. She was liberal in her gifts to servants and friends, and traded locally, buying fabrics and provisions from her tenants and neighbours. William Marshall, a tailor in Bongate, made her black cloth gowns which cost £1-9s-6d for materials and ten shillings for making up, totalling just under £2.[85] This was her dress "not disliked by any, yet imitated by none" and considered by George Sedgwick "very plain and mean, indeed far too mean for her quality."[48] Sedgwick also noted that "all the groceries, spices, stuffs, and the like which she used in her house, all wines, malt, hay, corn, and straw for her stables, she bought of neighbours and tenants near the place of her then residence, paying always ready money when they came for it. So she was a great support and help to those parts. Seldom had she anything from London, being desirous that the country might receive benefit from her. In whatsoever castle she lived, every Monday morning she caused ten shillings to be distributed among 200 poor householders of that place, besides the daily alms she gave at her gate to all that came."[48; 127] Outside the castle, the almswomen of St Anne's Hospital were her closest associates in Appleby, and she often dropped in for a chat, sharing their dinner. Every week some of them visited her at the castle, and they all came once a month.[129]

On the other hand she stood on her dignity. It is said that the inscription on the High Cross that now stands at the top of Boroughgate: "Retain your Loyalty – Preserve your Rights" was her personal motto, and it certainly sums up her approach to life. "She was at a vast charge in lawsuits to vindicate her rights" according to Sedgwick.[48] Her disputes with her tenants rumbled on and while anxious to be a just and generous landlord, she insisted that agreements were rigorously enforced. Fines of 8d were demanded when tenancies changed, and most tenants were also required to supply 'boon hens': some 800 of these birds came to Skipton Castle every year and a comparable number to Appleby.[48] Those that would not pay up were taken to court and in 1656 and 1657 she succeeded in getting some of the most obstinate Stainmore tenants ejected.[129] It cost her £200 to force a rich Halifax clothier named Murgatroyd, who took a property near Skipton, to pay her a hen, and his costs were comparable – but she won in the end. Sadly, the story that she then invited Mr Murgatroyd to dinner so that they could carve the hen up between them appears to be fiction, like the story that she sat face to face with Cromwell and defied him.[127] (The latter anecdote may well be based on her confrontation with General Harrison).

Some of Lady Anne's behaviour was a sheer abuse of power, and especially of her position as Hereditary High Sheriff of Westmorland. In 1650 she obstructed her cousins the Earl and Countess of Cork's resort to 'my County Court' of Westmorland. She packed juries at Appleby Assizes, and tried to favour a suit at Westminster by selecting the Westmorland jurors who were to hear it (though in both cases they asserted their independence and returned a verdict against her).[129] In 1663 she simply refused to serve or accept writs issued by the court in London against her and her son-in-law the Earl of Thanet in a long-running dispute over the Dorset estates. But, remote in Westmorland and protected by her age, she got away with it, while Thanet spent a month in the Fleet prison.[129] She was capable of great generosity, but it was on her terms. Cross what she believed to be her rights and she was as arrogant as any of her ancestors!

One reason why Lady Anne and Appleby town may have got on well together was that both were staunchly Royalist. The antagonism between them and the Parliamentarians of Stainmore and Kirkby Stephen is evident in the contemporary account by the Reverend Thomas Machell[9] [48] of what happened when a charter was imposed on the borough by Oliver Cromwell who also sent a proclamation proscribing King Charles II (who had escaped to France after the defeat at Worcester) as a 'traitor.'

When this arrived in Appleby, according to Machell, "no man there (either by reward or threatening) could be induced to act or to appear in so horrid a villainy. The Mayor withdrew himself, and the bailiffs (whose office it was to make proclamations) threw up their commissions

---

Note 9 - Like Sedgwick's memoir, this is quoted at length in Nicholson and Burn's first volume.

though but poor men, insomuch that the soldiers were glad to have recourse to a fellow in the market, an unclean bird, hatched at Kirkby Stephen, the nest of all traitors, who proclaimed it aloud whilst the people stopped their ears and hearts having nothing open but their eyes and those even filled with tears..."

"And the townsmen were not far behind this gallant example of their noble leaders; who when Captain Atkinson came down from the Castle with his musketeers to choose a Roundhead Mayor, and clapped his hand on his sword saying 'I'll do it by this,' yet made resistance; for they then conferred the office (to prevent bloodshed) on a moderate man who had acted on neither side except in bearing that office before, and so he was Mayor two years together. And though Oliver, through Captain Atkinson's means, in order to make himself more absolute, gave a charter to this ancient corporation which was rather imposed than accepted of, yet they preserved their old one to the last."[48] Captain Robert Atkinson, the commander of the Parliamentary garrison at Appleby Castle from 1645 to 1648, had earned the hostility of the Royalist gentry because he had been "active in securing the King's friends." Lady Anne described him as her 'great enemy' because he had managed a lawsuit against her on behalf of his fellow-tenants (which, of course, had made him popular with the common people).[139] These antagonisms helped to seal his fate in 1664.[139; 140]

On the king's return, Thomas Machell's father Lancelot was elected mayor, but "would not handle the staff of authority nor permit the oath of office to be administered unto him till he had sent for Oliver's charter, and in the face of the court cut it in pieces with his own hands, and then looking about he espied some tailors and cast it to them saying it should never be a *measure* unto him."

The Restoration was the occasion for a great party in Appleby. This was described with verve by Thomas Machell who wrote:

> *There were almost as many bonfires as houses, and two stately high scaffolds at each end of the town, hung with cloth of arras and gold; whither after service done at the church, the Countess of Pembroke with the Mayor, Aldermen, and all the other gentry of the country ascended, with I know not how many trumpets, and an imperial crown carried before them, where they proclaimed, prayed for, and drank, the health of the*

King upon their knees; the aged Countess seeming young again to grace the solemnity. The expenses of that day were very considerable. For throughout the town was kept open house, after the example of that noble Countess who thought not her gates were then wide enough to receive her guests, which before had been too wide for receiving armies of soldiers.[48]

Those two 'stately high scaffolds at each end of the town' may hold the answer to an Appleby puzzle – who built the High and Low Crosses, the one in the Market Place and the other outside the castle gates? They were certainly both standing by 1754, because they are shown on the burgage map made at the time of the election dispute between Lowther and Tufton.[61] The corporation minute books[141; 142] contain a reference to the High Cross in 1748, and to the Low Cross in 1712, 1718 and 1743. This is compatible with the Royal Commission on Historical Monuments'[9] conclusion that the south (High) Cross dates from the late seventeenth century, while their judgement that the Low Cross is 'a later copy of the eighteenth century' may be explained by the record that the Low Cross was rebuilt in 1817, and the High Cross 'likewise re-edified' in 1818.[59]

Given the expenditure records, it is very possible that both monuments originated in the late seventeenth century, even if they were partly rebuilt later, and they must stand near the sites of the two 'stately scaffolds.' It is tempting to speculate that the two pillars were erected after the Restoration as a permanent memorial to an event which caused so much popular rejoicing. If this is so, then Lady Anne may have had a hand in their erection (although there is nothing about this in her diaries). Even if the inscription on High Cross is a later addition, possibly due to John Robinson (see Chapter Seven), if it was indeed her personal motto it might have been carved in commemoration. There is a clear resemblance between the upper parts of the crosses and the upper parts of the Countess' Pillar at Brougham which is one of her most distinctive pieces of monumental architecture (figure 4).[129; 143]

The Restoration did not go unchallenged. In 1663 risings were planned by various groups of disaffected people, mainly with the aim of forcing the king to stand by his promise to grant religious freedom to all except Roman Catholics, to abolish unpopular taxes and to restore good magistracy and ministry (there are echoes here of the Pilgrimage of Grace). The rebels expected to take Carlisle and Appleby Castles without difficulty and to spark a popular uprising. The so-called Kaber Rigg Plot was one element in the conspiracy,[139; 140] and Captain Robert Atkinson – the same Atkinson who had tried to force the Roundhead Mayor on Appleby – was its chief leader. It was to be his task to take Appleby Castle, seize the excise money from the Clerk of the Peace and ride with his followers to Durham. The set date was 12 October 1663, and on that day a small band of armed men rode out from Atkinson's farm in Mallerstang. He expected 2,000 horsemen to rise at his signal, but news of the plan had already reached Sir Philip Musgrave and his fellow deputy lieutenants, Alan Bellingham and Daniel Fleming, and only 30 or 40 men arrived at the rendezvous. Disillusioned, Atkinson called the hopeless action off and the men dispersed – only to be hunted down and brought to trial. Atkinson himself was smuggled to London by his supporters, where, with the promise of a royal pardon before him, he confessed, incriminating a number of his confederates. Packed off to Westmorland in the power of his enemy, Sir Philip Musgrave, his king's evidence did not prevent his execution in 1664: the promised royal pardon arrived late. It is said that the messenger was deliberately delayed on the road, and this was doubtless convenient to both Musgrave and Lady Anne, who had old scores to settle.[131; 139; 140]

Lady Anne recorded the event in her diary with some satisfaction. "The 20th day of this August," she wrote, "did two Judges of Assize for this northern circuit come hither... to keep the assize here in Appleby... And they lay here in this Appleby Castle for 4 nights together, Judge Twisden in the Baron's Chamber and Judge Turner in the best room in Caesar's Tower. In which time they kept the Assizes in the Moot Hall in Appleby Town, where Robert Atkinson, one of my tenants in Mallerstang, and that great enemy, was condemned to be hanged, drawn and quartered as a traitor to the King, for having a hand in the late plot and conspiracy, so he was executed accordingly the first day of the month following."[131] Vendetta settled, Lady Anne seems to have been kind to Atkinson's widow and children, allowing them to remain on their farm at a nominal rent. Elizabeth Atkinson was one of the last visitors Lady Anne received in 1676, when she kissed her and made her a gift of two shillings.[131] Yet the memory still rankles: when I wrote of these events in 1956 I received a letter from one of Captain Atkinson's descendants in which he wrote of "Captain Bob's execution, which I call murder!"

During the years following the Restoration Lady Anne continued to live quietly in the north, dividing her time between different castles, but living in Appleby more than in any other. Her progressions were grand occasions, local gentry and retainers riding with her in an almost royal train.[129] It took 48 double carts (hired for 2s-6d each) to carry her goods from Appleby to Brough in September 1675. Furniture was also shifted from castle to castle when there was a special need, as when 4s-6d was paid for "three carts for carrying six beds from hence to Brough Castle, which were lately brought from thence hither against the Assizes here."[144] When she left a place, she gave gifts to the poor and to bell-ringers and waits who serenaded her departure. Largesse was also distributed along the way.[129] Keeping (in a sense) her own court in Westmorland, she declined suggestions that she might visit the other court in London.

Lady Anne was an indefatigable reader and had a good library. Her housekeeping is well documented in several account books which, as George Sedgwick put it, "were most exactly kept."[48; 144] On 15 August 1673 she recorded "this weeks expenses of my Housekeeping here at Appleby Castle" as £13-14s-3d. Other weeks were less expensive ranging from £9-19s-0d to £5-10s-5d. On 16 August she paid £8-2s-0d for "eight score and two loads of coals from my own pits on Stainmore, at 12d per load for firing my house at this Appleby Castle." On 7 October a further 122 loads cost £6-2s-0d and on the 24th 150 loads cost £7-10s-11d. These pits were in the small coalfield around Tan Hill, which supplied the greater houses at this time, while the fuel of the ordinary people remained peat or wood. From the accounts there must have been an unending procession of carts from Brough to Appleby to feed the capacious (and doubtless smoky and inefficient) chimneys of the castle.

The accounts are full of miscellaneous detail – oats for the stables at 2s-6d per bushel; £3-19s-9d for 'fine scarlet cloth' bought at Kendal; £2-10s for malt "for a brewing of beere for my house use at this Appleby Castle"; claret at four shillings a gallon; "a pound of the best Virginia tobacco for my owne taking,[10] four shillings" and numerous records of wages and of gifts of money and goods, including one entry "paid then to George Dent of Appleby for two great large stocklocks he made for me to give away, two pounds." One such lock, bearing the initials 'A.P.'

Note 10 - There are not many records of women smoking at this period, but Queen Elizabeth is said to have enjoyed a pipe and maybe Lady Anne was following an example she would have witnessed in youth.[145]

long remained at Great Asby Vicarage, while another can still be seen at Collinfield, Kendal, where George Sedgwick lived after his retirement in 1673 and one is still in use on the main door of the Bishop of Carlisle's palace, Rose Castle.[129; 144]

As Lady Anne got older, inevitably she became less mobile, but she still moved by coach or litter between her castles, living in each in her own room where she took her meals. Close relatives and friends might eat with her: others were entertained in a neighbouring room, joining her for talk after the meal. Like royalty, she kept a strict timetable, and her interviews followed a regal pattern: guests joined her at the time of her choice, stayed for conversation, were given a gift, and were escorted out again.[127]

Anne Clifford, Countess Dowager of Dorset, Pembroke and Montgomery, lived to the great age of 86, and died in 1676 "at her Castle at Brougham, Christianly, willingly and quietly having before her death seen a plentiful issue (by her two daughters) of 13 grandchildren." On 14 April her body was carried to St Lawrence's Church in Appleby where Edward Rainbow, Bishop of Carlisle, preached a sermon enumerating her virtues. "Thus fell at last this goodly Building; thus died this great wise woman; who while she lived was the Honour of her Sex and Age, fitter for an history than a Sermon."[127] An era had ended, but her reputation has endured. "In an age when women were merely their husbands' chattels, she remained steadfastly herself and her father's daughter. She defied King James, she defied Cromwell and she survived to see the restoration of King Charles II, leaving an indelible mark in the places and among the people who knew her well."[85] "It is but seldom that any personage who is not of first-class historical importance has succeeded in imprinting his or her personality upon a whole countryside or has transmitted, however superficially, a personal tradition through succeeding generations of a rural population. This is, however, the case with the Lady Anne Clifford."[9]

Her body lies in the vault under the north-east chapel of St. Lawrence's Church, and her tomb above is fittingly ornamented with the arms of the families of Clifford and Vieuxpont. The inscription records the details of her life, marriages, children, and death. In 1884 the vault below was entered, to see whether its masonry was in a sound condition to bear the weight of the tomb of the Dowager Countess of Cumberland, which was in that year moved from the east end of the sanctuary into the north chapel. A contemporary account records what was found there.[78]

> *[The vault] is 9 ft. 2 ins. square, strongly arched with stone to the height of 6 ft. 2 ins. and approached by a flight of eight steps. The coffin, which is deposited on rude stonework some 27 inches from the ground floor, is of lead attached to which are projecting handles on each side, apparently of iron, but much corroded, with one at the head and another at the foot. The length of the shell is a trifle over 6 ft. and the greatest width at the shoulder 17 ins. tapering to the bottom where there is a receptacle for the feet. It is fluted lengthwise, and bears the figure of a face and body terminating at the chest, below which is a brass plate engraved in the highest class of workmanship though like the handles a little corroded through the effects of the numerous invasions of the river Eden when in flood. The inscription reads, "Ye body of ye most noble, virtuous, and religious Lady Anne, Countess Dowager of Pembroke, Dorset, and Montgomery, daughter and sole heir to ye Right Honourable George Clifford, Earl of Cumberland, and Baroness Clifford, Westmerland and Vescey, Lady of ye Honour of Skipton in Craven, and High Sheriff by inheritance of Westmerland, who departed this life at her castle at Brougham, in ye county, ye 22nd March, 1676, having attained ye age of 86 years ye 30th of January before." The masonry is as fresh and as perfect as on the day it was executed, even suggesting that, having performed their labours, the workmen had just taken away their hammers and trowels and gone to dinner.*

A second visit in 1935 confirmed the details of this description but showed that the features are those of the Lady Anne herself, the body being wrapped in a closely applied lead sheet.

CHAPTER 7

Busy Market Town

THE late seventeenth century saw Appleby ticking along as a reasonably prosperous little market town, with added dignity because it sent two Members to Parliament, was the scene of the county assizes and had the best grammar school for miles around. And we know quite a lot about the detail of its life because the corporation minute books covering the period from 1614 to 1885 have been preserved, and considerable parts of them have been transcribed and published by the late Canon C M Lowther Bouch.[141; 142]

The population in 1674 can be guessed from the inventory of properties subject to a Hearth Tax in the Constablewick of Appleby.[142; 146] This lists 120 households, including the castle, gaol, school and the Hospital of St Anne. Most – 74 in fact – had only one hearth, as did each of the twelve almshouses in the hospital, but the castle topped the list with 40 (hence Lady Anne's massive coal bill, which must have been made even more enormous because Brougham Castle had 30 hearths, Brough 24 and Pendragon 12!)[59] Appleby constablewick did not coincide exactly with the old borough (Colby Laithes is included), but if 100 of the listed properties were in the town proper and each had five occupants, this would give a total population of 500.

This is not too incompatible with a diocesan survey in 1676 which indicated that there were 417 people "of an age to communicate" in the parish of St Lawrence, along with three Quakers.[147] Assuming that three quarters of these parishioners lived in the borough and that two thirds of the population were of an appropriate age, this would give 469 as the estimated total. The Hearth Tax lists a further 45 households in the Constablewick of Bongate, adding 225 people of whom perhaps half would have been in the borough. The figures thus fit with a total population of between 550 and 650. For comparison, the Hearth Tax statistics record 147 households in Kirkby Stephen.[125] In 1686 Appleby had 117 guest beds available for travellers, and 126 stabling places for their

161

horses, whereas Penrith had 136 beds and 214 stalls, Kendal 279 and 439, and Kirkby Stephen, on a less important road, only 52 and 70.[148]

The school received several important benefactions in the late seventeenth century, including a share in the revenues of the Temple Sowerby Trust established by Lady Anne in 1656. In 1671 three old boys of the grammar school, Dr Thomas Barlow (Provost of the Queen's College, Oxford, afterwards Bishop of Lincoln), Dr Thomas Smith (Dean and afterwards Bishop of Carlisle) and Dr Randal Sanderson (Fellow of Queen's) offered the governors £380 on condition that they transferred the right of appointing the schoolmaster to the Provost and Fellows of the Queen's College, Oxford.[101] This was accepted by the governors and the college on 23 April 1671, and immediately after that the three benefactors, together with Sir James Lowther (MP for Westmorland) gave a further £800 in cash or books.[101; 103]

This was an excellent arrangement, which guaranteed that the schoolmaster would be a man of learning and also strengthened the connection between the school and the college. Following this improvement in the school's finances, a new house for the master was built, in 1671 (map 5). A new headmaster, Richard Jackson, was appointed by the college soon afterwards, to be followed in 1686 by Jonathan Banks from St Bees who served for 35 years.[101] Banks was a close friend of Dr William Nicolson, Archdeacon and later Bishop of Carlisle, who sent both his sons to the school and commented in 1702 that it was "the best endowed school in this Diocese... and perhaps the most flourishing in the North of England, the present Master Mr Jonathan Banks... being a person of good learning and great industry."[101] Under this leadership, and closely tied to Queen's College, Appleby Grammar School was set for a flourishing eighteenth century.

Bishop Thomas Smith also made an important gift to the parish Church of St Lawrence. In 1684 a new organ was obtained for Carlisle Cathedral, and the chapter presented the old one to Smith who "freely bestowed it upon the Corporation of Appleby, for use in Appleby Church." It is still there, and is reputedly the oldest working organ in the country, incorporating parts dating back to before 1571 while its case was made in the early seventeenth century.[9] Bishop Smith also gave the borough "a convenient and decent market house or cloister, which fronts to the Market place." This stood on the site of the present cloister, and was particularly used as a covered market for butter.[48] Part of the cost of building it was borne by another old boy and benefactor of Appleby Grammar School, Dr Barlow, Bishop of Lincoln. The building was erected on the churchyard (one presumes that the Bishop of the Diocese had no difficulty in obtaining a faculty for this!) and in consequence the corporation paid the vicar an annual rent of five shillings.[59]

There were big changes at the castle following Lady Anne's death. It and the Clifford estates passed to her surviving daughter, Margaret, Dowager Countess of Thanet, and then, six months later to her grandson John Tufton. This by-passed his elder brother Nicholas, who was by then the Earl of Thanet, and sparked another family lawsuit! But Lady Anne's Tufton grandsons, who had all survived to adulthood, now fell like ninepins. Earl Nicholas died in 1679: Earl John in 1680 and Richard, the fifth Earl, in 1684 – all without offspring. However the fourth brother, Thomas, lived until 1729. This Earl of Thanet maintained Appleby Castle as his principal Westmorland residence, moving furniture there from Brough and Brougham.[25] It was the obvious choice, being the only castle to stand in a market and assize town. Lord Thanet's remodelling began in around 1695 and converted the eastern range into a spacious and well-lit modern house. The width of the north-west wing was doubled and the whole range was given a new neoclassical façade looking onto the main courtyard. Behind this façade the great hall, kitchen and many of the fifteenth century rooms were retained, although a fine new staircase was added. Dr W D Simpson[56; 57] described the result as "a fine essay in the pure neoclassical Renaissance. It is obviously the work of an architect of distinction, probably from southern England." Pevsner, with more restraint, terms it "a stately piece of late seventeenth century architecture."[149] The main range of the castle remains almost unchanged today apart from some mild Victorian Gothic additions to the south-east tower. The result is an interesting composite structure containing work of all periods from the twelfth to the nineteenth centuries (Plan 3).[9; 149]

It always used to be said that the remodelling of Appleby was achieved at the expense of the other Clifford castles which were demolished to yield lead, stone and timber. This does not seem to have been the case.[25] While lead stripped from Pendragon was sent to Skipton and its stone was sold in the 1690s, Brough and Brougham were maintained for a while. However in 1717, after the Jacobite rebellion had been seen off, the Earl of Thanet seems to have decided that the costs of maintenance far outweighed the benefits, and he sold the materials from both buildings. By

1730 they were just romantic ruins, attractive to antiquaries and poets. It was not until the 1840s that they began to be repaired, to halt further deterioration.[25] Lady Anne would surely have wished to give her grandson a severe ticking off!

Appleby, in common with many other boroughs, was summoned by King James II in 1685, to surrender its earlier charters. In response, the charter of King Charles II was sent to the king, who granted a new charter of incorporation quite unlike its predecessors. It says that "the said

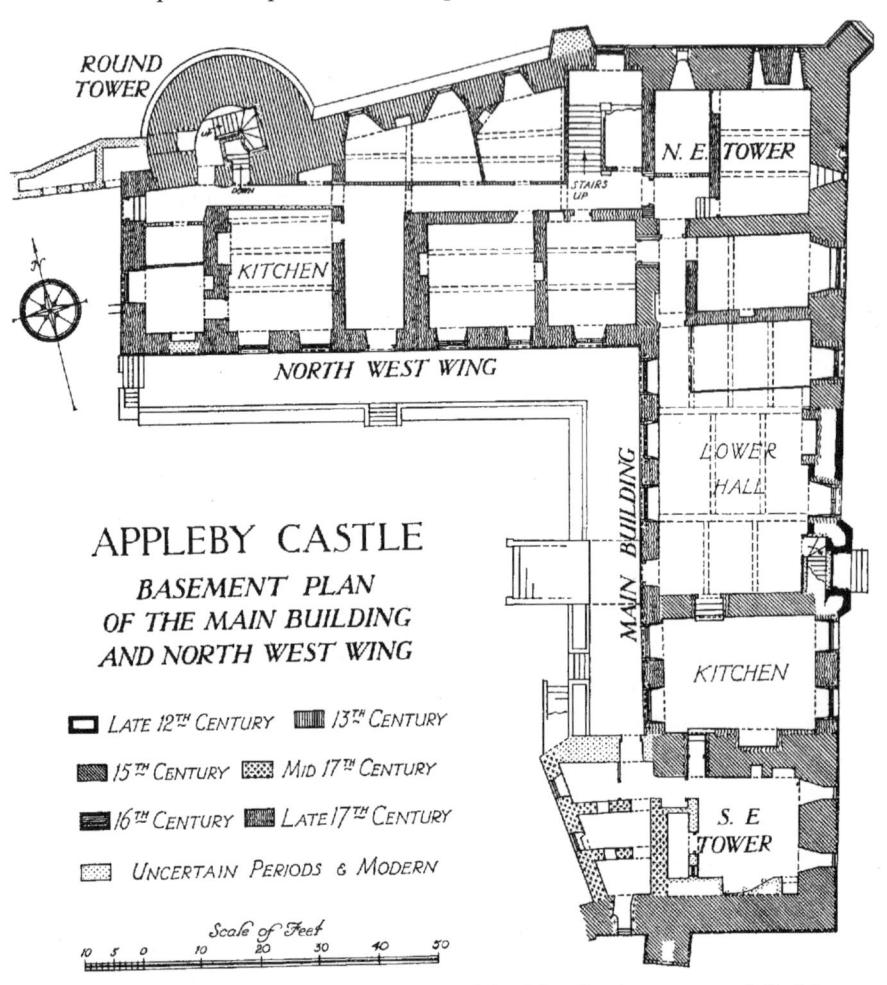

APPLEBY CASTLE
BASEMENT PLAN OF THE MAIN BUILDING AND NORTH WEST WING

- ☐ Late 12th Century
- ▦ 13th Century
- ■ 15th Century
- ▨ Mid 17th Century
- ■ 16th Century
- ▬ Late 17th Century
- ▒ Uncertain Periods & Modern

Plan 3 - The east and north west ranges of Appleby Castle, as re-modelled by the sixth Earl of Thanet in around 1695. From the Report of the Royal Commission on Historical Monuments, © Crown copyright.

164

town of Appleby... shall be and from henceforth for ever remain a free borough in itself, and that the Burgesses and inhabitants of the aforesaid town of Appleby... and their successors for ever... [be] constituted as a corporate body with divers powers."[74] It enumerates the officers as the mayor, recorder, twelve aldermen, one common clerk, sixteen capital burgesses, a coroner, bearer of the sword, sergeant at mace, two chamberlains and two bailiffs. John Atkinson is named as the mayor and Thomas, Earl of Thanet, as the recorder. The aldermen include Sir Christopher Musgrave, Edward Musgrave Esquire, Hugh Machell Esquire, Philip Machell, gentleman, and members of the Cole, Atkinson, Warcopp, Lowson, Jackson, Robinson, Coniston, Carleton and Hall families as other aldermen. Thomas Carleton was the first common clerk. Like others of its period, the charter reserved to the king the right to displace the mayor and councillors at his pleasure.[71] The town was granted a "fair or market for the purchase and sale of all and all manner of goods, cattle, horses, mares, geldings on the second Thursday in April, to last for two days." However this does not appear to be the antecedent of the present Appleby New Fair, for it was to be held within the borough whereas the New Fair is outside it.[150]

In 1688 this charter was also ordered to be returned to the king, but whatever was originally intended by this summons was not carried out and in the same year a proclamation was made restoring to all the corporations in England their ancient privileges. But no further charter was ever granted, and it was declared that the surrender of 1688 was void, never having been enrolled, so that the charter of 1685 remained in force. Lawyers argued that this charter had in turn been granted in consequence of the surrender of l685, and that this was also void, never having been enrolled. The result of all this confusion was that Appleby, after 1688, had no valid charter in force, and subsisted as an ancient corporation by prescription for the following century and a half.[48; 75]

As specified in King James II's Charter of 1685, the town was governed by a mayor, twelve aldermen, and a common council of sixteen burgesses. On the face of it, the system was reasonably democratic though not every citizen had a vote. The corporation was elected by the freemen of the borough, who numbered 180 in 1708 and 84 in 1795. People became freemen if they were born sons of a freeman, were nominated by the mayor on one occasion during his term of office, or purchased the privilege. They had to be Appleby people: in 1720 it was ordered that "no foreigner living out of the town to be made a freeman, under fine of £5. This to be a standing rule, except for the son of a Freeman."[141]

Freemen were exempted from the tolls which provided the chief revenue of the borough, so the position was both coveted and jealously guarded. In 1757 it was "ordered that no persons who deal in corn, grain, cattle, or anything whereby a toll would arise to the Borough shall be made a Freeman under a less fine than 20 guineas." The fine would have compensated the borough to some extent for the loss of revenue, which might be considerable since not only the man admitted but also his sons and their descendants would automatically be able to become freemen. As another guard against the appointment of too many freemen it was decreed in 1714 that "no Mayor to make more than one Freeman in one year, without the consent of the Common Council and Aldermen."[141]

The freemen elected the common council, who in turn appointed the mayor from among the aldermen. The aldermen took no part in the election "unless the Common Council be equally divided." This common council was called the Sixteen of the Borough, and was a separate body from the Sixteen who governed the business of the parish church. There was some overlap: in 1692 the charge of 3s-6d for "making the little Church gate" was borne by the town council, whereas in 1705 the church council paid 6d for "mending the Church gate." The Sixteen of the Borough were supposed to live within its boundaries, but in 1723 the Court of King's Bench reinstated three people who had been ejected for non-residence and displaced those that had been elected in their place.[141]

Being mayor was not cheap. 'By ancient custom' he (they were all men at that time) used to give a dinner at Christmas for the aldermen, common council and freemen and by 1673 this was held to be too expensive "and yieldeth no advantage to any" (a strange comment, given the corporation's fondness for special treats). The corporation decided on a rather bizarre alternative: each year the mayor would give £6, and the town £4, to purchase "a free plate of £10 to be run for every year at Sandford Moor." This was, presumably, a horse-race: circuses in place of bread! Prior to 1699 the mayor seems to have been paid £10 a year out of which he was responsible for funding all 'treats': one can guess it was not enough for, in that year the borough agreed to take over both the revenue and the expenses. In 1772 the mayor got an expense allowance of £20 and was exempted from a series of costs he had previously borne.

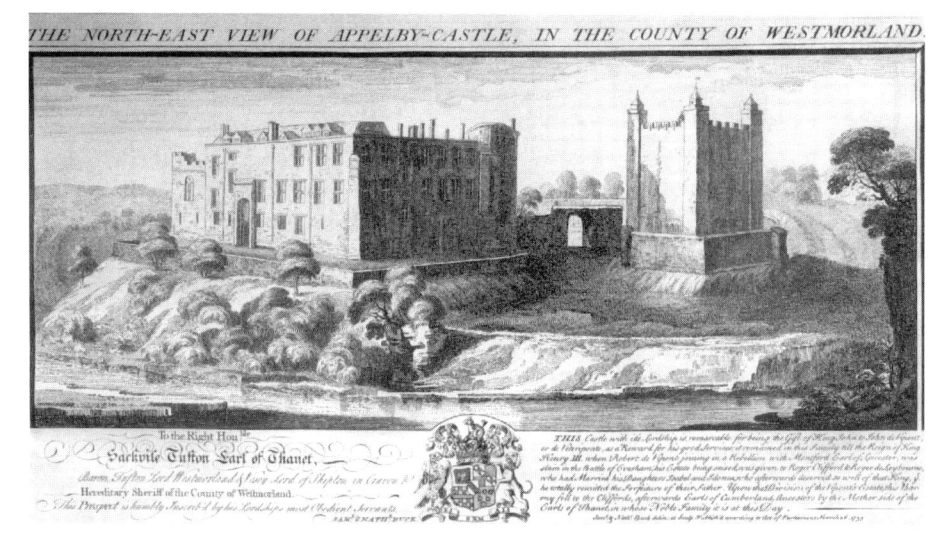

Figure 6 - Appleby Castle in 1761, as engraved by Samuel and Nathaniel Buck. The finest of the old views showing the castle, as remodelled by Lady Anne Clifford and subsequently by the Earl of Thanet.

And there was no easy way out of the mayoralty, for in 1674 it was decreed that any one who refused to take the job once elected would pay, if an esquire, £10; if a gentleman, £5 and if 'of any other degree' £3-6s-8d.[141]

The borough got its income from tolls paid by people using the market or selling goods elsewhere in the town, from the rents of certain tenements, and from fines. There was a separate endowment (Lady Anne's Temple Sowerby Trust) for repair of church, school, bridge and Moot Hall. Tolls on the sale of grain were especially important because Appleby was the principal corn market in the area. The Metley Toll was taken by volume from each sack of corn, using a brass measure, and the Gatley Toll was weighed out using iron weights. In 1699 these tolls brought in £35, and stallage and rents added £6-19s-4d: in 1799 the total had risen to £92-17s-8d. In 1758 it was noted that "the ancient measures or dishes by which toll of grain taken [are] much worn; new ones, duplicates of old ones ordered."[141]

By their early charters the burgesses of Appleby were themselves exempted from tolls throughout England except the city of London, and this immunity was still prized and defended in the eighteenth century. In 1741 there was a complaint of "Mr William Gorst, Steward of the Earl of

Thanet, having seized the goods of John Bainbridge and other freemen of the Corporation, in pretence of their being liable to pay toll and stallage at Kirkby Stephen, this was deemed a great infringement of the rights and privileges of this Corporation. In due course Mr William Gorst inspected the grants and was satisfied that the freemen of the Corporation are by the same exempt from tolls not only in Kirkby Stephen, but in all England." In 1746 it was protested "that toll at Carlisle unjustly demanded from burgesses of this borough" and a similar complaint against Lancaster followed in 1750.[141]

Just as the corporation were at pains to preserve their own immunity in other towns, so they were concerned to exact the revenues due from people passing through Appleby itself. In 1757 there was a "complaint that persons have of late denyd to pay toll of corn sold in Bongate, which has been immemorially paid; ordered farmers of Metley and Gatley tolls demand toll on all such grain, if not paid action to be started." (This only makes sense if the reference is to sales in the part of the borough lying within St Michael's parish: the corporation would have had no jurisdiction over sales within Bongate proper). Tolls of money were taken for passage of certain highways, and in 1793 it was ordered that the "several persons who assaulted the constable in assisting the toll gatherers in taking the Bridge Street ½d toll be prosecuted."[141]

The market provided other revenues. The letting of the shambles – butchers' stalls and slaughter houses which stood in the middle of Boroughgate – brought in 21 shillings in the year l699-l700. These shambles were carefully supervised, and fines were levied if they got out of repair and were not put in order despite an instruction to the tenants. Any extension to these premises required permission. In 1736 Charles Robinson applied for "leave to extend the shamble he now has by 2 yards and to take in a shamble or shambles adjoining on the S.E. of the same which has not yielded any profit for many years." In 1792, however, George Bowness, butcher, was fined £1-10s-0d "for erecting a Shamble in front of his house, and extending it upon the Corporation street about 7 feet towards the channel and near the front path, which we deem a great nuisance having viewed the same."[141]

Like the shambles, the meat market – which was the largest in the district – was in Boroughgate, above the Moot Hall: no butcher was allowed to sell meat below the shambles under pain of a fine of 20 shillings. Sale of meat not in fit condition was also punished by a fine, thus in 1749

"John Dent of Birkdale" was fined one shilling "for exposing unwholesome meat." In 1763 "Thomas Smith, for killing and selling part of one sheep not being exposed in the market" was also fined a shilling. In 1681 James Spedding was fined 6s-8d for "offering Tupp mutton upon sale after Michaelmas," at which time the meat was likely to be in poor condition. The use of the street by butchers caused problems of sanitation and in 1748 it was ordered that "no butcher shall empty the baggs of any beast cattle that they kill, or lay garbage, in any part of the street."[141]

Regulations were especially numerous in connection with the sale of bull beef. It was ordered that no bull might be butchered and the flesh offered for sale unless the animal had been baited with dogs. In 1746 James Orton of Kirkby Stephen, butcher, was fined 3s-4d for exposing bull beef not baited, and in 1765, "George Bowness for selling a bull in the market not being set to the ring" was fined 6s-8d. Bull baiting was certainly a noisy business and this may have been the reason why in 1772 "John Shepherd and Joseph Nelson, for baiting a bull about the hour of 3 o'clock in the morning contrary to order," were fined 13s-4d.[141]

The bull ring and rope for tethering the animal were maintained by the corporation, and the ring is still to be seen let into a stone in the market place. A new rope cost ten shillings in 1700. The custom was maintained until 1812, in which year a large and ferocious red roan bull snapped the rope and careered around the town with an equally ferocious bull mastiff firmly gripping its nose. "The High Cross was rounded" so one account goes,[78] "and the massive beast then tore away down the street and, pursuing his wild career amid the loud cries of the crowd, he galloped down the High Wiend and along Doomgate, where he fell exhausted." By 1812 opposition to bull-baiting was growing and the obvious danger of such incidents was probably enough to cause the corporation to impose a ban: the practice was prohibited throughout England in 1835.[151] By then the citizens of Appleby had probably concluded that the main street of the town was not really the most desirable location for slaughterhouses.

The butcher's market above the Moot Hall was segregated from the general market lower down around the Low Cross, where corn, butter, cloth, leather, eggs and other goods were traded (presumably bulls were not baited here on market days!) After the cloisters were built, in around 1696, they became the only place where butter was permitted to be sold and then only after 10 o'clock in the forenoon. Various orders were made against forestalling, that is the buying up of produce before it had reached the market, and its subsequent sale at a higher price. In 1788 Matthew Johnston of Stainmore was fined 13s-4d for repeatedly offending in this way and in 1799 John Taylor of Crosby Ravensworth was fined 9d for "regrating in market by buying a quantity of potatoes and immediately retailing them out again at an advanced price."[141]

There was also a complaint "against persons monopolising the potatoes brought into the market so that the inhabitants of this Borough and more particularly the poor thereof have of late been deprived in manner of their chief support; ordered that no potatoes be sold in large quantities before 10.30." To reinforce this last decree it was further ordered "that any person refusing to sell by the bushel or any quantity under a bushel be fined." The giving of short weights in the market was also punished by fines, as was the sale of poor quality leather. The latter was tested by the official 'sealers and searchers of leather,' of whom the corporation employed four in 1688. The types and weights of loaf sold were also regulated and the profit which could be taken on each of them was firmly controlled.[141]

Income from the market would have been boosted at the time of special fairs. Most of these were held in the town, allowing it to draw revenue from tolls and taxes on animals and goods. The first fair in the year, granted by King James II's Charter of 1685, was held on two days in April. There was another two-day fair on Whitsun-eve and Whit Monday, and a third on St Lawrence's day (10 August). But some fairs were held outside the borough. In 1750 the mayor is recorded as approving a "show of horses and sheep and also of black cattle if it please God to cease the distemper" (probably foot and mouth disease) "that now rages among them, to be held in Battleborough on Gallow Hill and Brown Bank on 1st and 2nd June and 29th September." Before 1744, when it was enclosed, Gallows Hill (which was the county's site for executing felons condemned by the assizes held in Appleby) formed part of Bongate Moor. After its enclosure the Earl of Thanet and other owners took exception to the Corporation of Appleby presuming to advertise fairs on it although a compromise must have been reached as the site continued in use.[150] Fairs held here were popular because, being outside the borough, they escaped the tolls charged in the town. The June fair, described in the nineteenth century as for 'cattle, sheep, horses and merchandise' was probably the fore-runner of the New Fair that continues to this day.

It is difficult for citizens of the twenty-first century to imagine the smell, noise and mess of an eighteenth century town. With animals being penned and killed in the streets, many others regularly driven through the town, and horses the universal means of transport, a high state of cleanliness was not to be expected, and the roadways seem to have been a dumping ground for household rubbish of all kinds. There were no sewers, slops being emptied into gutters and runnels like the Doomgate Sike. Most of the muck must have ended up in the Eden. The corporation employed a scavenger, and took some measures to keep the filth under control. In 1674, for example, it was "ordered that all the dung hills be clearly removed out of the street called Briggatt (Bridge Street) before 21st December, that John Bainbridge scour and dress his gutter at Farbarend, that every person clean his frontage upon the back street; that every person in the Wiends do cleanse their own front every month, that the swine lookers go about every month." In 1748 a fine of 6s-8d was decreed on any "who do not lead their dung hills clean away four times in the year," and the town scavenger, John Graveson, was fined ten shillings for not keeping the gutters and pavements in Boroughgate clean. Then in 1760 it was ordered that "dunghills to be removed from the shambles before 2nd February or fine 13s-4d," and three years later "dung and other nuisances to be removed by the Scavenger at the Low end of the New Building and also at the High end of Mr Robinson's slaughter house."[141] Such conditions were commonplace in English towns of the period, and visitors to Appleby would not have found it unusual.

However, the town's swine seem to have been a special problem. It sounds as if they were allowed to roam the streets, perhaps scavenging amongst the household refuse, and the corporation employed three swine lookers to control the nuisance. In 1717 "any persons that have any swine in the town" were ordered "to shut them up every market day between 9 and 4 of ye clock," presumably to stop them foraging among the stalls! Again in 1760 "all swine" are ordered "to be well ringed and on every market day to be kept in their stalls or houses." In 1783 it was noted that "Thomas Outhwaite does keep two sows which go at large and are a common nuisance – fine 5 shillings."[141]

What with dung and refuse in the streets, no proper sewerage and animals wandering everywhere, it is not surprising that the water supplies were polluted. In 1714 it was ordered "that wells in Dungate

(Doomgate) and... before Jane Addison's door be cleansed, and conduits made to carry all corrupted and filthy water from about it; that the runnel coming down Dungate be well scoured and dressed." Four years later the maintenance of the same wells was raised again, when it was "ordered that the Chamberlains do repair Dungate Well, commonly called Sowerby well, so as to hinder beasts and horses to drink in it. Well before Jane Addison's door to be made good."[141]

There are several references to the town pumps. In 1757 it was noted that "considerable sums of money having been spent in repair of the Pump at the Town Head, which has not answered the intended purpose and is now out of use – £5-5s-0d to be spent on making it a good going pump." In the same year there is a note that "as a pump at the Low End of the Town Hall would be of singular advantage to the inhabitants of Bridge End and others near to, Thomas Wilson contractor agreed for 30 shillings down and £1-1s-0d per annum for 7 years to sink such a well and to keep the pump going for 7 years." Another pump in Scattergate was ordered to be repaired in 1761, and in 1769 the shambles pump was to be inspected. The pump at the Town Head seems still to have been in a bad state, and in 1785 it was finally ordered that "the materials of the High Town Pump be taken up, sold, and the well filled up and secured."[141] The system of wells and pumps continued to supply Appleby until 1877, when a more efficient source was found and the whole service modernised.

Besides regulating trade, trying to keep the place clean and maintaining wholesome water supplies, the corporation also helped the unfortunate. In 1699 £4-16s-0d was paid to 'the poor' and in 1704-05 a 'traveller that was robbed' was given 3s-4d. In 1706-07, 4s-8d was paid out to 'travellers' and 1s-0d to 'a decayed gentleman traveller.'

In the seventeenth and eighteenth centuries Appleby had quite a tally of officials. In 1688 the full list was: mayor, town clerk, coroner, sergeant-at-mace, two chamberlains, two attorneys, two bailiffs, three informers (who brought charges against wrong-doers), three ale-tasters, four sealers and searchers of leather, three hedge and swine-lookers, two house-lookers, one cutter of peeks (?peats), two appraisers, two surveyors of highways and two constables. These were paid an annual salary of about £1 apiece, while the church organist got £5 and his 'blower' five shillings.[141] The officers also got liveries of office, and in 1700-01 £2 was paid for eight yards of broad red cloth for the officers' coats while in

The Story of Appleby in Westmorland

Photographs 17 and 18 - Appleby Assizes - above showing the Judge's procession and below the Judge at the cloisters, circa 1920. Photographs from old postcards, courtesy of D. Furniss.

The Story of Appleby in Westmorland

Photograph 19 - Appleby Market Place - the two buildings in the foreground are the old Shambles, the butchers' premises demolished in 1883.

Photograph 20 - The Moot Hall and Boroughgate in 1853 showing the original steps up to the council chamber.

Photograph 21 - The cheese market and the High Cross, circa 1890.

Photograph 22 - Market day, circa 1900, showing the thatched building which stood where the Post Office is today.

The Story of Appleby in Westmorland

Photograph 23 - Queen Victoria's Diamond Jubilee celebrations, 1897

Photograph 24 - Boroughgate from the tower of St. Lawrence's Church. The lime trees, planted in 1876, are still young. From the Valentine postcard series.

The Story of Appleby in Westmorland

Photograph 25 - The Market Square, Low Cross, St. Lawrence's Church and the cloisters in about 1900.

Photograph 26 - Proclamation of King George V, 1910, on the steps of the courthouse, from a postcard, courtesy of D. Furniss.

177

The Story of Appleby in Westmorland

Photographs 27 and 28 - Two views of Appleby's New Fair on the Sands. Photographs believed to date from the 1920s.

The Story of Appleby in Westmorland

Photograph 29 - Battlebarrow, circa 1900.

Photograph 30 - Appleby signal box, circa 1910.

The Story of Appleby in Westmorland

Photograph 31 - The River Eden in flood on the Sands, 1968.

Photograph 32 - Her Majesty the Queen leaving Appleby in a rain storm in 1956, holding a specially bound presentation copy of the original edition of this book. Photograph by Eric Davidson.

Busy Market Town

1712 £9-6s-0d was paid for the "cloth and trimming for the bailiffs coats and waits cloaks and for making the coats and cloaks." The tally was much the same in 1700 when Sir Richard Sandford was mayor, but the list for that year includes a deputy mayor and several people held more than one job (and doubtless took more than one income): Robert Wharton and John Hewetson the bailiffs were also the informers, aletasters and hedge and swine-lookers and Hewetson was the cutter of peeks. George Dent doubled as chamberlain and appraiser, while Robert Bolton and Henry Richardson, the surveyors of highways, were also two of the four searchers of leather and sealers.[142]

The surveyors of the highways were certainly among the busiest of the officials. It was their duty to note where repairs were needed, to guard against trespasses and illegal building on the roads, and see that the bridges were kept in repair. Much money was spent on the upkeep of the roads; in 1756 for example £50 was spent on the paving and flagging of 'the street,' and in 1764 it was ordered that "Town Street to be new paved and levelled and to be flagged with fell flags." There were clearly the rudiments of what we would now call 'town planning', for fines were levied for such things as 'an unlawful hedge,' and permission had to be obtained for the extension of houses onto the streets.[141]

The corporation were themselves responsible for the upkeep of the Moot Hall, which was used regularly for the assizes in Lady Anne's time.[131] In 1769 the county suggested that the borough join with them in building a new Court House which might also do for a Moot Hall. The borough dissented, because they did not want to move their Town Hall out of the principal street, but agreed that if a convenient site could be found they would go along with the proposition even though they would lose rent from the shops under the hall. Four years later however they declined to grant land adjoining the hall because it would reduce the size of the market, but they did agree that the hall should be pulled down and rebuilt in a more convenient place.[135; 141] A grant of £100 was approved and Lord Thanet, Sir James Lowther, General Sir Philip Honeywood and Mr Fletcher Norton – the two Parliamentary patrons and the two sitting MPs – were invited to subscribe. But for some reason – perhaps shortage of funds – nothing happened and the Moot Hall remains today much as it was in the eighteenth century, still with the shops on the ground floor which are recorded as having brought in a rent of £9-10s-0d in 1769.[135] It was, however, enlarged in 1800, when a house and a place to keep the public scales and to store grain was built onto the northern end.[135]

The income of the corporation in the eighteenth century was more than sufficient for its needs, and the surplus was generally disposed of in 'treats', to which the members were very partial. In most years the expenditure ran at between £5 and £10, and the breakdown for 1704-5 is typical.

	£	s.	d.
For a treat at the Bridge, and for Sir Christopher Musgrave's family		14	9
8 March. Ale at the Moot Hall, Tobacco and pipes	1	11	2
5 Nov. Ale in Moot Hall		19	0
Tobacco and pipes, a fire 9d		2	4
Wine to treat my Lord Bishop (Nicolson) 12s-0d; ale at Sankeys		13	0
Spent on the first news of the Victory in Germany in ale	1	7	0
To the Soldiers, 5/- Tobacco, pipes and fire 2/6		7	6
On the Thanksgiving day for the said Victory Ale 47s; Brandy 12s	2	19	0
Lime Juice 3s; Sugar 3s-2d		6	2
Tobacco 2s; pipes 6d; fire 1s		3	6
Treat to two Mr Musgraves		17	2
	£10	0s	7d

Bishop Nicolson clearly enjoyed the wine, recording in his diary that "I was kindly treated by Mr Mayor (Mr Atkinson) and ye Corporation at ye public Expence."[152] It will be noted that the corporation, by celebrating the 'Victory in Germany' (Blenheim) when the news arrived, and then on the official day of Thanksgiving, got in two celebrations of the one event! But the expenditure in this year was nothing to that in 1713 when the Peace proclamation was celebrated to the tune of £18-15s-10d, the total bill for the year came to £38-4s-5d and the result was a debit balance on the year's accounts of over £1. That deficit may be one reason why it was ordered that "arrears of £77-3s-3d due to the Corporation be paid: defaulters to be prosecuted."[141]

We do not know whether Appleby had a collection of municipal silverware before the Civil War, but if it did it is quite likely that it was sent away to be melted down to help pay for the royal armies. Certainly a lot of the old plate belonging to Oxford and Cambridge Colleges went that way, and it is suggestive that most of the notable articles now belonging to the corporation date from the late seventeenth and eighteenth centuries. The ceremonial sword was presented by John Dalston, who sat as MP for the borough in 1660 and again between 1661 and 1678; it is 50 inches in length and richly ornamented. The first recorded appointment of an official sword-bearer occurs in the year 1709, although £2-10s-6d was spent on 'the sword' in 1700-01[141] and ancient tradition would carry the office back to the twelfth century.[84] The borough mace appears to have been purchased by subscription, and in 1722 the chamberlains acknowledged the receipt of "twenty six pounds, being moneys paid into Mr Robinson's hands for ye use of ye town for a mace." Again, in 1733 there was a minute ordering that "all that are in arrears in their subscriptions to the mace pay them forthwith to the chamberlains." The mace then acquired is of silver gilt, 42 inches in length, the head is ornamented with the royal and the town arms (as then used), and the date 1733.[153]

The corporation also owns a large silver loving cup, which was presented by Colonel James Graham of Levens Hall in 1703, on the occasion of his admission as freeman and alderman of the borough. The donor was MP for Appleby from 1702 until 1708 and for Westmorland between 1710 and 1727,[154] and was Mayor of Appleby in 1705 and 1717. The punch bowl of silver was obtained in 1785, in exchange for a number of pieces of older silver plate which had been presented by various donors. Finally there is a silver punch ladle, having at its bottom a Queen Anne shilling dated 1711, and an exceptionally fine bronze bushel measure which dates from the reign of Queen Elizabeth I.[153]

It was probably in the eighteenth century that the borough began to use the coat of arms of three leopards or lions, *passant guardant* 'differenced' by placing ducal coronets on the beasts' heads.[84] The seventeenth century carved wooden escutcheons in St Lawrence's Church bear the uncrowned leopards of the old royal coat, as represented on the borough seal, and so does the wrought iron sword-rest by the corporation pew. Possibly the 'differenced' animals were taken from a seal of Robert de Vieuxpont, first Baron of Westmorland, which shows a single crowned leopard or lion *passant guardant*.[71] This was not, however, his armorial bearing, which was a device of six rings or annulets, arranged in rows of three, two and one – a coat later adopted, with changed colouring, by the local families of Lowther, Musgrave and Helbeck.[71] The Appleby arms with the crowned beasts appear on maps by Bickham (1743-54), Kitchen (1753) and other authors in 1761 and 1786 and in the representation on the Moot Hall, and these arms are also described by Nicholson and Burn, in 1777.[48] The supporting dragons, the crest of the 'salamander enflamed' and the motto *nec ferro nec igni* (neither by iron nor fire) were probably added at the same time as signs of the town's resilience despite the ravages of fire and the sword.[84]

In the eighteenth century, towns had some responsibility for their own local defence and Appleby Corporation spent money on repairing the Butts – presumably used by then for musketry rather than archery practice – in 1700 and again in 1741. There are also records of payment to the Train Band – the corps of local youths trained in basic soldiery. Defences were needed, for these were still unsettled times. In 1715 rebellion broke out in Scotland, with the aim of restoring the Stewart monarchy. The Earl of Derwentwater (a grandson of King Charles II) raised an army in Cumbria, being reinforced by a few thousand Scots. The High Sheriff of Cumberland, with the Earl of Carlisle and Viscount Lonsdale, mustered the Government's forces – including the Cumberland and Westmorland Militia – on Penrith Fell. Bishop Nicolson of Carlisle was there to provide spiritual encouragement. Although numbering between 3,000 and 4,000 men, the motley array was ill-prepared and ill-equipped and melted away when Derwentwater, with 1,700 troops, was reported to be approaching.[59] Lord Lonsdale made a hasty retreat to Appleby while the bishop's wig was blown off as he yelled out of his coach window to his coachman who was making all speed for Rose Castle![2]

Passing through Whinfell – where they helped themselves to the Earl of Thanet's rabbits and deer – the Jacobite forces arrived in Appleby, where the Old Pretender was proclaimed as King James III, a public collection of money was made, and the vicar joined in Roman Catholic prayers. However, the rebels attracted very few supporters among the gentry, perhaps because the government had taken the precaution of locking up known sympathisers in Carlisle.[2; 59] Only one man joined the army as it marched from Penrith to Appleby – and he deserted next day at Kendal. Fate dealt harshly with him for he was later executed, not for treason but for stealing the horse on which he joined the rebels![59] In Appleby, about a hundred Jacobite troops quartered themselves at the Crown and Cushion Inn in the Market Place, the property of a former mayor, Richard Baynes. Mr Baynes, who was bailiff to Lord Wharton, was locked up in the Moot Hall for refusing to say where the excise money was or to drink the health of the claimant king.[59] He later complained that he had been "kept close confined and put to great expense and in danger of his life,"[138] and blamed this treatment for the loss of Lord Wharton's estate deeds and papers, which had been in his custody.[155] However, he seems to have suffered no lasting harm for he was mayor again in 1716! The rebels got no further south than Preston before all was over. James Radcliffe, last Earl of Derwentwater, was the most distinguished local casualty, being executed on Tower Hill in 1716.

On 9 November 1745 Charles Edward Stewart, 'Bonnie Prince Charlie,' reached Carlisle to find it poorly defended by just 80 soldiers, some of them 'old and infirm,' plus ill-equipped local levies. The 249 men from Westmorland included the local militia for which Appleby was the headquarters. They surrendered on 16 November and the Prince then marched south, levying hay and oats from local estates. Like Charles II in 1651, he followed the old Roman road from Brougham to Tebay and onward to Preston and Derby, reached on 4 December. Many people have speculated about what would have happened if the invaders had kept their nerve and carried on towards London, but they did not, turning back through a countryside that swiftly distanced itself from the lost cause. On 17 or 18 December the Hanoverian Prince William, Duke of Cumberland, caught up with the Highlanders at Clifton Dykes, south of Brougham and ten miles from Appleby and the last battle fought on English soil followed. It is a curious coincidence that this must have happened close by where Cerialis and Agricola sorted out Venutius nearly 1,700 years before! Both sides claimed victory, but it only proved a temporary check in the prince's retreat. On 30 December the Jacobite garrison of Carlisle surrendered.[156] By then, Cumberland had sent 63 Highland men and nine Highland women who were in their company to 'the Keeper of the Jail of the Town of Applebee' for safe keeping – "hereof you are not to fail, or you will answer the contrary at your peril."[157] Curiously, the gaoler's receipt refers only to '70 rebel men and women' so perhaps some slipped away in transit! We do not know the fate of the captives, but most of those taken at Carlisle were transported overseas, although the leaders were executed.[2]

In 1745 the old gatehouse at the west end of the bridge, extended in Lady Anne's time, still served as the county gaol: the county paid the borough a rent of 6d a year for it.[59] Even with its extension it had been described as unsatisfactory as early as 1683 and in 1714 it had become ruinous (although £2-14s-0d had been spent on its repair in 1712). In 1765 it was again condemned as unfit for the purpose and beyond repair.[59] Richard Burn, the county historian, described it as "a little, mean, incommodious building without one inch of ground out of doors wherein the prisoners might receive fresh air."[48] It seems most unlikely that it could have accommodated 63 male and nine female Jacobites, so that we can guess that the castle was pressed into service after the '45.

In 1769 the county started the dialogue with the borough about building a new court house to replace the cramped upper room in the Moot Hall. It was resolved that this be done "at the cheapest cost to the inhabitants" of Appleby, and that the buildings were also to incorporate a new county gaol. Robert Adam, the famous architect, prepared plans but these probably failed to meet the criterion of 'least cost' and the gaol built in 1771 was designed by Robert Fothergill of Wharton while the work was supervised by his son Edmund.[158] In 1773 the Shire Hall and County Court were built next to the gaol by a prominent Cumberland builder, Daniel Benn of Whitehaven.[159] These buildings still front the road on the Sands, though their uses have changed down the years and later extensions to the prison have been demolished.

While the renewal of the gaol was certainly motivated by concern for the welfare of the prisoners, punishments for the latter were none the less savage. Executions took place on Gallows Hill a mile north of the town, while vagrants and thieves often received a public whipping from the High Cross to the Low Cross, or in severe cases from the gaol to the High Cross and back again. Sentences of transportation were recorded from time to time, and the stocks, the pillory, and the ducking stool were all in use. In 1743 there was an order "that the stocks and pillory be removed to the end of the open hall facing the Low Cross, that being deemed the proper place for the same. And that there be a whipping post and convenient place for burning criminals in the hand likewise erected there."[141] The 'burning in the hand' refers to the law that all persons convicted of felonies should be branded on the base of the thumb with a hot iron, the mark being a letter M (for malefactor). Disorderly women, scolds and dishonest traders were liable to find themselves in the ducking stool, by the river on the north side of the bridge: a new stool was bought by the corporation for £1 in 1705-06.[138; 141] Maybe because of the tough penalties, escapes from the gaol were not uncommon. Several were recorded between 1771 and 1799, the most startling, in May 1799 being by William Dennison who actually tunnelled under the huge encircling wall.[160]

Appleby was important because it was the assize town, the judges coming regularly to hear serious cases in the Moot Hall. Its prosperity seems to have stemmed from its role as a trading centre, for unlike Kendal it was not a centre of manufacture of cloth (the celebrated 'Kendal Green') and unlike Kirkby Stephen it was not famous for woollen stockings.[125] When John Speed published his *Theatre of the Empire of Great Britain* in 1611, Kendal rather than Appleby appeared as the chief town in Westmorland.[161] Daniel Fleming, writing in 1671, commented disparagingly that Appleby was "so slenderly inhabited, ye buildings (for ye most part tho' of late much amended) so mean, and ye Inhabitants generally so idle (having no manufacture of note amongst them) that were it not by reason of ye antiquitie... it would be little better than a village."[162] In contrast Kirkby Stephen was "a market town, well known – the market much improved of late by the trade of making stockings."[162] The seventeenth and eighteenth centuries were also a period when mining was expanding in Cumbria, but Appleby had no mineral wealth to exploit.[2]

There are several pointers to a decline in Appleby's population in the eighteenth century. In 1771 Nicolson and Burn refer to it as "a handsome small town, containing between 70 and 80 families," and elsewhere say that its population was about 400 in 1772.[48] This may be an underestimate, or it may only refer to the centre of the town around Boroughgate, but if there were really some 127 households in 1563, 123 at the time of the 1674 Hearth Tax,[146] but only 80 in 1772 the decline is obvious. The number of freemen did halve between 1708 and 1795. The 1754 burgage map and inventory confirm the contraction of the borough for they record many empty burgages in the Castle Park (including all those in the original top section of Boroughgate), with more along the north side of Scattergate, on both sides of Doomgate, in the Sands and in Battlebarrow.[61; 63] Even if Nicolson and Burn's figures are too low, it seems clear that Appleby was no longer the pre-eminent settlement in the

The Story of Appleby in Westmorland

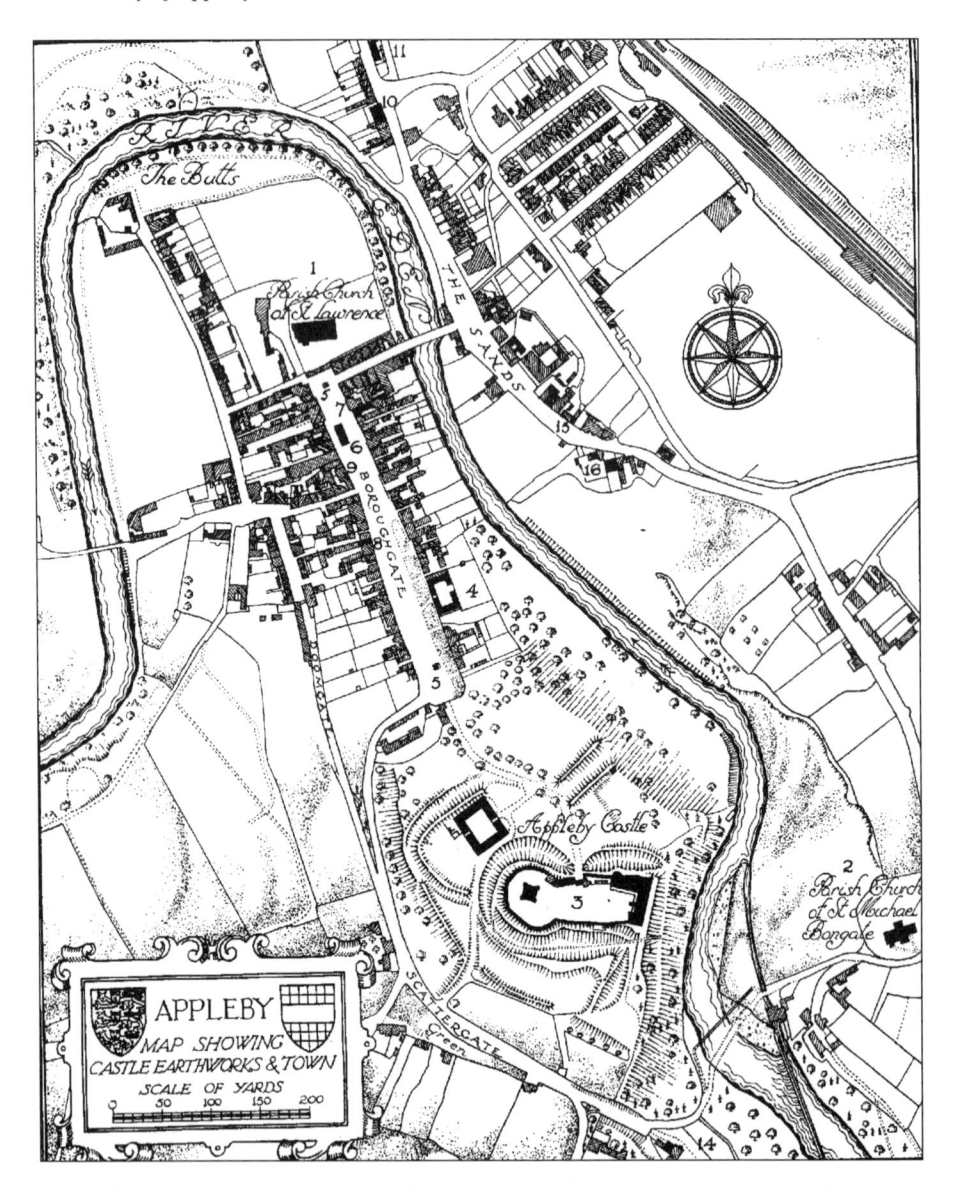

Map 6 - Historic monuments in Appleby. From the Report of the Royal Commission on Historical Monuments, 1936, © Crown copyright. Numbered buildings date from before 1714.

upper Eden Valley that it had once been.

None the less, it shared in the local prosperity that followed the political stabilisation after the end of the Scottish wars. The period between 1650 and 1750 was (as Daniel Fleming noted) an era of rebuilding in stone, replacing the old and highly combustible timber-framed housing. In Appleby, a few buildings like the Moot Hall and the house and shop that face it on the east side of Boroughgate date from the late sixteenth century. There are at least five houses incorporating date stones from between 1660 and 1690, as if Lady Anne's example sparked off a wave of reconstruction by other citizens[9] (Map 6). Much of the character of Boroughgate and the other main streets depends on buildings erected between 1700 and 1800. The Red House near the High Wiend was built in 1717 by Thomas Carleton, steward to the Earl of Thanet and mayor in 1707 and 1710.[189] The even bigger White House, facing the opening of the Wiend, is due to John Robinson in 1756.[189] The Red House has a broad frontage because Carleton was able to combine several burgages he owned at the junction of High Wiend and Boroughgate. Although Robinson also owned several burgages, his house was squeezed into one of the original Boroughgate blocks and – as in New York – he was forced to build upwards rather than sideways. The King's Head Inn in Bridge Street was described as 'new' in 1746 and was then the biggest such hostelry in the town and the place where banquets were held for visiting judges.[138] The architecture reinforces the corporation records in suggesting that the town was doing well in this period.

In the second half of the eighteenth century, the town's prosperity may have been boosted by agricultural improvement. Prior to 1750 much of the land around was rough moorland common, used only for summer grazing. Cumberland and Westmorland had more of it than most counties, because of the ruggedness of the terrain and the turmoil of the Border wars. But after the 1745 rebellion had been put down and peace seemed assured, not only did local landowners begin to improve their farms, especially by draining, but the move to enclose the commons gained momentum. Between 1763 and 1800 42,000 acres in Cumberland and 10,500 in Westmorland were enclosed, and the process accelerated in the nineteenth century when a further 234,000 acres in Cumberland and 90,500 in Westmorland were parcelled up.[163] It was this process of enclosure that gave us the now familiar pattern of large fellside 'allotments' bounded by great lengths of magnificent drystone wall.

The enclosures did not affect Appleby's own lands because the borough was small and owned no commons, but the Earls of Thanet were keen enclosers of their manors, and gained great wealth through the process. One of the motives for enclosure in the Eden Valley, moreover, seems to have been the creation of arable land. The 1773 and 1774 enclosure awards for Ormside, Bongate and Burrells Moor stipulated that sheep should be kept out of the new fields for at least seven years. This not only helped the young hedges to grow to the stage where they could be successfully 'cut and laid', but gave an incentive to cereal cultivation which was further encouraged by a tax concession: tithes of grain were halved for the first seven years after enclosure.[163] As Appleby was the chief grain market in north Westmorland at this time it must have benefited from the increase in trade.

The other big change was to the roads. Before around 1750 a network of tracks did link the various settlements in Cumbria, and they were served by pack-horses but the system was slow and the surfaces notoriously bad.[2] Pack horses could travel no more than 25 miles a day, each carrying loads of about two hundredweights in panniers: at the height of this traffic some 350 such beasts arrived or left Kendal each week.[134] Lady Anne Clifford's diaries give a fair picture of the slow progress that even rich people expected to make when travelling to London or other towns. The Duke of Cumberland's army had real trouble moving its supplies as it chased the Young Pretender's forces northwards in 1745.

But in the 1750s the turnpikes – a system of improved toll roads – made their appearance. An Act of Parliament in 1741-2 paved the way for the road from Bowes over Stainmore to Brough to be improved, and in 1752 a second act allowed its continuation via the end of Appleby Bridge to Lowther Bridge and Penrith. Sadly, a good deal of the original Roman Road was destroyed in this process.[59] The route from Kendal to Appleby via Grayrigg and Orton became a turnpike in 1782 (the Scattergate toll bar cottage which collected £101 in 1814 remains at the foot of the hill immediately south of Appleby).[59] In 1818, when the Reverend John Barwis travelled, there were six turnpike gates on the 29 miles from Skelton (near Penrith) via Appleby to Brough, one charging 9d for his carriage and the others 7d.[164] In 1821 the average annual income from the 22-mile turnpike from Brough via Appleby to Eamont Bridge was £1,041 and the expenditure £962, while the 44 mile road from Appleby through Orton to Kendal brought in £310 and cost £262.[134]

Coach travel grew during the eighteenth century, and became more reliable when regular stages were introduced, allowing relays of fresh horses to be applied. Appleby was on the route from Glasgow via Stainmore and Scotch Corner to London, and there was a daily mail coach in each direction. In 1795 the northbound service halted for 25 minutes for breakfast at the Spital Inn on Stainmore and took two hours from there to the King's Head at Appleby, two hours more from there to Penrith, and two hours and twenty minutes for the onward journey to Carlisle. In 1829 there was an express (stage) coach from Carlisle via Appleby to York on Mondays, Wednesdays and Fridays, while the Newcastle-Lancaster service passed through Brough and Kirkby Stephen. In 1773 it took three days to travel from Carlisle to London by coach: by 1837 this was reduced to a jolting 32 and a quarter hours at an average speed of nine mph, broken by brief 'comfort and refreshment' stops.[134] Local carriers provided onward and connecting services for people, mail and goods.

In the eighteenth century Appleby Grammar School reached the pinnacle of its achievements. Under Jonathan Banks (1686-1721), and then Richard Yates, who was master for 50 years (1723-1781), it provided nearly half the foundation (fellows and scholars) of the Queen's College Oxford. The connection with that college was strengthened by the endowment in 1720 by Thomas Tufton, sixth Earl of Thanet, of five exhibitions for "poor scholars who have had their education for three years immediately before their going to University in the free grammar school in Appleby. None to be entitled to any share therein who were not born in Westmorland."[101] In 1739 Appleby Grammar School was one of twelve northern schools to benefit from a further series of exhibitions endowed by Lady Elizabeth Hastings. The list of old boys, between 1670 and 1870, includes six Provosts of Queen's College and seventeen fellows. It also includes eight bishops, three Members of Parliament, a high court judge, an admiral, a commander in chief and a Lord Mayor of London. It is especially noteworthy that the majority of these men were locally born, like Cardinal Bainbrigg and Bishop Langton before them. In the eighteenth century, during Richard Yates' long and distinguished tenure as headmaster, the scholarly library continued to expand and the curriculum was broadened to embrace English, Mathematics, Science, French, Geography and History as well as the traditional Latin and Greek.[101]

The fame of the school was such that it attracted pupils from a distance. They came regularly from all four northern counties, and sometimes from even farther afield. Among them were the Washington family, originally from County Durham. Captain Lawrence Washington of Westmorland County, Virginia, died in 1698 and within the following two years his widow married George Gale of Whitehaven who was then the agent in Virginia for a family tobacco company. The Gales returned to Cumberland in 1700 and John and Augustine Washington, Captain Lawrence's sons, became boarders at Appleby. They left in 1704 following a dispute over their custody, but Augustine clearly had happy memories of his schooling for in 1729 he sent his elder son, Lawrence, to Appleby. His younger boy, Augustine (Austin) followed in 1733, and they returned to Virginia in 1738 and 1741 respectively. Their father planned that his youngest son George, who was Lawrence and Austin's half brother, would follow the older boys in his turn. Unfortunately, Augustine Washington senior died in 1743 when George was only eleven and his mother wanted him to remain with her. So Appleby Grammar School was deprived of the chance of counting the first President of the United States among its alumni.[101; 165]

However George Washington could not have escaped hearing a lot about the town, and this is confirmed by what happened on 18 October 1781 when the British frigate *Guadeloupe* surrendered following the capitulation of Yorktown. The Captain, Hugh Robinson, belonged to a distinguished Appleby family and his elder brother, John, had been at school with George Washington's brother Austin. When Captain Robinson surrendered his sword, General Washington asked him where he came from. "Appleby, in Westmorland" he answered. "I am very glad to meet a Westmorland man," said Washington. "My family sprang from that county and my brother was at Appleby School." An invitation to dinner, and considerable personal attention followed.[101] They probably worked it out that if George Washington had followed his brothers to Appleby, they would have been contemporaries at school.[165]

Hugh Robinson's brother John had a notable career in English politics. After qualifying as a lawyer in the practice of Richard Wordsworth, grandfather of William the poet, he became Sir James Lowther's chief law agent and land steward. He served as mayor of Appleby in 1760-61 and again in 1770-71 (a portrait of him still hangs in the Moot Hall), became MP for Westmorland in 1764 and was Secretary to the Treasury in Lord North's Government of 1770-1782. Although he fell out with Lowther, and in 1774 switched his Parliamentary seat to Harwich, Robinson remained an Appleby man. He built Appleby's White House, which still dominates Boroughgate, and is credited by some with the inscription on the High Cross outside the castle gates. He is above all famous for being at the receiving end of a popular saying. Early in 1784 when he was using his celebrated skills as "a master of political intrigue" to help William Pitt build up his power base, he was viciously attacked by a fellow Member, the playwright Richard Brinsley Sheridan.[166] "A Member is employed to corrupt everybody in order to get votes!" stormed Sheridan. "Name him! Name him!" came cries from the floor. "I shall not name this person," replied Sheridan, addressing the Speaker. "It is an unpleasant and invidious thing to do. But don't suppose, Sir, that I abstain through any difficulty in naming. I could do that, Sir, as soon as you could say Jack Robinson!"[166] For the incident to make sense, the saying must have been in popular usage at the time, and it has been suggested that it refers to an earlier Sir John Robinson who was Commanding Officer at the Tower in 1660-1679, and to the speed of beheading with an axe.[167]

Although he never represented Appleby in Parliament, Jack Robinson was involved in some of the complicated (and murky) manoeuvres that affected the borough's elections in the middle of the eighteenth century. The two MPs had, since the thirteenth century, been elected by the holders of the burgage tenements. Originally this had meant more or less free elections, usually of members of families prominent in the borough such as the de Goldingtons. But as time passed, and especially after the restoration of King Charles II, more and more burgages were bought by the larger landowners, and they gained increasing control over the governance of both Appleby and Westmorland. Lady Anne had controlled the Parliamentary elections in 1661.[129] In the eighteenth century Musgraves, Lowthers, Whartons and Tuftons and their agents like Richard Baynes, Thomas Carleton and John Robinson appear frequently in the list of Appleby Mayors, Lord Wharton himself serving in 1707 and Viscount Lonsdale in 1723.[74]

The Tuftons inherited Lady Anne's properties in 1676, and with them came her power base in Appleby. Between 1690 and around 1720 the Whartons were also powerful landowners and controllers of elections.[154] The Lowther family, who had been prominent in Westmorland since the fourteenth century and gained great wealth through their virtual ownership of the port of Whitehaven,[2] rose as the Whartons declined.[168] The Lowthers of Whitehaven and the Lowthers of Lowther both wielded great influence (their roles are readily confused, not least because at one time both branches were headed by a Sir John Lowther MP).[71] By the 1720s the family had acquired the Wharton burgages in Appleby, and by 1725 they and the Tuftons seem to have shared control not only over Appleby's representation in Parliament but over the appointment of the mayor, aldermen and councillors as well.[168; 169] Under a 'gentlemen's agreement' between Viscount Lonsdale and Sackville Tufton, the Earl of Thanet, each nominated one of the borough's two MPs, they took it in turn to name the mayor, vacancies among the twelve aldermen and sixteen councillors were likewise to be filled in turn and burgages were not to be purchased without prior notice to the other party.[168] The implication is that the freemen (who elected the councillors) must have been controlled by the two noble parties, and that must have meant either financial inducement or direction from landlord to tenant. Those burghers of Appleby who had so triumphantly asserted their independence from the castle back in 1296 would surely have shuddered to see how profoundly that independence had been eroded!

By 1751 the Lowther share of the power had become consolidated in the hands of Sir James Lowther, fifth baronet. Although stemming from a junior branch of the family (his grandfather was the untitled and relatively impoverished squire of Maulds Meaburn), Sir James inherited wealth and land from his father, formerly Governor of Barbados, his cousin the third Viscount Lonsdale of Lowther who died unmarried in 1745, and subsequently from his more distant cousins the Lowthers of Whitehaven in 1756.[169] One of the richest and most powerful men in the north west of England, Sir James was also domineering and politically ambitious, and it may be because of his personality that the 'gentleman's agreement' with Thanet came unstuck in 1752. It was Lowther's turn to choose the mayor – but his man was not only voted down by the Thanet faction but the latter also pushed in one of their own aldermen. The Lowthers retaliated by buying six burgages for £490.[168] In 1753 they still failed to prevent the election, on Thanet's recommendation, of Anthony Ward who had been mayor three times previously.

So battle lines were drawn as the 1754 election loomed. The Thanet faction was in some disarray as a new earl succeeded in 1753 and inherited only nine burgages (apart from 28 long swallowed up in the Castle Park but of doubtful value as they had been held ineligible to confer a vote in 1723, and four absorbed by the Hospital of St Anne). The new Earl of Thanet went on a spending spree and between 11 December 1753 and the election in April 1754, 65 burgages were bought on his behalf for £19,500 - an average of £300 each. Mrs Lowther, Sir James' mother, spent £7,883-18s in buying a further 21.[168; 169] Even pigsties are said to have changed hands at enormous prices. Both parties hastily enlisted allies among the burgage-holders who would not sell. The result was that when the election came, the Castle Park burgages held the balance. The question was whether they would be allowed a vote!

The candidates themselves were distinguished enough. The Lowther nominees were Sir John Ramsden (a relative of Sir James Lowther) and one of Ramsden's connections, Fletcher Norton (later, as Sir Fletcher, caricatured as 'Sir Bullface Doubleface').[154; 168; 169] In the Castle corner were Lt. Col. Philip Honeywood (later General Sir Philip), then of Mark's Hall, Essex, whose brother had inherited thirteen Appleby burgages from Sir Richard Sandford, and William Lee, son of Sir William Lee, a former Lord Chief Justice. Before the voting started on 17 April both Thanet and Lowther conveyed the freeholds of their burgages for one year to their most trusted supporters. This gave an appearance of propriety, but as voting commenced the eligibility of each burgage was scrutinised. As the scrutineer was Anthony Ward, the mayor, and he was Thanet's man, the omens were not good for Lowther![168]

Voting was slow – only six votes being admitted on each side during the first day. After ten days the score was level at 63 votes each. Quite a few Lowther burgages had been rejected, and when the Castle Park ones were put forward and accepted, the result was settled. The mayor declared Honeywood and Lee the winners with 121 votes each, as against 108 for Ramsden and Norton.[168] But the rumpus grew louder as analysis suggested that many of the burgages owned by Lowther and disqualified by the mayor were more credible than a number owned by Thanet that he had accepted. Petitions were laid before parliament and an undignified public row loomed. The Prime Minister wanted the whole business tidied up quietly, and Thanet suggested reversion to the old system of one MP each, and alternate nomination of mayors and aldermen. Lowther refused, insisting on his 'right' to the whole borough! John Robinson, speaking on his behalf, argued that the Lowther family and their friends had represented Appleby in parliament since the time of King Edward II (which was stretching the truth, although Robert de Lowther did sit for the borough in 1318). It was all very unseemly. In the end the result was declared void and Sir Philip Honeywood and Fletcher Norton were returned in a fresh election. And the governance of Appleby was stitched up again – Lowther and Thanet would nominate an MP each; they would recommend the mayor alternately, and the council would be split down the middle, each party filling vacancies on its own side.[168] No wonder that places like Appleby became known as 'pocket' or 'rotten' boroughs!

Sir James Lowther did not stop at Appleby. Two years later he spent £58,000 buying control of Cockermouth. In the years that followed he became celebrated (notorious might be a juster word) for returning nine members to parliament. He was one of the nine until 1784, when he was made first Earl of Lonsdale. Wits called these members his 'nine pins' because if they did not vote as he instructed he bowled them over.[154] But power did not bring popularity. Lowther became known as 'the bad Earl' and 'Jimmy Grasp-all, Earl of Toadstool.' Alexander Carlyle described him as "more detested than any man alive... an intolerable tyrant... truly a madman, though too rich to be confined."[169] Local legend records him as a gloomy despot travelling in a neglected coach at whose coming the streets fell silent, whose corpse was buried with difficulty, and whose turbulent ghost was eventually exorcised and 'laid' under Walla Crag near Haweswater.[151]

The stitch-up between the Lowthers and the Tuftons continued in operation until 1832 when the borough lost its representation. Deplorable though it may have been, under it Appleby returned some very distinguished people to parliament, including three future Prime Ministers. Charles Jenkinson (nick-named 'Jenks'), later Baron Hawkesbury and President of the Board of Trade, sat for the borough in 1766-68. He became the first Earl of Liverpool in 1796. His son Robert Banks Jenkinson, 'young Jenky', was made member for Appleby by Lord Lonsdale in 1790 even though the candidate was under age and had not asked for the appointment![170] There was one condition – that he voted as his father did! But the younger Jenkinson only sat for Appleby for a few months, migrating to Rye in December 1790: in the early nineteenth century, as the second Earl of Liverpool, he was to serve as Prime Minister for fourteen years.[170] The Appleby seat was also held very briefly by yet another future Prime Minister, Charles Grey, then Viscount Howick, this time through the good offices of Lord Thanet. Grey seems to have been reluctant – he had lost his seat in Northumberland, was deeply unpopular, and protested against the Thanet nomination, but accepted it for the period between July and November 1807. He then moved to represent Tavistock.[170]

Appleby's most famous MP was undoubtedly William Pitt the younger, who first entered parliament in January 1781 as the Lowther nominee.[170; 171] The nomination was suggested by the Duke of Rutland, who had been at Cambridge with Pitt and was friendly with Sir James Lowther. Pitt wrote to his mother in November 1780 that "Appleby is the place I am to represent and the Election will be made (probably in a week or ten days) without my having any trouble, or even visiting my constituents."[171] It is somewhat ironic that on 7 May 1782 he spoke out for parliamentary reform, commenting that "when the representative ceased to have connection with the constituent, and was either dependent on the crown or the aristocracy, there was a defect in the frame of representation..."[171] Mr Pott was clearly calling Mr Kettle black – but despite these laudable sentiments, there is no evidence that he ever visited Appleby or took any interest in the place. None the less, he was re-elected without difficulty when he became Chancellor in 1782 and Prime Minister on 19 December 1783 at the age of 24, and no doubt Appleby basked in some reflected glory. In 1784 he resigned the seat, being returned for the University of Cambridge (the seat he had first contested in 1780, and had always coveted).[170; 171] Pitt's portrait hangs today with that of Jack Robinson and a host of mayors in the Moot Hall.

The late eighteenth century was a time of political sensitivity, sparked by the French Revolution. Fear that the upheaval might trigger a rising in Britain led to severe measures to deter public unrest and drove the movement for parliamentary reform underground. In Cumbria, the 'blue' Whigs were seen as the party of reform, opposed by the 'yellow' Tories headed by Sir James Lowther, by then the first Earl of Lonsdale. The watchword of the 'blues' was 'Freedom and Liberty,' and they accused the Tories of 'Tyranny and Corruption.' In 1792, as Britain moved towards war with France, 'Associations for Preserving Liberty and Property against Republicans and Levellers' sprang up, backed by William Pitt's Tory government. One such association was established in Appleby: there were others in Kendal and Carlisle. The Reverend J R

Sproule, Vicar of St Lawrence's Church between 1789 and 1797, wrote to the Home Secretary about the risk that revolutionary principles would lead to popular tumult in the northern manufacturing towns, and was asked to make a note of any revolutionary societies in the neighbourhood, any inflammatory publications being circulated, and any suspicious people in the district. He was to communicate this intelligence secretly to the Government. There was indeed serious unrest in the Carlisle area in 1795, but no record of trouble in Appleby.[172]

Sproule's predecessor as vicar of St Lawrence's was the most famous incumbent in the history of that church. Dr William Paley, whose *Evidences of Christianity* argued that the intricate design of the universe proved the existence of God just as surely as a watch found on a beach provided compelling evidence of the existence of a watchmaker, was appointed in 1777 and stayed until 1789. He may, therefore, have had something to do with a 'proclamation for the Observance of the Lord's Day' which was made by the Justices of Appleby in 1781.[151] This stated that "the Lord's Day has for some time past been shamefully profaned by persons exercising their calling, doing all servile work, opening ships, using boats or barges, driving stage coaches, diligences, wagons, carts and other carriages, travelling for hire, drovers driving their cattle, and carriers travelling and following their business on a Sunday with impunity and in such manner as gives great scandal and bad example and calls loudly for redress," and ruled that persons thus offending should be "punished with the utmost severity." Thomas Ferguson was duly fined 20 shillings on 18 October 1824 for driving cattle in Bongate on the Lord's Day, and William Irving was fined in 1827 for travelling with, and driving, sheep. Such orders for Sunday observance were common at this period and one of the more amusing (made in 1749) provided that "any barber or perriwig maker that shall, after Martinmas, exercise his trade or business on the Lord's Day, be fined 3s-4d."

Neither Paley nor Sproule could vie as preachers with John Wesley, who first visited Appleby in 1766 and returned in May 1786. He does not seem to have been impressed, describing it as "a county town worthy of Ireland, containing at least five and twenty houses." On his first visit it poured with rain, and although invited to preach, he went on to Brough. On his second call he records having preached "in a very large room." The tradition that he spoke under a large sycamore tree on Scattergate Green (blown down in 1959) seems to have no foundation; perhaps there has been some confusion with Brough where he spoke under "some shady trees which covered both me and most of the congregation."[173]

John Wesley was but one of many travellers who took advantage of the improved turnpike roads and began appearing in the north of England. The fashion of visiting the Lake District was begun by the poet, Thomas Gray, in 1769, followed by William Gilpin in 1771 and the naturalist, Thomas Pennant, in 1773. Gray has little to say about Appleby, but he gives a vivid description of Brough Hill Fair, one of the great livestock sales of the north, describing "a great army encamped, ...myriads of horses and cattle in the road itself and in all the fields round me, a brisk stream hurrying cross the way, thousands of clean, healthy people in their best party-coloured apparel: farmers and their families, esquires and their daughters hurrying up from the dales..." Gray noted that the crowd reached on as far as Appleby.[174] Appleby Fair at the period was no less massive, with an estimated 40,000 animals in June 1781. This was still the era of the drover, moving large numbers of beasts slowly from Scotland and the north of England to London and other major towns along the green 'drove roads' that still criss-cross Cumbria and Yorkshire – a way of life that the railways were to destroy in the mid-nineteenth century. One estimate is that in 1853 alone, 270,000 animals moved through Carlisle.[134]

William Gilpin was concerned with landscape rather than fairs, and his book *Observations relative chiefly to Picturesque Beauty* was pungently parodied by Thomas Rowlandson in *Dr Syntax's Tour*. His account of Appleby is a fair sample of his style and an illustration of how well he lent himself to parody.[175]

> *The situation of Appleby castle, which belongs to the Earl of Thanet, is magnificent. It stands on a rocky eminence, falling precipitately into the river Eden, which half circles it. The banks of the river, and the sides of the precipice are finely hung with wood. The castle is still in good repair, and is a noble pile. But, in a picturesque light, it loses half its beauty from its being broken into two parts. A smaller break from a grand pile removes heaviness; and is a source of beauty. We have seen the same principle exemplified in mountains and other objects...*

Gilpin has little to say about the town itself, being content to moralize upon it from across the Eden, and then to abstract particulars concerning the life of the Countess of Pembroke from the account by her secretary, George Sedgwick. Pennant was more thorough. He came to the town from Brough in 1773.[80] The castle first attracted his attention, and his book includes an engraving of it, with St Michael's Church in the foreground (figure 7). This drawing preserves for us the appearance of the church as it was after Lady Anne's rebuilding, but before the well-meant but drastic 'restoration' of the nineteenth century which completely altered its character. Passing northwards, Pennant reached the borough. "After crossing a bridge guarded by a gateway, since pulled down," he wrote, "I entered the small town of Appleby, consisting of a single street irregularly built on the steep slope of a hill; on the summit is the Castle."

From this account, it seems clear that the gatehouse at the west end of the bridge was demolished soon after 1773, and we know that a new court house and gaol on the Sands were under construction at this period. The bridge gate had been damaged in 1771 by a great flood which poured along Bridge Street and through the churchyard, tore up flags in the cloisters and the pavement in the streets, caused two arches in St Lawrence's Church to subside, and made the furniture float about and collide in the houses so that "many lost great store of liquors."

Nicolson and Burn's monumental *History of Westmorland and Cumberland* provides another contemporary eighteenth century account.[48] They describe Appleby as:

> *a handsome small town... consisting principally of one broad street terminated on the north by the church, and rising by an easy ascent to the castle on the south, with two handsome crosses or obelisks, one at each end. On the upper cross is this inscription:*
> RETAIN YOUR LOYALTY. PRESERVE YOUR RIGHTS.
> *The shambles and town hall in the middle of this street greatly incommode it. If these were taken away, and removed to more proper places, the street, from its natural situation and openness would be very grand and elegant.*

As the nineteenth century began, old prints show an Appleby that looked very much as it does today (frontispiece; figure 3). However it was clearly very different in many ways from the old, independent merchant borough. Most of the burgages belonged to the Castle or to the

Busy Market Town

Figure 7 - Bongate Church and Appleby Castle in 1773, as drawn by Thomas Pennant's servant Moses Griffith. The church is in the form it was given by Lady Anne Clifford.

Lowthers, and many of the remainder to well-to-do local landowners. The selection of MPs, the mayor, and even aldermen and councillors was in Tufton and Lowther pockets. Members of these ruling families regularly held office in the borough and acted as governors of its school. In 1782, for example, the minutes of the meeting to elect a headmaster of the grammar school in succession to Richard Yates are signed by Sir Philip Musgrave, Thomas Baynes, Richard Machell, Christopher Morrison, Edward Milward, John Thompson, the Right Honourable Sackville Tufton Earl of Thanet, John Ward, Gilpin Gorst and Thomas Heelis who was the Thanet land agent. A real mixture of 'top families' and 'town worthies.'[101]

But reform was in the air in the nineteenth century, as England passed through a revolution in wealth and power. Over the century the constitution of the borough, its communications, its buildings and its way of life were to change profoundly.

CHAPTER 8

Into the Modern World

THE nineteenth century was a time of profound change in many English – indeed European – towns. Not far to the south of Appleby, communities were being transformed by the industrial revolution. Powerful commercial magnates planned new settlements with a vigour that matched that of feudal lords in the twelfth and thirteenth centuries. Places that had once been comparable in size with Appleby – like Liverpool – mushroomed into great cities.

Amidst it all, most of Cumberland and Westmorland remained a rural hinterland. A few towns on the west coast – especially Workington and Barrow in Furness – were touched by the new industrial dynamism and expanded into medium-sized mining and manufacturing communities. The new-found prosperity, linked to the railways, also brought plans for grand holiday resorts at places like Seascale and Silloth.[2] The smaller and quieter resorts of Keswick and Windermere promoted clean air and healthy walking amid magnificent scenery, and this was also the line taken by several places in the Eden Valley later in the nineteenth century. But these developments scarcely touched the district between the 1780s and the 1860s, and Appleby jogged along as a small market town, serving the local farming community as it had done for centuries.

In 1829 the town was said to have a well attended market "supplied with corn, provisions and coal" (from Stainmore). As well as normal tradesmen like blacksmiths, cloggers, tailors, shoemakers and carpenters the town had two breweries, three bellows-makers, a rope and twine manufacturer and a bag maker.[134] There was also a small centre of clockmaking, headed by George Wilson of Bridge Street, John and Robert Powley, John Hutchinson, Joseph Barker, members of the Savage family and James Weyman or Wemyss.[176] Two linen manufacturers operated in Bongate. As befitted a county town, there were also marks of culture. A book club had existed since 1810, and the King's Head had a News Room and Assembly Rooms.[134] The Appleby Pitt Club was founded in

1819 under the presidency of the Hon. Henry Cecil Lowther MP.[59]

Provision for education expanded and broadened. The grammar school flourished under a succession of headmasters, all of them graduates of Queen's College, Oxford. In the early years of the nineteenth century the school was attended by nearly a hundred scholars, and in 1826 a new boarding house was built so that 'country boys' did not have to live in lodgings in the town.[101] However the grammar school catered only for promising boys, and, outside wealthy families, most girls were illiterate. Something needed doing, and soon after 1800 other schools began to appear. A British and Foreign Schools Society's School was built in Chapel Street in 1808, and the quaintly (and rather condescendingly) entitled National Society for Promoting the Education of the Poor in the Principles of the Established Church founded the Institute of St Michael's Church School in Bongate in 1811.[78] The latter had room for 150 pupils, with a schoolmaster's house next door: the buildings still remain. In addition, the *Directory* for 1829 records five private academies in Appleby, two being schools for girls, and a third taking both sexes.[134]

The investment brought benefits. Literacy seems to have been significantly higher in Westmorland in the early nineteenth century than in southern counties like Cambridgeshire and Hertfordshire.[134] In 1849 81% of males and 65% of females were able to sign their names in the marriage register. Assuming that they were aged 21 and over, they must have been at school in the 1820s and 1830s. In Cambridgeshire the figures were 55% and 48% respectively and in Hertfordshire, 48% and 43%.[177]

In 1832 Appleby lost its two Members of Parliament, in consequence of the Reform Bill which abolished the so-called 'pocket' boroughs, and thereafter its representation was merged with that of the county. While this must have pushed the town a little further into obscurity and made it less important to the Earls of Thanet and of Lonsdale it probably did not affect the townsfolk much. By 1841 there were faint signs that the textile industry, already strong in Kendal, might invade the county town for Appleby had a twine spinner and several linen manufacturers and weavers. There was a woollen mill with sixteen staff two miles out of town, at Coupland Beck. There were also basket-makers, chair and cabinet makers, curriers, printers, horn dealers, a barber and hairdresser, a banker and a bank agent and two breweries. The first public utility, the

Appleby Gas Company, built its works at the end of Chapel Street in 1837 and by 1851 the streets were lit by eighteen lamps.[134] The Appleby and Kirkby Stephen Agricultural Society was founded in 1841, holding its shows alternately in the two towns until 1890, when separate societies were formed.[59] In 1848 the Mechanics' Institute was established, and there was a library at the Shire Hall.[134]

The 1841 census recorded a total population of 1,342 in St Lawrence's Parish, including Scattergate, Colby and the outlying hamlets and 1,159 in Bongate (including Crackenthorpe and Murton), and these totals changed very little over the following 50 years.[134] In 1851 the three settlements of Appleby town, Bongate and Scattergate had 1,697 residents, rising to 1,795 in 1861 and 1,999 in 1881.[74]

The census returns show what people did for a living.[134] In 1851, 213 male inhabitants of Appleby and Bongate (43.4%) were engaged in some kind of craft or industry and 51 (10.4%) in trade. Twenty eight (5.7%) were judged professional, 23 (4.7%) were servants and only eight (1.6%) were involved with transport. There were 25 hotels and inns, some being kept by people who had other jobs including those of farmer, butcher, shoemaker, carpenter and auctioneer. A quarter of the male population - 123 people - were farm workers and a further eighteen were described as farmers. No doubt most of these lived in the villages within Bongate parish, but some farm workers may have lived in the town and walked to work from there.

During the nineteenth century Appleby continued to have the county gaol, which had been moved from the bridge gate to the new buildings erected on the Sands in 1771. In 1844 Thomas Thwaites was governor, and his report for one quarter is illuminating:[78; 151]

> *Since my last report 11 prisoners have been committed, viz. 2 for larceny, 4 for poaching, 1 for vagrancy, 1 for want of sureties, and 3 debtors. Unfortunately one of the youths for poaching has been killed on the tread wheel.*
>
> *The prisoners have continued healthy under the new dietary. The greatest number at any one time has been 16, the average number 14. Contracts for provisions have been entered into for the next 6 months at the following prices, best Wheaten Bread 2½d per lb., Beef 3½d per lb., Oatmeal 1s-7¾d per stone, Coals 7d per cwt.,*

Onions 1s-4d per stone, Barley 2d per lb., Soap 5s-10d per stone, Cocoa 10d per lb., Molasses 3½d per lb., Pepper 1s-4d per lb.

The prisoners, being young and healthy, have been kept on the tread wheel labour. They have also ground 148½ quarters of malt for which was obtained 1d per quarter from the local public brewery. Nothing has been done amongst wool this last quarter. The prisoners have conducted themselves satisfactorily. The prison rules have been strictly attended to, and instructions have been afforded to all the juvenile prisoners in reading and writing and the Church Catechism.

The 'hard labour' routine in 1823 sounds distinctly unpleasant:[59]

At 6.0 in the morning the prisoners commence work on the mill, and remain there until 8.0; half an hour is allowed for breakfast and from 8.30 until 9.0 they work at the mill; from 9.0 to 9.20 they are at Chapel and then at the mill till 12.0; one hour is allowed for dinner and from 1.0 till 5.30 they are upon the mill; they then attend chapel for one quarter of an hour and are again placed upon the mill till lock up time which is at 7 o'clock.

The regime was not only dull and tiring but dangerous (there was no safety brake on the treadmill until after the fatal accident involving the young poacher), but the result was considered satisfactory in that "everyone committed during the last quarter have paid their fines rather than continue on the tread wheel." Maybe the tough regime was also a factor in escapes, of which two were recorded in 1842, two more in 1850 and one in 1859.[160] Each prisoner cost 4½d per day to feed. The governor's salary was £100, the matron's £20, and there was also a turnkey. The school teacher, chaplain and medical officer visited regularly. The prison was divided into three sections: felons, debtors, and females. Upon special occasions such as elections and at Christmas the prisoners received extra fare, and on Queen Victoria's Coronation "the prisoners in the County Gaol return thanks for the treat upon Coronation Day and also to Mrs Herd, King's Head Hotel, for the crumbs from the rich men's tables."[78]

Not all the prisoners, however, had a hard time. In 1854 John Atkinson the 25-year old church organist eloped with a thirteen-year-old pupil from the boarding school for young ladies that then occupied Ivy House in Boroughgate. As the newspaper of the day put it, in language worthy of Jane Austen, "Mr Atkinson was engaged by Miss Bishop to give lessons in music to her pupils, and had availed himself of the opportunities this position afforded him to trifle with the youthful affections of Miss Ward." They were duly married at Gretna, but the husband was arrested in Carlisle on their return and sentenced to spend nine months in Appleby gaol. The judge was lenient, recording the crime as a misdemeanour, so that, as the local newspaper put it, "he may lie on his own featherbed, find his own provisions, drink a butt of wine a day if he can, and have an unlimited supply of books. A rumour is got abroad that his piano is allowed him." Presumably the young wife was excluded from the permitted comforts, but the story had a happy ending, for on 12 September 1859 John Atkinson and Anne Jane Ward were married at St Marylebone Church in London.[178]

In 1867 Appleby and Kendal had a quarrel over the county's prisons. Kendal had the house of correction, while Appleby had the gaol, and neither of these came up to the standards required by the Prisons Act of 1865. Kendal, "because it provided most of the prisoners" wanted one gaol for the county, on grounds of economy, and proposed that it should be at Kendal. But the Appleby magistrates were afraid that the loss of the gaol would also mean the loss of the assizes, held in the Shire Hall next to the gaol, and of the revenues that they brought into the town. As a result in 1873 Appleby prison was reconstructed to meet the new regulations. But only five years later it went out of use, and was converted to serve as the East Ward Union Vagrancy Ward and Divisional Police Headquarters.[78] The greater part of the gaol was demolished in 1971, when the front of the building was restored to its original appearance.[158]

Appleby was transformed in mid-century by the coming of the railways. The process started on 24 May 1844 when a Bill to authorise the construction of the Lancaster and Carlisle Railway passed both Houses of Parliament in one day (what a contrast with today's long-drawn-out planning process!)[59] The line opened on 15 December 1846, linking the west of the Eden Valley to London. The South Durham and Lancashire Union Railway across Stainmore followed in August 1861, making it possible to transport coal and coke from the Durham mines to the iron ore fields of Furness, and iron back to the factories and ship-builders of the north-east. At Kirkby Stephen this line connected with the Eden

Valley Railway, opened in June 1862, which ran through Appleby to Penrith, with connections to Keswick, Cockermouth and the West Cumberland mines. In May 1876 the completion of the Carlisle and Settle line brought London itself within a day's direct journey from Appleby.[59; 134; 179]

Railways meant employment. In 1881 the transport industry employed ten men in Appleby and 35 in Bongate, but by 1891 the total had risen to 72, including 66 railway workers and a bus driver. In contrast, the proportion of the population working on the land had dropped significantly.[134] Two railway companies meant two stations – Appleby Midland (later re-named Appleby West), served by the Settle-Carlisle Line, and Appleby North Eastern (later Appleby East) on the Eden Valley Line. They stood close to one another at the top of the slope above the Sands. The new, fast, rail connections allowed the import of fresh foods such as fish, and the despatch of local produce (including Eden salmon) to places as far away as London. They also enormously increased the movement of people. In 1878, 14,629 passengers passed through Appleby Midland station and in 1882 the total was 18,882. The employment and prosperity generated by the railways prompted the building of new streets on the hillside below the two stations.

Railways also meant tourists. Appleby began to promote itself as within six hours' journey from London. Hotels began to offer accommodation for 'families, commercials and tourists.' A *Guide to Kirkby Stephen* had appeared in 1884, and the first *Guide to Appleby,* by the Vicar of St Lawrence's Church, Canon W A Mathews, followed in 1890.[134] Appleby proclaimed itself a centre for road and rail excursions and for fishing, while Dufton was commended as a base for 'long or short walks, pure water and bracing air' and Kirkby Stephen even hoped to become 'a second Harrogate.'[134] Whatever their ambitions, these communities never took off as major tourist resorts, and indeed depended for their appeal, as they still do, on their quiet rural character.

By 1894 there were only around a dozen hotels and inns in Appleby, but temperance hotels, apartments and refreshment rooms had also sprung up. By that date also a wide range of shops was established. Merchants sold flour, butter, eggs, lime, manure, seeds and poultry. In the Market Place there was a branch of Wilson, Jespers & Co., merchant tailors, clothiers and sewing-machine suppliers, who also had shops in Carlisle and Penrith. There were grocers, greengrocers, brewers, gasfitters, paperhangers, mechanical and agricultural engineers, a fishmonger, a chemist (who was an Associate of the Pharmaceutical Society), an umbrella repairer, a mineral water manufacturer, eight insurance agents and agents for sewing machines, rifles, ammunition and agricultural implements! Some local merchant families like the Whiteheads had done well enough to live in a large modern house in Bongate.[134]

The railways brought about a big change in the trading of cattle, sheep and horses. In 1851 fairs were still held in Appleby on the second Thursday in April and the Friday following it (King James II's fair), on Whitsun-eve and Whit Monday ('Whit Fair'), on St Lawrence's Day in August and on the second Wednesday in June. This June fair was held on Gallows Hill one mile from the town, and it seems to have been known at the time as Brampton Fair, no doubt because it was held on the road to Brampton, or even within Brampton township. But these periodic fairs became much less important when the railways replaced the drovers and when new auction marts appeared – as Appleby's did on 29 May 1876.[150] In 1878 some 837 trucks carrying livestock either arrived at or left Appleby Midland Station: in 1882 the total was 794. This was more than twice the tally at Kirkby Stephen.[134] By 1885 Appleby's traditional Whit Fair was still an event, but not long afterwards all the fairs except the early June Brampton Fair seem to have ceased and the latter, moved for a time off the traditional site and then back again, became renamed 'New Fair.'[150] The name may have changed because it took the place of the borough's traditional Whitsun Fair. By then Gallows Hill (which was last used for a public execution in March 1829 when William Jennings of Kendal was hanged for rape) had also changed its name to the more cheerful-sounding Fair Hill.

As county town, Appleby had special civic, ceremonial and social status and it was the place of residence of a number of Westmorland officials, including the clerk of the peace, a coroner, a high constable, the county bridgemaster and an inspector of weights and measures.[134] The county town was also the base for the Royal Westmorland Militia, which held its annual training week at Brackenber Moor, and in 1874, 1,400 men in camp there were visited by the Earl of Lonsdale and Viscount Lowther together with a large crowd of other visitors who came by train. The militia band was called upon to play at many functions including balls and agricultural shows: sadly for the town recruitment fell off and the headquarters of the militia was moved to Carlisle in 1880.[134] Sports, agricultural shows and 'hirings,' when young farm workers sought new employment and there were sideshows, entertainments and dancing, added to the social life of the district. Brass bands, bell-ringing, choral societies and both visiting and local dramatic companies were found in almost every community and were certainly well-established in Appleby by the latter part of the century.[134]

Sometimes the entertainments took bizarre form. On May Day in 1868 the old bridge over the Eden was the scene of one of Appleby's more entertaining hoaxes. A large crowd gathered for a demonstration by 'Professor De Greaves of the Royal Marine Academy of Le Havre', who promised to walk a mile up the river Eden on his patent Kamptullicon Boots! At the stated time, however, Tom Graham the local postman appeared and "after a shrill blast on his horn, gravely announced to the motley throng that it was the first of May, and they had unfortunately been duped into a flock of May goslings." The first day of May rather than 1 April was the day for such practical jokes in Cumbria and north Yorkshire.[138]

The nineteenth century was a time when friendly societies, designed for mutual help and support in bad times, proliferated. The first Friendly Society of Appleby had, in fact, appeared in 1794, meeting at the King's Head.[59] By 1864, Appleby had one of the ten Westmorland branches of the Manchester Unity of Oddfellows, and the Ancient Order of Foresters was also well established. The Eden Valley Freemasons' Lodge was in action by 1861, holding monthly meetings at the King's Head. A Co-operative Society was formed in 1868, followed in 1873 by the Vale of Eden Agricultural Co-operative Society, based in Appleby. Recreation and advancement of knowledge were the themes of the Mental Culture and Mutual Improvement Societies and Mechanics Institutes: the latter had lectures in Appleby in 1857 on 'the pursuit of knowledge', 'candles and light' and 'the history of printing.' The Temperance movement was also strong in the district, as was Primitive Methodism to which it had close ties, and by the 1880s the White Hart and Black Boy Inns in Appleby had become temperance establishments (King Richard II, whose badge was the white hart, might have approved but Charles II, nick-named 'the black boy,' might not!) The town's Mutual Improvement Society was connected with the Church of England Temperance movement. From 1857 onwards the Band of Hope held well-attended festivals, one in Appleby in June 1874 attracting 890 people to march in its procession and 1,600 children to attend the event. In 1875 over 1,200 members attended a demonstration.[134]

Nineteenth-century Appleby was still a modestly-sized market town without any major manufacturing industry: indeed the local linen businesses had failed by 1870 leaving only the small woollen mill at Coupland Beck.[134] There was some small-scale local brewing and milling, and various crafts, but these too declined in the face of easy import from larger urban factories. None the less, the century saw some substantial rebuilding in the town centre. The cloisters that had served as a covered butter-market from 1696 onwards were replaced in 1811 by the present structure, designed by Sir Robert Smirke, the architect of Lord Lonsdale's grand new Lowther Castle. In the late nineteenth century there was a public bath house in the eastern side of the Appleby Cloisters: cold, warm, hot or vapour baths cost a shilling for a 'first class' hour of use or sixpence for a 'second class' half-hour. They were reserved for ladies on Monday afternoons. The Tufton Arms Hotel, which now dominates the Market Place, was erected in 1873 in the place of an earlier inn, the Crown and Mitre.[138]

There were also improvements in the amenities of the borough. The first fourteen lime trees along the upper part of Boroughgate were planted in 1876 thanks largely to a donation of £5-5s-0d from the bell-ringers of St Lawrence's Church. When the last of the shambles was removed in 1883 four more trees were added.[138; 180] In 1886 some new (and ugly) iron steps were put up in place of the stone ones that used to give access to the upper floor of the Moot Hall: fortunately, they were demolished by a motor van in 1931 and replaced by the present stone flight, paid for by a legacy from the former town clerk, Mr William Hewitson.[135] In the 1880s the Butts, where once the citizens practised archery, were laid out as a recreation ground, and connected to the bridge end by a footpath constructed along the river bank on a strip of ground acquired from the vicar of St Lawrence's Church. The Vicar's Croft, or glebe land, adjoining the church, was taken over on lease and made into a cricket ground in the same period.

The accelerating pace of development in the late nineteenth century placed increasing strain on Appleby's antiquated system of government. This had not been affected by the Municipal Reform Act of 1835, and remained dependent for its income on the rents of municipal properties, tolls and fines. These provided an unpredictable cash flow, and receipts totalled only around £200 per annum - quite insufficient to pay for the modernisation the citizens were demanding.[78] In 1861 the tolls were challenged by the farming community which successfully argued for reductions.[134] In 1875 it was recorded that the corporation's total annual receipts were £50, that interest on loans took £30 of this, and that the assets were £60 and a quantity of broken stone![78] In 1877 the Municipal Corporations Committee paid a visit and noted disapprovingly that Appleby was a 'closed borough' with a council appointed solely by the freemen (presumably no longer under the direction of the Lowther and Tufton families!)

By then the very existence of a mayor and corporation in such a small town was being questioned in some circles, and in 1874 they were made fun of in a local newspaper which described a civic procession as "pomp and ceremony and childish displays... in mimic rivalry to the Lord Mayor [of London]... as a few feeble and tottering old men in gowns headed by... sword and mace bearer accompany the enterprising Town Clerk."[134] None the less, the ancient borough clung to its ceremonies (as it continued to do throughout the twentieth century), and it may not be irrelevant that the newspaper in question was based in Penrith!

Fortunately, the corporation was no longer responsible for water supply or sewerage. By 1874 dissatisfaction with the system of wells and pumps – recorded as giving rise to problems a century before – came to a head. The corporation told the East Ward Guardians – the district administrative body – that the water in the centre of the town was not fit to drink.[134] Eighty three houses in Appleby and Bongate, with 366 inhabitants, relied on their own wells and a further 113 houses with 502 residents depended on public wells or those of their neighbours. Only one public well was considered fit for use. The East Ward Sanitary Authority agreed that a new supply, providing 80,000 gallons a day for the town and a further 20,000 for the railway was essential. Hilton and Murton becks were rejected as sources because they were polluted by mine drainage, and instead springs of soft water issuing from the red sandstone at George Gill, three miles away, were tapped.[78; 134] The scheme cost £5,500 but it proved so efficient and economical to run that there was no general water rate until the undertaking was taken over by the Eden Water Board in 1963! The need for sewerage to replace the open gutters in the streets was equally compelling, but it was not until 1882 that a proper scheme was carried out, at a cost of £4,000, extended thereafter as the borough grew.[78]

Although it was able to improve Boroughgate by demolishing the last of the shambles, the corporation could not afford to re-pave all the streets, which were in a wretched state after they had been dug up, first to lay water mains and then to install sewers.[78] It was therefore with some alacrity that the borough availed itself of the Municipal Corporations Acts of 1882 and 1883 and petitioned for a new Charter of Incorporation. The old corporation was dissolved, and in 1885 a new charter granted by Queen Victoria established Appleby as a municipal borough with a mayor and a corporation of four aldermen and twelve councillors elected by all householders.[74] It held its first meeting in November 1885.[181] The new body inherited a debt of £8,600 from the old corporation, but was now able to levy rates rather than depend on tolls, and this transformed the finances. It was only after this reform that the corporation was really able to set to work to repair the roads and footpaths throughout the borough.[78]

These administrative changes were paralleled by others outside the borough. Before 1885 district government rested with the Board of Guardians of the East Ward Union, which was, among other things, the governing body for the East Ward Sanitary Authority. The police came under a joint Constabulary for Cumberland and Westmorland.[78; 134] In the late 1880s a 'three tier' system of local government came into being. The reformed Appleby Corporation was the bottom tier, responsible for local affairs within the town. The East Ward Union was replaced by a new Rural District Council (although for a time both bodies operated, with overlapping functions). Westmorland County Council, the top tier local authority, was set up in 1889, and the county courts, held like the assizes in Appleby, were under its jurisdiction.

The reform of Appleby Corporation brought a fundamental change to the status of the freemen. They were not exempted from rates, nor had they any special privileges under the new charter. After 1885, therefore, no more ordinary freemen were appointed. Instead, as in many other towns, people who had given special service were awarded the honorary freedom of the borough. The last ordinary freemen under the old system, Mr James P Shepherd and Major John Nanson, lived on until 1925 and 1932, but both gave years of faithful service, the former as town clerk from 1869 to 1885 and the latter as treasurer from 1857 to 1904 and mayor in 1904, 1905 and 1906. The first honorary freeman, Sir James

Whitehead Bart., Lord Mayor of London in 1888-9 and a great benefactor to Appleby Grammar School and to St Michael's Church, was elected in 1888. The freedom of the borough was granted next to ten Appleby men who served in South Africa in the Boer War, and then to a succession of mayors, aldermen, councillors, town clerks and surveyors. In 1952 the Border Regiment was given honorary freedom and the right to march through the town with drums beating and bayonets fixed.[78]

The nineteenth century saw an astonishing burst of church building and church restoration throughout England. In Appleby, St Lawrence's Church got a new ring of six bells in 1833[138] and a full refurbishment in 1863, when many of the windows were given new tracery and the ancient organ was removed from a gallery at the west end to a position on the north side of the choir-stalls (it went back to its original place at the west end in 1976). St Michael's Church in Bongate followed in 1885, and was treated much more drastically. A tower was added on the north side, the windows were mostly renewed, the arcades were re-tooled, and many old carved stones including an early fifteenth century tomb canopy were cast out and built into the garden wall of the vicarage (now the Courtfield Hotel).[9; 138] A new organ was presented by the first Lady Hothfield, a carved oak pulpit and screen by Sir James Whitehead, Bt. and a font by Lady Whitehead.[78] Sadly, despite all this generosity, by 1975 St Michael's had been declared redundant, and after standing empty for ten years it was converted into a private house in the 1980s. Lady Anne would have been horrified!

The name of Hothfield is a reminder that the nineteenth century saw a major change in the ownership of Appleby Castle. Despite the prolific production of six sons by Lady Anne's daughter Margaret, three of these died without children and the legitimate line of the Tufton Earls of Thanet and hereditary High Sheriffs of Westmorland ended with Henry, the eleventh Earl, who died unmarried in 1849. His supposed illegitimate son, Richard Tufton, who had been born in France in 1813,[100] inherited the estates but the line of hereditary high sheriffs ceased with the earldom, the crown assuming responsibility for appointing high sheriffs for the county year by year. Richard Tufton married a French wife in 1843 and only became a British subject in 1849, the year in which he inherited the family estates. He was made a baronet in January 1851, and his son Henry, who lived from 1844 to 1926, was created first Baron Hothfield (of Hothfield in Kent) in 1881.[100] The Earls of Thanet had not been regular residents at Appleby (the under-sheriff lived in the castle) but Lord Hothfield became deeply involved, restoring the Countess' Pillar at Brougham in 1883,[25] joining the Cumberland and Westmorland Antiquarian and Archaeological Society, taking an interest in his castle ruins and serving as mayor of Appleby in 1895-96. The present wrought-iron entrance gates by the High Cross bear his initials and baronial coronet.

In 1886 the corporation decided that the new streets that had been built below the railway stations needed a direct link to the town itself. Up to that date, their only connection was round about, via Station Road, or by a single footpath across an open field called Lady Garth which incorporated the abandoned burgages along the Sands and had been bought up by the Lowthers in the 1750s. The corporation applied to the local government board for a loan, in order to buy this field and lay out footpaths across it. The loan was refused, whereupon several burgesses bought the field privately from Lord Lonsdale's trustees, and carried out the work themselves. They financed the building of the paths by selling off plots as building sites, and when all was done had enough money left over to pay for seats to be placed at suitable viewpoints in the borough, and to present the corporation with a new badge and chain for the use of the mayor and his successors.[78]

This was just part of a surge of development on the east side of the borough. The Primitive Methodists had built their 'Chapel on the Rock' there in 1872, perched on the red sandstone cliff above Howgate and largely using stone quarried on site (the building was converted to serve as the Jehovah's Witnesses' Kingdom Hall in 1995).[182] The Wesleyan Methodists needed to replace their original building in Chapel Street which dated from 1823 and had become too small, and also decided to move east. They bought a site at the foot of Lady Garth, fronting on the main road along the Sands: the foundation stone was laid in 1888, and the building completed soon after (it was extended in 1904).[78] In 1898 the road to the stations was linked to Bongate by the construction of the Garth Heads Road, which more or less follows the line of the ancient 'back lane' behind the old burgages along the Sands. Soon the Sands road became lined with houses, as it had been in the days of the borough's wealth.

The ancient stone bridge was the only link between the centre of the borough and these developments around 'railway Appleby' and the

Sands, and in the 1880s this was in a fairly shaky condition after centuries of use. It had been damaged by many floods, not least in 1822 when the water poured along Bridge Street and onward down Low Wiend, standing three feet deep in the grammar school and St Lawrence's Church and causing the abandonment of services. In this same flood a wooden bridge behind the King's Head Hotel, which linked the latter to its stables across the river, was carried away.[59] By 1885 the old bridge was once again in need of repair. A detailed survey was ordered, and this took place in 1887.[59; 87] It recorded that the stone was sandstone, that the two arches each had a span of about 45 feet and had five sandstone ribs, and that the original width of the bridge had been thirteen feet, which was quite wide for a structure of such antiquity.

There was a wrangle between Appleby Corporation and the county council over who should pay for either repairing or replacing the bridge. In the end, it was ruled that the county must foot the bill. They were told that repair would cost £831-10s-0d, but this, of course, would do nothing to adapt the structure for modern traffic. They were also quoted £3,562-12s-0d for a new stone bridge with two arches, £3,869-12s-0d for an iron single-span structure, £3,400-0s-0d for a two-arched iron bridge and £3,595-12s-0d for an iron girder bridge with a single span. Despite the feeling that this was the age of iron, the traditionalists won the day and a new stone bridge was commissioned: the actual cost was £3,624-14s-0d.[59]

The demolition of the old bridge began in the summer of 1888, and in the same year the foundation stone of the new centre pier was laid. In the demolition, so Canon Mathews recorded, three fragments of carved stones were found in the central pier of the old bridge, together with a bottle of antique form which appeared to contain a piece of parchment. It was thrown by the workman finding it to the foreman on the bank; he failed to catch it and it fell back into the river and was lost.[58] If these anecdotes are true they give a broad hint that the structure demolished in 1888 was – like the bridge at Kirkby Lonsdale to which it has been compared – a rebuilding from the fifteenth or early sixteenth century, rather than the 'stanebrigg' of 1382. The 1880s also saw the building of a new footbridge over the Eden alongside Bongate ford, in commemoration of Queen Victoria's Golden Jubilee in 1887. This lasted only until 1968 when it was severely damaged in yet another great flood, to be replaced in 1970 by the present footbridge.[138]

In 1886 the old buildings of Appleby Grammar School by Low Wiend also fell victim to modernisation. The school had been under scrutiny since 1864, when Mr D C Richmond had inspected it on behalf of the Schools Inquiry Commission and criticised deficiencies in teaching, curriculum and facilities. Numbers had fallen from the hundred or so pupils at the turn of the century to only 23 dayboys and ten boarders. The emphasis was on classics and mathematics, with some French, history and geography. There was no playground. The headmaster, John Richardson, had been appointed in 1839 and was described as 'somewhat infirm' though he still had a high reputation for classical scholarship. The report noted that the governors still clung to the tradition of the school as a 'classical seminary' and resisted the idea that it might be "adapted more completely to the requirements of the tradesmen and farmers of the district." None the less, its scholastic record in competing for exhibitions at Queen's College Oxford remained good, and pupils had also been going to the new university at Durham and to universities in Scotland.[101]

Mr Richmond's inspection was followed by a visit from a Mr Durnford, Assistant Commissioner to the Charity Commissioners, in 1869. The Schools Inquiry Commission's report was being implemented by a new Endowed Schools Act, so it is natural that Mr Durnford again raised the question of whether the grammar school should continue as a high-grade classical establishment or have a broader curriculum with more emphasis on mathematics, modern languages and science. By this time Mr Richardson had died and been succeeded by Mr Colin Threlkeld, a picturesque character nick-named 'Old Baccy', but pupil numbers had fallen to only sixteen in 1868, all except two from the town itself.

Mr Durnford concluded that if the school was to be revived the buildings must be improved and a boarding hostel provided (something must have gone wrong, for the 1826 boarding house should have been adequate for the tiny population of pupils).[101] The governors clearly took the question seriously, and under Mr Threlkeld's leadership pupil numbers rose to 37 in 1869, 53 in 1870 and 83 in 1881. Plans were drawn up for new buildings in Low Wiend, but in 1881 the governors concluded that the old site was too cramped and that it would be better to move to a new location on the outskirts of the town. In 1884 a site at Battlebarrow was chosen and it was decided to go ahead in 1886. Colin

Threlkeld did not like it and resigned.[101] By the end of 1887 the new buildings were ready. The Charity Commissioners were annoyed over what they felt was inadequate consultation and sent Mr Durnford back on another inspection in 1888, but all moved forward smoothly and the School re-opened on its present site under Mr A F Davidson's headmastership.

So ended several centuries of teaching close by St Lawrence's Church. In 1886 the old buildings were auctioned off: the headmaster's house was later demolished, and the schoolhouse was converted to dwellings (now numbers 27, 28 and 29 Chapel Street). Reginald Bainbrigg's classical inscriptions were taken from the original schoolhouse and set in the wall of Broad Close, where they continue to decay. The lintel of Bishop Smith and Randal Sanderson's school of 1671 was placed above a doorway in the new school, supported by carved stone pillars and surmounted by an inscription commemorating Bishop Smith, also transferred from the old building.[101] Faint humps and hollows in the King George V Memorial playing field opposite the old schoolhouse may mark the site of the 'Little Schole' (Map 5).

Two Appleby Grammar School old boys achieved special distinction in the second half of the nineteenth century – James Whitehead and John Percival. Whitehead, whose family moved to Appleby after farming near Sedbergh, was at school between 1843 and 1848 and then moved to London. He became an Alderman of the City of London, was Lord Mayor in 1888-1889 and was made a Baronet in 1889 not least because he had negotiated an end to a damaging strike in London Docks.[101] But he kept close to his Appleby roots, making generous gifts to St Michael's Church, endowing a science laboratory and scholarships at the grammar school and creating the Whitehead Trust. John Percival, also a farmer's son (from Brough), went from Appleby school to Queen's College Oxford in 1855 and became a fellow in 1858 before embarking on a teaching career. He rose to be headmaster of first Clifton College and then Rugby, served for a period as President of Trinity College, Oxford, and in 1895 was appointed Bishop of Hereford. In his will he left £1,000 to the grammar school to endow bursaries.[101]

In Appleby, as elsewhere in England, the first decade of the twentieth century was an almost seamless continuation of the closing years of the nineteenth. Public services, amenities and education came top of the town agenda. In 1905 the corporation bought (for £5,600) the undertaking that had supplied the town with gas since 1837.[78] They ran into trouble, finding that about a fifth of the gas produced was lost by leakage and that it was difficult to persuade townspeople to accept gas cookers and coin-in-the-slot meters.[183] The retiring mayor, John Nanson (one of the last two ordinary freemen) promoted the merits of gas, telling people that they could now cook breakfast in record time for almost nothing, instead of wasting half an hour sizzling the bacon and eggs over an open fire! Fortunately, promotion seems to have worked for by 1908 gas production had doubled and losses were down to about seven per cent – to be cut to a bit over four per cent by 1910. But there was trouble with the smell – described in 1911 as "suggestive of decomposing codfish and doubtful eggs!" and this was not sorted out until 1913.[183] None the less, the corporation battled on, and continued to run the gas works until nationalisation in the 1940s.[78] By then, some of the equipment was pretty archaic, and the last gasholder was eventually transferred to the Beamish Open Air Museum.[138] Appleby's fire service, which operated from an adjacent building, was also fairly antique, the first fire engine being horse-drawn with a steam-driven pump. It is recorded that if the jolting and jarring on the road put out the fire in the pumping engine's fire-box the engineer would stop to commandeer burning coals from the most convenient house along the route.[138]

Amenities and facilities also received attention. In 1902 the golf club, which had been founded in 1894 and had laid out its first 9-hole course at Minsceugh, moved to its extensive 18-hole course among the heather of Brackenber Moor. A bowling green was laid out on the bank of the Eden in 1913. In 1910 a new cemetery was laid out in Bongate, and in the same year a gift from Lady Hothfield allowed the inner hall of the Market Hall to be altered for public entertainments and the showing of films. St Michael's Institute and the British School also merged in 1910 into Appleby County Primary School not far from the railway stations; a master in the British School, Mr William Harris, becoming the first headmaster of the new venture.[184] In 1912 a new post office was built, the last thatched building in the town being demolished in the process, and in the same year the cobbles were removed from the Market Place.

A decade of peaceful progress was shattered by the outbreak of the First World War in 1914. Throughout the country, men rushed to join up and Appleby was no exception. The town's detachment of the 4th Battalion Border (Territorial) Regiment soon found itself in Burma, and

Into the Modern World

was later transferred to upper India, where it was joined by the Reserve Battalion. However, the majority of Appleby men enlisted in the Battalion of the New Army which Lord Lonsdale raised from the hills and dales of Cumberland and Westmorland, and this force, after training at Carlisle, Wensleydale, and Salisbury Plain, sailed for France in November 1915. In July 1916 it suffered heavy casualties during an attack at Authuille Wood near Thiepval, and among those killed was the Commanding Officer, Lieut. Colonel P W Machell CMG of Crackenthorpe Hall.[78] John Sackville Richard Tufton, who was to become the second Lord Hothfield in 1926, also played an active part in the First World War although not in the local regiment. In 1915 he was a Major in the 3rd Battalion of the Royal Sussex Regiment where he was mentioned in despatches, and won a DSO and the Croix de Guerre.[100]

The whole community at home backed up the war effort. The Red House in Boroughgate, which had been placed at the disposal of the Red Cross by Lord Hothfield, was converted into a convalescent home. Alderman E A Heelis remained in office as mayor for the entire war period, from 1913 to 1920, and Mrs Heelis, the mayoress, was at the heart of the wartime charitable effort. The town clerk, Mr W Hewitson, kept the administration running smoothly despite the absence of so many men at the front. The election of Alderman and Mrs Heelis to the honorary freedom of the borough in 1921 was in recognition of their outstanding services throughout the war, while Mr Hewitson was made an honorary freeman in 1923 in recognition of the 37 years during which he had guided Appleby "with wise counsel and sound judgement."[78]

With the return of peace, Appleby relapsed into a state of tranquillity in which disputes over housing sites, water supplies and gasometers provided the chief disturbances. The borough's War Memorial was built in the new Bongate cemetery in 1920: it now commemorates the dead of both World Wars. But in 1923 the tranquillity was rudely broken when the Lord Chancellor's Committee recommended that the Westmorland Assizes which had been held at Appleby from time immemorial should be abolished on grounds of economy. The corporation protested loudly, and was supported by Westmorland County Council. The argument went on for several years, but in the end Appleby won and the assizes were saved! It was, however, agreed that the judge was only to visit the town when there were cases for trial instead of coming, as had often happened in the past, merely to be presented with a pair of white gloves and to compliment the county on its freedom from crime.[78]

At the turn of the twentieth century, Appleby had only two small manufacturing industries – one making corsets and the other producing butter – and both ceased to exist during the First World War. However, the expansion of dairy farming – based, at the time, on the dual-purpose Northern Dairy Shorthorn whose red-roan cows were a universal sight in the meadows – allowed the opening of the Express Dairy Company's Milk Collecting Depot on 1 January 1931, and this gave a great boost to the local economy. An egg collecting station was added in 1935.[78]

It is hard to see how this could have happened without electricity, but this service, now considered the most essential of all, was astonishingly slow in reaching Westmorland. Great Asby set up its own local supply (powered from Rutter Falls) in 1929, but a contract for supply to Westmorland as a whole was not granted until 1931.[78; 185] Although Appleby had had a gas supply since 1837, electricity did not reach the town until 1934, and some buildings were not connected until much later. Indeed it was not until after the Second World War that a supply was proposed for the Hospital of St Anne. Lord Hothfield offered to pay for it, but was politely turned down by the occupants because "Lady Anne would not have liked it!"[131; 143]

In the 1920s and 1930s, the grammar school continued to evolve, with a broadening curriculum and an enlarged governing council (the membership, curiously, included the owner of Appleby Castle, ex-officio, plus two members appointed by Appleby Town Council, two by Westmorland County Council, one by Queen's College, Oxford, and one by the Temple Sowerby Trustees, plus five co-opted members, all local worthies). In 1928 a new science laboratory was built and equipped from funds left in trust by Sir James Whitehead.[101] It remained a selective school for local boys, while girls went to Kirkby Stephen Grammar School – a far from ideal arrangement because pupils had to commute quite long distances, mostly by rail.

In 1932 the town was also affected by a further modernisation of local government, the three authorities covering north Westmorland (the East Ward Rural District Council, the West Ward RDC and the Shap Urban DC) being amalgamated as the North Westmorland Rural District Council. Although this reorganisation did not affect the borough it was at Appleby that the first meeting of the new authority was held, in April 1935.[181]

The Second World War took Appleby men back to France, the

Borough Platoon of the 4th Battalion, The Border Regiment, going across in November 1939. The regiment was broken up at Fecamp and St. Valery, and its members escaped by various routes, leaving some 200 behind in France as prisoners. After the evacuation of France, the battalion saw service in Syria, Tobruk, India and Burma, under the command of Lieutenant Colonel G B Harker of Appleby. Back home, paralleling the situation between 1914 and 1918, the town retained the same mayor – the second Lord Hothfield – for the entire war period, with councillor (later alderman) J F Whitehead as deputy mayor.[78]

The town itself had a very quiet war. The nearest bombs were dropped – almost certainly jettisoned – at Drybeck one night, and the local air raid warden who knew that no damage had been done thought so little of the event that he did not report it until the next day. More excitement was caused by the rumour of a landing of enemy paratroops at Asby, and many fictitious but entertaining stories went round the district! As in the First World War, Appleby people joined in many local charities and the borough ran a series of gift sales and special appeals. A hospital supply depot was run for the Red Cross, and over 20,000 garments, all locally made, were handled there during the war period. Another useful service undertaken by many residents was the entertainment of airmen from Commonwealth countries for their leave periods.[78]

Being such a safe area, the district received children and parents evacuated from many places, including Newcastle, South Shields, Barrow-in-Furness and London. The majority of the evacuees were unaccompanied children, and most of those parents who did come found it hard to settle in the district and soon returned home. A special and privately-organised evacuation took place in 1941 when Wagon Repairs Limited of Birmingham removed their entire office staff and their families to Appleby. Accommodation was found for 120 in and about the town, and Bongate Hall and Eden Grove at Bolton were purchased as offices. This firm brought much life and trade to the borough, and gave strong support to local charities. The company returned to Birmingham in 1945.[78]

Victory in 1945 was celebrated with thanksgiving services, parades, sports and bonfires. The town soon settled down to normal peacetime activities, but the return of men from the forces created one major problem; a housing shortage. The corporation responded by buying a site extending up the slope on the south side of Scattergate Green, capable of taking some 70 to 80 houses. Despite the delays and hindrances that were familiar in the post-war period, the first of these new houses was ready for occupation in 1949. They were just the start of a major expansion around Scattergate and along the Colby road which continued throughout the second half of the century as Appleby's population grew from 1,704 in 1951, to 2,020 in 1975 and 2,851 by the summer of 2003.

The formal memorial to the eight Appleby men who were killed in the Second World War is in the cemetery in Bongate. In 1946 an appeal was launched for funds to build a modern swimming pool, as an appreciation of the services of all those who had served in the war. A site by the river in the Butts was leased by the corporation. Money flowed in, Wagon Repairs Ltd giving £1,500 in appreciation of Appleby's war time hospitality; however a shortage of materials and lack of government assistance held the scheme up, and it was not until 1959 that a new, heated, open-air pool was completed.[78] In 1994 it was reconstructed as an indoor facility.[138]

The pool was only one of several new amenities. In 1944 the Broad Close was purchased by the corporation, and laid out as the King George V Memorial playing field. It was opened by the Princess Royal (Princess Mary, Countess of Harewood, daughter of King George V and Queen Mary) in August 1956. By curious coincidence, this was the first of two royal visits in the same month, for later that August Queen Elizabeth II and the Duke of Edinburgh paused on their way to the Lake District in a downpour of rain worthy of Borrowdale at its wettest! This may well have been the first visit by a reigning monarch since Edward I stayed at the Friary in 1300!

The post war-period saw a number of other new features. The Roman Catholic Church of Our Lady of Appleby was built in Garth Heads Road in 1958.[138] In the 1960s, a plot of land adjacent to the gaol field, which had been a garden since 1935, was presented to the corporation by Alderman J F Whitehead, who had it laid out as a children's playground. A legacy of £5,000 left by Mr J. Ingram Dawson of Barnard Castle because he had always found those of Appleby 'a most friendly people,' and because of his liking for the town, was used to improve 'the walks and river banks.' A new clock was installed in St Lawrence's Church in 1964, to mark the retirement of Alderman Whitehead from the council. In 1970 the northern end of the Moot Hall was redesigned. A new health centre and library were built in Low Wiend on the site of the headmaster's house of the original grammar school.

Appleby Grammar School also underwent a major transformation after the war. The 1944 Education Act required the provision of secondary education throughout the country, but this threw up a serious problem in the upper Eden Valley. There were only two secondary schools – Appleby Grammar School, catering for boys and Kirkby Stephen Grammar School as a girls-only establishment. The segregation meant a lot of unnecessary travel. Changes were clearly needed and although both schools retained their ancient title of 'grammar' school, both became co-educational and comprehensive.[101] At Appleby there was new building in 1945 and 1954, and there has been more since, as pupil numbers have risen to around 560 in 2005. Although it is a quite different establishment from the selective and highly academic institution of yesteryear, it has maintained the old link with Queen's College, Oxford, sending three pupils there in the 1990s.

Communications have always been the key to prosperity in fairly remote places like Appleby. Turnpikes, regular coach services and finally railways transformed the town in the nineteenth century, and in the twentieth the transformation of the road network changed things again. The progressive improvement of the A66 along the old Roman corridor has given Appleby a fast new by-pass, linking to the main motorway network. Most people and freight coming to the town now come by road, and that has brought the now-familiar problems of congestion, parking, wardens and road rage. As the road network grew, so the railway network withered. The Eden Valley branch of the old London and North Eastern Railway closed in 1962, and for many years, questions hung over the future of the Settle-Carlisle line, despite its appeal as the finest scenic railroad in England. Thanks in considerable part to an energetic band of Friends, the railway has survived so that Appleby still has a rail link to London via Leeds and to Scotland via Carlisle and more and more freight is also passing through. Appleby (West) station, like others on the line, has been refurbished as an important part of our railway heritage.

Appleby is unique in England in that, for one week in the year at least, the horse comes back into its own. The New Fair remains the largest and most important horse-market in the north of England, but since the Second World War it has been a focus of debate. Immediately after the war some people argued for its abolition, but the protests were such that in 1948 it was reinstated on Fair Hill, and the corporation pressed the county council and North Westmorland Rural District Council to provide the site with a water supply, sanitation and a track where horses could be shown instead of being trotted up and down the public road.⁽¹⁵⁰⁾ Money proved an obstacle, and nothing happened except talk (including strong words from the Medical Officer of Health about the insanitary conditions). It was not until 1966 that the travellers went back onto Fair Hill after many years of camping by the roadside, and even then horses continued to be put through their paces along the Long Marton Road rather than on the 'show track' built for the purpose. Arguments continued about facilities, policing and cost, but the New Fair had become a self-perpetuating event, drawing travellers from all over the country, and as such it operated independently of Appleby Borough though it still bore the town's name.⁽¹⁵⁰⁾ The fair still remains an important social gathering for the travelling community and stands as a monument to old times: one of the last of a kind of event that used to be commonplace but has vanished from much of the country. And controversy continues: in 2005 there were renewed calls for abolition following allegations of mess and loutish behaviour.⁽¹⁸⁶⁾

In the second half of the twentieth century agriculture – and especially dairying, stock-rearing and hill sheep farming – remained the dominant industry in the upper Eden Valley, but Appleby was no longer the main market for farm produce that it used to be. In the immediate post-war period, the Express Dairy Depot was still a significant centre of employment, drawing on herds of black-and-white Friesian cattle that progressively replaced the dairy shorthorns. A fleet of eleven road tankers collected from farms to the factory, which in 1969 handled over 21 million gallons of milk, some of it sent by rail to several northern towns and to London, while more was made into 'Cheddar' cheese. In 1969, 3,283 tons of cheese were produced, and 70,000 dozen eggs were handled in peak periods,⁽⁷⁸⁾ while by 1981, when the factory employed 190 people, it was taking in 30 million gallons of milk a year and making 12,000 tons of cheese. In 1994 the business was re-named the Cheese Company Ltd, and in 1996 it was modernised. But, perversely, this marked the end rather than a new beginning and later in 1996 the cheese-making business was transferred to another factory at Lockerbie, the Appleby creamery finally closing in 1997.⁽¹⁸¹⁾ The site, and a new industrial estate nearby, are now occupied by various service industries.

Between 1950 and 1980 there were also four major 'happenings' that affected the status and image of Appleby. The first came in 1958, when Alderman J F Whitehead asked the College of Arms about the armorial

Into the Modern World

bearings of the town. They confirmed that Appleby had no authentic, approved, arms and that the three leopards/lions *passant guardant or* on a field *gules* were far too similar to the royal device for England to be acceptable, even with the ducal coronets added in the eighteenth century, while the crest and supporting heraldic beasts used by the borough would also require change since they had previously been granted to others. The Earl Marshal finally granted the town arms of "*azure semee* of apple leaves proper three Lions *passant, or,* in pale each resting the dexter fore paw on an apple *or*." Put simply, this means that the three gold lions pace a blue field scattered with apple leaves, and rest their right paws on a golden apple. The enflamed salamander still bursts from an ancient crown as crest, and the supporters on either side are green and pink dragons resting their claws on more golden apples. The motto '*nec ferro nec igni*' endures. So, after seven hundred and fifty years, apples have come back to figure prominently in the official arms of Appleby.

Figure 8 - Appleby's old and new Coats of Arms.
Left: The old unauthorised coat used from the 18th to the 20th century. Three golden 'lions' with gold coronets on a red ground.
Right: The new coat granted in 1958. The three lions are still golden, but they pace more decorously and each rests a fore-paw on a golden apple. The ground is blue, scattered with apple leaves.

In 1962 there was another major break with ancient history, after the death without children of the third Lord Hothfield. The title passed to one of the grandsons of the second baron from his second marriage,[100] but Appleby Castle did not pass with it and was sold. Many of the family portraits and documents were sent for safe keeping to museums and the County Record Office. The 'great picture' commissioned by Lady

Anne has been bought by the Lakeland Arts Trust and is kept at Abbot Hall Gallery in Kendal, where, however, there is no room to show the immense central section.[11] While these important objects are safe and remain available for study, many people will regret their separation from the fabric within which they had been housed for so long, and the passing of that fabric from the ownership of a family which had held it since 1204. That family has, however, remained local for the sixth Lord Hothfield lives at Drybeck Hall, some four miles south of Appleby.

The third profound change in Appleby's status really began in 1949, when there was yet another proposal that all civil cases should be heard in Preston rather than at the Westmorland Assizes. Although this was fought off, as previous proposals had been in 1923, the critical drips slowly wore away the stone. And with reason, for however pleasant it may have been for judges and counsel to have a day or two's break in a small market town, it was difficult to justify bringing all the panoply of law to so tiny a place, to hear so short a list of cases. Finally, economy triumphed over history and the last assize was held in 1970.

A fourth and even greater change followed in 1974. Local government reform merged Westmorland, Cumberland, a corner of Yorkshire and Lancashire 'north of the Sands' into a new county of Cumbria. Carlisle reasserted its authority as the dominant local city, and Appleby ceased to be a county town. The Westmorland Shire Hall on the Sands lost its traditional function, and has yet to find a new role.

As millennium and century succeeded one another, therefore, Appleby was a very different place from the small, rural market town of 1900. Various kinds of tourism have become dominant, alongside agriculture, in the local economy. The town itself has changed in response. As late as 1960 it had a comprehensive range of shops that served the local farming community. You could buy almost anything there. The 1970 *Town Guide*[187] records four grocers, two greengrocers, two bakers and confectioners, a sweet shop, a tobacconist, three butchers, a fishmonger, a dairy, two drapers and outfitters, two shoe shops, two hairdressers, three ironmongers and general hardware stores, two booksellers, stationers and newsagents, two joiners and decorators, a smithy, two electrical engineers (also covering radio and television), a coal merchant, an insurance agent, three garages, two taxi services, a sawmill and two builders.

Note 11 - Indeed, it is too big to get through the doors – and Abbot Hall is a listed building!

Newly-built retirement bungalows were on offer for £1,680. Visitors were welcomed to three cafes and eleven hotels and guest houses, but only two concerns advertised themselves as gift shops and there were no advertisements for antique or curio shops or art galleries. Thirty years later many of the specialist stores have succumbed to competition from larger undertakings in Penrith, thirteen miles away, and souvenir shops and galleries have taken their place.

Some things do not change. The lower part of Appleby, along the Sands and within the loop of the river, has suffered from recurrent floods down the ages and they remained a problem during the twentieth century. There was a serious one in 1929, and an even worse inundation in 1968 when Bridge Street, St Lawrence's Church, the Police Station, the Methodist Church on the Sands and many houses were flooded. The water stood three feet deep on the Sands and cars and vans floated about: one mini took off down the river for an unknown destination.[188] The Jubilee Bridge at Bongate was irreparably damaged. There may not have been the loss in wines and spirits that depressed the citizens of 1771, but the bill for repairs was far longer. With such a record it is not surprising that new flood defences were demanded and in 1995 – after further floods that winter – a new alleviation scheme was completed. Yet January 2005 again saw water pouring through houses and shops on the Sands, on its way to cause even worse disaster in Carlisle. The new scheme did give partial protection to Bridge Street and Chapel Street, but the flood underlined the vulnerability of the lowest part of Appleby and brought calls for yet more work to protect it.

In 2005 Appleby is probably less important as a market town for the upper Eden Valley than at any time in the past 800 years. The closure of the Cheese Factory created a manufacturing void, and the new firms giving employment are almost all in the service sector. Such prosperity as the borough enjoys today rests largely on its attraction as a historic riverside town with its handsome main street, tall castle and green river banks, set in a wide tract of unspoiled countryside. But Westmorland is changing around it, not least as hill farming comes under ever-greater economic pressure. Now, climate change also threatens to transform the landscape. The twenty first century could well see alterations as great as any in the town's thousand years of turbulent history.

CHAPTER 9

If you require their Monuments...

ONE of the chief objects of a history of this kind is the better understanding of the present by reference to the past. The Appleby of today is the result of events spanning ten centuries of human occupation and extending back into still more remote ages. War and pestilence, the conflict of kingdoms, the ambition of powerful lords, the industry of thousands of merchants and tradesmen, the zeal of priests and scholars have all interacted to give us the patchwork of buildings and activities that we now see. It is fitting, therefore, to close this account of its history with a brief description of the town as it now is, and to use this description to bring together the different threads of narrative which have occupied the preceding pages.[12]

Suppose that you enter Appleby by the road from Brough. Until you are just under two miles from the town you are following the line of the road that the Romans made from Stainmore to the Solway in the first century AD. Then you branch off to enter Bongate. Here the first settlement to bear the name of Appleby was built in about 930; here in 'Old Appleby' the bondmen dependent on the castle lived in the thirteenth century. The former Church of St. Michael, on the left of the road, bears witness in its walls to many phases in the development of the present town. Over the north door in the nave there is the 'hogback' tombstone which is all that remains of the original settlement: the wall in which it is set was built during the first century of the new Norman borough. The south aisle, south transept, and porch date from the thirteenth century, and in the south wall of the nave there is an effigy, said to be that of the widow of the sixth Lord Clifford, who died in 1424.[13] The church as a whole was repaired by Lady Anne Clifford,

---

Note 12 - When this chapter was first written there was no good guidebook to Appleby. Now there is an excellent one by Barry and Vivien McKay which should be used as an accompaniment to the present chapter.
Note 13 - But the arms on the slab are of Vieuxpont, not Clifford.

whose work is commemorated by her initials and the date 1659 carved on a stone high in the north wall. The nineteenth century added the tower, and the twentieth saw the building made redundant as a place of worship and converted into a house. Fortunately, that conversion has been done sensitively, most of the living accommodation being contained in the Victorian tower, and the nave being retained as a single space used occasionally for concerts and exhibitions. The historic features like the hog-back tombstone have been protected, but can only be seen by private arrangement with the owners.

Across the road from St Michael's, the Courtfield Hotel was once Bongate vicarage. It has a tithe barn, and its garden wall includes various carved stones ejected from the church during the restoration of 1885. The road between it and the church drops to the Eden, with views to the castle (Figure 6 is the best of the old engravings of it). This is the view over which William Gilpin moralised in 1772, and which Moses Griffith, servant to Thomas Pennant, drew in the year following (Figure 7). Griffith was a self-taught artist, which may explain why his drawing suggests buildings in the south east corner of the bailey which, so far as we know, never existed! The east face of the castle, which from this aspect almost conceals the keep behind, contains work of all periods from 1170 to the nineteenth century, but most of what you see is due to Thomas, eighth Lord Clifford, in the 1450s. If you descend from the church to the footbridge you will see how effectively the castle commands the river crossing at this point. Wordsworth's 'statelier Eden' here flows swiftly over the broken weir and the shallows below it, to wash the base of the steep bank below the castle wall. The slopes, as when Gilpin viewed them, are still, "well hung with wood" and Bongate Mill, close by the footbridge, cannot be far from the site of the castle mill where the Cliffords tried to force the burghers to grind their corn in 1276.

The track through Bongate ford may well follow the line of a prehistoric roadway, and explain why the Romans may have built a fortlet or guard post where the castle now stands. The track climbs steeply past the old house of Castle Bank – which is said to incorporate the walls of a stout ancient tower – and joins the Orton road. This became a turnpike in 1782, with its own monument in the shape of Toll Bar Cottage, on the far side of the hill to the south where the road passes Slosh, 'the muddy farm.'

Scattergate, Appleby's southern suburb, was there in 1230 and some say its name 'schitergate,' 'sewer street,' describes the filth that once ran in the little stream that drained it and continued into Doemgate, 'muck street.' There may once have been tanneries in Scattergate, which would explain the smell and mess. Today, though there are still fine trees on Scattergate Green, the sycamore that legend (falsely) identified as a preaching-spot for John Wesley in 1786 has gone, as have the burgages that once lined the castle side of the road. New houses are, however, much in evidence for it is here that Appleby's first post-war housing estate was built in the late 1940s.

When I wrote my first *History of Appleby*, fifty years ago, the land to the west of Scattergate, along and above the Colby road, was green fields and there was a market garden where Glebe Road and Murton View now stand. Part of this land was anciently church property, known as Banks Gardens and Greater Vicar's Banks. The sprawl of new building dates from the period between 1950 and 2000, but the historic setting of Appleby has been maintained because the slope west of the road from Scattergate into Doomgate – where there were also burgages in early mediaeval times – has been kept as green space. The green space of the Castle Park extends east of the road too, and there were other burgages here in the days of Appleby's flourishing. Above, the castle rises above its earthworks, and in order to reach the centre of the town the road is forced to make a great loop to the west. Shaw or Shaw's Wiend is an ancient link between Boroughgate and the 'back lane' of Doomgate and it, too, was once flanked by burgages. 'Shaw' comes from the ancient word for a copse.

Standing on Shaw Wiend and looking over Doomgate, you can still speculate over whether there were once defences in the gap between the castle and the river to the west. The shortest route would have been straight across from the castle, down into the defile, up to the knoll where Murton View now stands, and down the steep river bank opposite Holme Farm – but had there been even an earthwork there, the ditch and bank would still be evident, so we can dismiss that possibility. The other option would have been a palisade along the scarped bank that extends from the castle on the east of Doomgate, and thence beside the mucky little stream, the Doomgate Sike, to the river by the bridge to Holme Farm – and again, there is no sign of anything here. We can conclude that Appleby was never rich and powerful enough to defend even its inner core with a wall or rampart.

Shaw Wiend leads to the High Cross and the gates of the castle. On the left hand side as you reach Boroughgate the house known as Goldington Hall once stood – presumed residence of the de Goldington family who were so prominent among Appleby's chief citizens in the thirteenth and fourteenth centuries. A few grassy mounds may mark its foundations. On the other side of the wiend, new houses mask the view of the rectangular sandstone stable block built in the time of Lady Anne Clifford in 1652-53. The castle gates and lodge are of course much newer, the gates bearing the monogram of Lord Hothfield who set them up in the 1880s. What is less obvious is the fact that the castle grounds encroach on the ancient borough at this point, the Borough Stone being clearly marked on the celebrated map of 1754 some 70 metres within today's park. No trace remains of any of the mediaeval burgages that once stood on this ground, but away to the left and overlooking the river bank there is a curious small building known as Lady Anne's beehive. It stands on the foundations of an old tower, and she probably had it built as a place to walk to, look out from and be quiet in. There is a story that she copied it from a similar little oratory in the grounds of Knole where she spent many years during her marriage to Richard Sackville, Earl of Dorset.

If the castle is open (and one day we may hope that it will be, for it is Appleby's most historic building and potentially its greatest attraction) its bailey is entered on an earthen mound that spans the deep northern ditch and leads to a partly modern gatehouse. In Lady Anne's time the gate was a massive structure, ornamented with the arms of Vieuxpont, Clifford and Percy, and the approach would have been across a drawbridge rather than a mound. The curtain wall to the left runs to a round tower built in the thirteenth century, originally with two smaller siblings in the middle of the south curtain wall. As you enter the castle courtyard the contrast in the buildings is startling. On the west (right) the tall keep (which Lady Anne called Caesar's Tower) is pure mediaeval fortress. Most of its outer walls probably date from the time of Ranulf le Meschin, Hugh de Morville and Ranulf de Glanville in the twelfth century, before and after the taking of the castle by William the Lion of Scotland, while the interior, turrets and roof are the work of Lady Anne in the mid-seventeenth century. On the other side, the grand house that fills the east of the bailey, while it incorporates the original twelfth century sally port with its portcullis arch and additions

The Story of Appleby in Westmorland

from the thirteenth and fifteenth centuries, hides these ancient structures behind the new front built by Lady Anne's grandson the sixth Earl of Thanet in the late seventeenth century. Its fine interior rooms are very much of that period.

The finest prospect in Appleby is the view to the north from the castle gate, looking down Boroughgate.[14] This is the ancient axis of Ranulf le Meschin's 'planned borough' of 1110, leading from the castle on the hilltop to the church below. Now that it is lined by trees and by pleasant houses built in limestone and the mellow local red sandstone, the street justifies Nicolson and Burn's prediction that it could be 'very grand and elegant.' The High Cross in the foreground may well date from Lady Anne's time, and mark the site of one of the 'stately scaffolds' from which the restoration of King Charles II was hailed. The words on it – 'Retain your Loyalty; Preserve your Rights' are said to have been her personal motto, although some attribute the carving to John Robinson whose White House dominates the middle section of the street.[(189)] Nearer to and on the right, the Hospital of St Anne bears the arms and dedication of Lady Anne, as Countess of Pembroke, and the quiet central courtyard is overlooked by further panels carved with the shields of arms of the families of Vieuxpont and Clifford. Boroughgate's houses still mark the sites of the original mediaeval burgages, and narrow passageways that open between them lead to small courtyards surrounded by buildings – developed by in-filling within the confines of the original plots.

The Moot Hall today stands squarely in the middle of parked traffic, except on market days. Still used for council meetings, it carries many memories of the old corporation, and the days when it rose above the noisome bustle of the eighteenth century market. Inside, there are portraits of John Robinson and of William Pitt, Appleby's greatest MP, alongside those of many of the town's mayors. The bull ring, set in a stone in the middle of the Market Place beyond, still reminds one of eighteenth century butchery though the shambles and the dunghills have been cleared away. The Cloisters beyond, even in the Gothic form in which Sir Robert Smirke left them in 1811, probably do not differ very much from that 'convenient and decent market house' which Bishops Smith and Barlow gave to the town in 1671. Behind them, St. Lawrence's Church stands on a site which has been occupied by a church since the foundation of the

---

Note 14 - It is actually better still from the top of the keep, but that is not available as I write.

new borough and its fabric bears witness to successive Scots' incursions and to the destruction which they brought.

Only the tower remains of the late twelfth century building which rose after the occupation of 1174, but the thirteenth century arcades and walls speak of the borough's greatest prosperity and the clerestory and upper stage of the tower were reconstructed after the sack of 1388. Lady Anne cannot be forgotten here, for her tomb stands beside the magnificent effigy of her mother in the north chapel, and her body lies in the vault below. The organ, restored in 1976 to its original place below the tower at the west end, is one of the oldest working instruments in the country. It was given to the church by Bishop Smith and had a good deal of history behind it when it was brought to Appleby from Carlisle in 1684. The case is surmounted by the arms of Lord Lowther, Colonel Graham and Sir Richard Sandford who paid for its installation in the church in 1722. The rests for the sword and mace in the corporation pews bear the old royal arms without the ducal coronets that Appleby added when it usurped them in the eighteenth century. The faded banners behind glass in the north chapel are the colours of the short-lived Westmorland East and West Wards' Militia, which were consecrated in the church in 1810 and returned here from the Tower of London in 1914. Alongside them are the colours of the Royal Westmorland Militia, 4th Battalion, the Border Regiment.

The grammar school has been mentioned many times in this book, although there is not much to see on its former site near the church, and the Low Wiend, leading from the Cloisters westward into Chapel Street is no longer called School House Lane as it was in 1453 (Map 5). Chapel Street itself bears a recent name, being formerly simply 'the lane leading to the Butts.' However the houses that form numbers 27, 28 and 29 are built within the old schoolhouse and several of the inscribed stones which Reginald Bainbrigg collected in the late sixteenth century can be seen in the wall of the Broad Close. The 'Roman' inscriptions, now scarcely legible, all seem to date from Bainbrigg's own time, although some may be copies of older texts. Beyond Broad Close lies the river, looping in its great arc around the flat land (the scene of recurrent floods down the centuries). Just across the river to the west, over the bridge at the end of Holme Street, stands the Holme Farm, on the site of the Leper Hospital of St Nicholas, established in 1235 and suppressed in 1541.

The footpath around the Butts testifies to the natural defence provided by the swift-flowing river, while at the same time raising a question: was there ever any bank or palisade to make a naturally strong site even stronger? The question has added force when the river is low, for it is then easily forded. The bridge had the elaborate defence of a gatehouse, but this was probably for toll-collectors and the mediaeval equivalent of traffic policemen: a military structure would make little sense when a determined thrust across the Eden could easily out-flank it.

Bridge Street, anciently Briggate, runs east from the Market Place, making a right angle with Boroughgate. It is an ancient feature of the borough's layout, following the line Ranulf le Meschin decreed in around 1110. The bridge, too, stands on the original site and though the present structure is only 120 years old, part of the inscription which once surmounted the arched gate of its ancient predecessor is still visible in the wall of a nearby house. East of the bridge, the Sands – perhaps anciently 'Bridge End' – had a row of mediaeval burgages stretching from the roadway to a 'back lane' where Garth Heads Road now runs, but all seem to have been abandoned in the years of Appleby's decline. The Shire Hall where the county assizes were held between 1778 and 1970 and magistrates courts continued until 2000, stands prominently (and vacantly) beside the road along the Sands: as I write, county and town are locked in argument over its future. Next to it, Appleby Police Station incorporates the front part of the county gaol built in 1771 to replace the cramped and insanitary conditions in the bridge house, although the Victorian prison buildings that once stood behind it have gone. Higher up the slope, the Victorian expansion of the borough marks the influence of the railways, whose two stations stand at the top of the hill. Beyond the railway there is a labyrinth of new housing estates, while a new industrial estate flanks the Murton road.

South of the Sands the road runs in a cutting through the soft red sandstone to the Borough Stone at Drawbriggs Lane. This marks the boundary between Appleby Borough and the castle lands of Bongate, though all the ground east of the river, in or outside the borough, was in St Michael's parish. North of the Sands the road climbs up the hill called Battlebarrow. Some have held that this name means 'the hill or tumulus where some specially noteworthy battle was once fought' and others derive the 'barrow' part of the word from 'borough' or 'burgh', meaning a fortified town. One mediaeval deed calls the place, in pseudo-Latin that no Appleby Grammar School boy would have got away with, *vicus de fyte.* However the authoritative *Place Names of Westmorland* derives it from *battel beorg* 'the fertile hill.'

Battlebarrow is important because it was here that the Carmelite Friary of St Mary was founded in 1281, and the grammar school was re-located in 1887. Unfortunately virtually nothing of the Friary now remains above ground, apart from a fishpond in a garden and a spring that still feeds a trough behind the new housing estate. Geophysical surveys suggest that there may be foundations below the turf, but most of the stone was undoubtedly taken to build other structures and various fragments are incorporated into houses nearby. Friaries were commonly placed on the outskirts of mediaeval towns, and if this was the case at Appleby, the summit of Battlebarrow may be taken as defining the northernmost limit of the old town. Today the new grammar school, standing back in its own grounds west of the road, marks that limit. The building dates from 1887, with later additions, but it incorporates the door pillars and lintel of Bishop Smith and Randal Sanderson's School, built in 1671, and houses an outstanding library, including books collected by Reginald Bainbrigg and a volume bearing the autograph of St John Boste the English Martyr. The school gates were erected by Old Applebians in 1955 to commemorate those killed in the two World Wars.

Appleby's buildings, then, provide a complete record of its history. There is the stone in St. Michael's Church to remind us of the first Danish settlers, and of the time when England came near to being a Scandinavian country. There are the castle earthworks to tell of the hasty fortification of a land newly won for the Norman kingdom and re-taken by King David of Scotland less than fifty years later. The heart of the town preserves the layout planned by Ranulf le Meschin in 1110, and the keep may well be partly his work, perhaps extended later in the twelfth century by Hugh de Morville, assassin of Archbishop Thomas Becket. The churches contain many relics of the succeeding years of prosperity, with phases of rebuilding that suggest, like tree-rings, the alternation of success and adversity. Successive generations of Cliffords are commemorated in the eastern range of the castle, while the last great member of that line has left us the Hospital of St. Anne, and her tomb and that of her mother in St. Lawrence's Church. The seventeenth century is commemorated by the two crosses and the eighteenth by the White House and other buildings of the same age in Boroughgate. The nineteenth century has left many buildings, but Appleby has been fortunate because almost all of them harmonise well with their setting and with the older structures around them. As to the twentieth – well, at least its sprawling housing estates have left the heartland of the ancient town unscathed, and they are, indeed, almost invisible from it.

Appleby is a microcosm of northern England. It began as a Danish farmstead amid earlier Anglian and Celtic settlements. It was caught in the conflict between English and Scottish Crowns. Today's town was planned by a Norman baron, chartered by a Plantagenet King, prospered through trade, suffered in war, and emerged as a modest and peaceful market borough. The castle that dominates it has belonged to lords who have shaped national history, fallen in famous battles and been guilty of dark and evil deeds. Others among them have been generous benefactors whose good works are still to be seen in the town's buildings. The town itself has bred scholars and saints, warriors and merchants. It sent Members to Parliament for over 500 years – one of England's most famous Prime Ministers among them. Its ancient grammar school has turned Westmorland boys into archbishops, generals, ministers and lord mayors – and narrowly missed educating the first President of the United States. As an ancient chartered borough, former assize town, seat of a great barony and once the smallest county town in England, Appleby is unique. Few communities of its size – for, remember, it has never had more than three thousand inhabitants – have been caught up in so much history. Will it, as the years unfold, remain only a place with a great past – or will it find a way of pulling above its weight as it helps to build the future?

Some Notable Dates in the History of Appleby

70 (about)	Roman armies under Agricola and Cerialis occupy the Eden Valley
650 (about)	Anglian settlers create 'Westmoringaland'
930 (about)	First Danish settlement in 'Old Appleby'
1058 (about)	Appleby and the Eden Valley under Scottish rule
1092	King William II (Rufus) occupies the Land of Carlisle. Appleby granted to Ivo Taillebois
1110 (about)	Appleby Castle and the new Borough begun by Ranulf le Meschin
1135-1157	Westmorland, including Appleby, again part of the Kingdom of Scotland. Hugh de Morville lord of Westmorland
1157	Henry II of England recovers the Land of Carlisle including Westmorland
1174	Carlisle and Appleby briefly re-taken by King William the Lion of Scotland
1179	Henry II's Charter granted
1200	King John's Charter. Beginning of Appleby as an independent borough
1204	Appleby Castle and the Barony of Westmorland granted to Robert de Vieuxpont. Borough of Appleby grows in prosperity
1232	Charter granted by Henry III
1264	Appleby Castle and lands granted to Roger de Clifford. Master William de Goldington Appleby's first Mayor
1276	Burgesses successful in lawsuit against the Lords of the Castle

1281	Carmelite Friary founded in Battlebarrow
1286	Charter granted by Edward I
1295	Robert de Goldington and John de Carlisle Appleby's first Members of Parliament
1314, 1322	Appleby looted in Scots raids. Liberties of the borough forfeited for debt. Robert de Lowther 'Keeper of the Town'
1332	Charter granted by Edward III
1348-49	The Black Death hits Westmorland. Perhaps a third of the people die
1380	The town impoverished by pestilence, removals, and the wars with Scotland
1388	The town sacked by the Scots in August and perhaps again in December
1454	Major rebuilding of Appleby Castle by Thomas, Lord Clifford
1515	"The greater part of the town as yet lies in ruins." Fee farm reduced
1528	Charter from Henry VIII
1536	Pilgrimage of Grace affects Westmorland
1539	"Appleby is but a poor village, with a ruinous Castle"
1543-48	Suppression of the Friary and Chantries
1553	Charter granted by Queen Mary Tudor
1574	Queen Elizabeth's Charter granted to the Grammar School. St John Boste the English Martyr, headmaster
1590	Birth of Lady Anne Clifford, afterwards Countess of Dorset, Pembroke and Montgomery
1587-88 and 1597-98	Severe outbreaks of plague
1618	Charter granted by King James I
1628	Charter granted by King Charles I
1643	Death of last Earl of Cumberland. Lady Anne Clifford, Countess of Pembroke inherits Westmorland estates

Some Notable Dates

1648	The Castle surrendered to the Parliamentary army
1649	Lady Anne Clifford arrives in Appleby
1651	Appleby Castle repaired by Lady Anne. Confrontation with General Harrison the regicide at Appleby. Hospital of St. Anne founded
1655	St. Lawrence's Church restored by Lady Anne. St Michael's follows in 1658
1663	Kaber Rigg Plot led by Captain Robert Atkinson, subsequently executed at Appleby in 1664
1676	Death of Lady Anne Clifford, Countess of Pembroke
1685	Charter granted by James II
1686	The eastern range of the castle rebuilt by the sixth Earl of Thanet
1715	Jacobite army passes through Appleby
1752	Turnpike road links Appleby to Carlisle and London
1754	Fierce struggle between Sir James Lowther and the Earl of Thanet for control of Appleby's Parliamentary seats, mayor and council
1771	New County Gaol built on the Sands, followed by Shire Hall and County Court in 1773. Bridge gatehouse then demolished
1776	John Wesley's first visit
1781	William Pitt became MP for Appleby, becoming Chancellor in 1782 and Prime Minister in 1783
1786	John Wesley's second visit
1812	Last bull baiting in the market place
1828	Last public execution on Gallows Hill
1830	Stocks removed from Moot Hall
1832	Appleby loses its two MPs
1837	Appleby Gas Company commenced operation
1849	Death of last Earl of Thanet. Appleby Castle passes to Richard Tufton, created Baronet

1862	Eden Valley Railway line opened
1863	St. Lawrence's Church restored
1875	New water works opened
1876	Carlisle and Settle Railway line opened. Auction Mart opened. First trees planted in Boroughgate
1881	Henry Tufton, son of Sir Richard, created first Baron Hothfield
1883	Last of Shambles removed from Boroughgate. Last four trees planted in Boroughgate
1885	First meeting of reformed Corporation. St. Michael's church 'restored'
1886	Charter granted by Queen Victoria.
1887	Grammar School rebuilt. Jubilee Bridge built.
1888	Appleby Bridge re-built
1890	First *Guide to Appleby* published
1898	Garth Heads Road opened
1931	Express Dairy Co. opened Appleby depot
1932	North Westmorland Rural District Council formed
1934	Electricity scheme for Appleby
1956	Visit of Queen Elizabeth II and the Duke of Edinburgh
1958	Coat of Arms granted by Earl Marshal
1959	War Memorial Swimming Pool opened (rebuilt in 1994)
1962	Eden Valley Railway line closed. Sale of Appleby Castle
1968	Jubilee Bridge destroyed by flood
1970	Jubilee Bridge replaced. Last Assize held at Appleby
1974	Appleby ceased to be a Borough and County Town
1975	Last service held at St. Michael's Church
1976	Town incorporated 'Westmorland' into its name
1981	By-pass opened

References

(1) Pearsall, W H and Pennington, W (1973) *The Lake District: A Landscape History* London: Collins (New Naturalist)
(2) Rollinson, W. (1978) *A History of Cumberland and Westmorland* London and Chichester: Phillimore
(3) Quartermaine, J. (2002) Upland Survey: Neolithic and Bronze Age Sites. Chapter 4 in *Past, Present and Future. The Archaeology of Northern England* ed C. Brooks, R. Daniels and A. Harding. Durham: Research Report 5 of Architectural and Archaeological Society of Durham and Northumberland
(4) Bradley, R. (2002) The Neolithic and Bronze Age Periods in the North – Some Matters Arising. Chapter 5 in *Past, Present and Future. The Archaeology of Northern England* ed C. Brooks, R. Daniels and A. Harding. Durham: Research Report 5 of Architectural and Archaeological Society of Durham and Northumberland
(5) Waterhouse, J. (1985) *The Stone Circles of Cumbria* Chichester: Phillimore
(6) Fell, C (1950) The Great Langdale Stone Axe Factory *Transactions of the Cumberland and Westmorland Antiquarian and Archaeological Society, New Series,* Vol. L, p. 1
(7) Bradley, R., and Edmunds, M R (1993) *Interpreting the axe trade.* Cambridge: University Press
(8) Wheeler, R E M (1936) Prehistoric and Roman Westmorland in *An Inventory of the Historical Monuments in Westmorland* Royal Commission on Historical Monuments, England: London: HM Stationery Office
(9) Royal Commission on Historical Monuments (1936) *An Inventory of the Historical Monuments in Westmorland* Royal Commission on Historical Monuments, England: London: HM Stationery Office
(10) Fell, C (1940) Bronze Age Connections between the Lake District and Ireland *Trans. C & W A & A Soc, NS,* Vol. XL, p. 118
(11) Wells, C. (2003) Environmental Change in Roman north-west England: a synoptic overview of events north of the Ribble. *Trans. C & W A & A Soc, Third Series,* Vol. III, pp 67-84
(12) Shotter, D (2004) *Romans and Britons in North-West England* Revised and expanded edition. Lancaster University: Centre for North-West Regional Studies.

(13) Haselgrove, C. (2002) The Later Bronze Age and the Iron Age in the Lowlands. Chapter 6 in *Past, Present and Future. The Archaeology of Northern England* ed C. Brooks, R. Daniels and A. Harding. Durham: Research Report 5 of Architectural and Archaeological Society of Durham and Northumberland

(14) Shotter, D C A (2000) The Roman Conquest of the North West. *Trans C & W A & A Soc, NS,* Vol C, pp 33-53

(15) Richardson, A (2003) The possible historic contexts of some Roman camps in Cumberland. *Trans C & W A & A Soc, Third Series*, Vol III, pp 91-95

(16) Margary, I D (1973) *Roman Roads in Britain*, 3rd Edition. London

(17) Collingwood, R G (1937) Two Roman Mountain-roads. *Trans C & W A & A Soc, NS*, Vol XXXVII, pp 1-12

(18) Richardson, A. (2002) Some probable Roman Roads in East Cumbria. Notes. *Trans C & W A & A Soc, Third Series*, Vol. II, pp 307-309

(19) Jones, G D B and Woolliscroft, D J (2001) *Hadrian's Wall from the Air.* Stroud, Gloucestershire: Tempus

(20) Holmes, M (1974) *Appleby Castle* Newcastle upon Tyne: Ferguson Industrial Holdings

(21) McCarthy, M (2002) The Archaeology of Roman Non-Military Sites. Chapter 10 in *Past, Present and Future. The Archaeology of Northern England* ed C. Brooks, R. Daniels and A. Harding. Durham: Research Report 5 of Architectural and Archaeological Society of Durham and Northumberland

(22) Huntley, J P (2002) Environmental Archaeology: Mesolithic to Roman Period. Chapter 9 in *Past, Present and Future. The Archaeology of Northern England* ed C. Brooks, R. Daniels and A. Harding. Durham: Research Report 5 of Architectural and Archaeological Society of Durham and Northumberland

(23) Jones, M J and others (1977) Archaeological work at Brough under Stainmore, 1971-72. I: the Roman Discoveries. *Trans C & W A & A Soc, NS,* Vol. LXXVII, 17-47

(24) Richmond, I A (1936) Roman Leaden Sealings from Brough under Stainmore. *Trans C & W A & A Soc, NS,* Vol. XXXVI, pp 104-125

(25) Summerson, H, Trueman, M, and Harrison, S (1998) *Brougham Castle, Cumbria. A Survey and Documentary History.* Cumberland & Westmorland Antiquarian and Archaeological Society Research Series, No. 8. Dorchester: The Dorset Press.

(26) Chadwick, H M (1954) The End of Roman Britain *in* Chadwick, N K (ed) *Studies in Early British History* Cambridge: University Press

(27) Chadwick, H M (1948) *Early Scotland* Cambridge: University Press

(28) Lynch, M (1991) *Scotland: a New History* London: Pimlico

References

(29) Phythian Adams, C. (1996) *Land of the Cumbrians. A Study in British Provincial origins, AD400-1170* Aldershot: Scolar Press
(30) Loveluck, C (2002) The Romano-British to Anglo-Saxon Transition – Social Transformations from the Late Roman to Early Mediaeval Period in Northern England. Chapter 12 in *Past, Present and Future. The Archaeology of Northern England* ed C. Brooks, R. Daniels and A. Harding. Durham: Research Report 5 of Architectural and Archaeological Society of Durham and Northumberland
(31) Morris, J (1993) *The Age of Arthur* London: Weidenfeld & Nicholson
(32) Kirby, D P (1962) Strathclyde and Cumbria: a survey of historical development to 1092. *Trans C & W A & A Soc, NS* Vol. LXII, pp7
(33) Barrow, G W S (1973) *The Kingdom of the Scots* Edinburgh: University Press
(34) Bromwich, R (1954) The Character of the Early Welsh tradition *in* Chadwick, N K (ed) *Studies in Early British History* Cambridge University Press
(35) Williams, Sir Ifor (1952) Wales and the North. *Trans C & W A & A Soc, NS,* Vol. LI, pp 73-88
(36) Hunter Blair, P (1954) The Bernicians and their Northern Frontier. In Chadwick, N K (ed) *Studies in Early British History*. Cambridge: University Press
(37) Bede (1955) *A History of the English Church and People* Harmondsworth: Penguin Classics
(38) Chadwick, H M (1954) Vortigern. In Chadwick, N K (ed) *Studies in Early British History*. Cambridge: University Press
(39) Jones, Gwyn (1968) *A History of the Vikings* Oxford: University Press
(40) Stenton, F M (1936) Pre-conquest Westmorland. In *An Inventory of the Historical Monuments in Westmorland* Royal Commission on Historical Monuments, England: London: HM Stationery Office
(41) Fellows-Jenson, G (1985) Scandinavian settlements in Cumbria and Dumfriesshire. The place-name evidence. In Baldwin, J R and Whyte, I D (eds) *The Scandinavians in Cumbria* Edinburgh: Scottish Society for Northern Studies.
(42) Ziegler, Philip (1982) *The Black Death* London: Penguin Books
(43) Smith, A H (1967) *Place names of Westmorland* Cambridge: University Press
(44) Garmonsway, G N (Ed.) (1953) *The Anglo-Saxon Chronicle* London: Dent
(45) Collingwood, W G (1902) The battle of Stainmore in legend and history. *Trans. C and W A & A Soc, NS,* vol 11, p. 32
(46) Walton, J (1954) Hog-back tombstones and the Anglo-Danish House. *Antiquity,* 110

(47) Collingwood, W G (1907) The Lowther Hogbacks. *Trans C & W A & A Soc, NS*, VII, 152-164
(48) Nicolson, J and Burn, R (1777) *History and Antiquities of the Counties of Westmorland and Cumberland,* 2 vols., London
(49) William of Malmesbury *De Gestis Regum Anglorum* ed. Stubbs London: Rolls Series
(50) Size, Nicholas (1930) *The Secret Valley. The Real Romance of Unconquered Lakeland* London and New York: Frederick Warne
(51) Symeon of Durham *Gesta Regum* (ed. Arnold). London: Rolls Series II.
(52) Casson, T E (1937) Horn Childe and the Battle on Stainmoor. *Trans C & W A & A Soc, NS*, Vol XXXVII, pp. 30-39
(53) Holinshed, R. (1577) *The Chronicles of England, Scotland and Ireland* London: Bishop
(54) Sharpe, R. (2006) Norman rule in Cumbria, 1092-113. C & W A & A S Tract Series, Vol XXI
(55) Beresford, M W (1967) *New Towns of the Middle Ages* London: Lutterworth Press
(56) Simpson, W D (1949) The town and Castle of Appleby: a morphological study. *Trans C. & W. A. & A. Soc, NS.*, XLIX
(57) Simpson, W D (1950) Appleby Castle, In Mathews, W A and Whitehead, J F (1950) *History of Appleby*. Appleby: J Whitehead & Son
(58) Mathews, Canon W A (1890) Appleby Old Bridge. *Trans C & W A & A Soc,* XI, 54-57
(59) Curwen, J F (1932) *The later records relating to North Westmorland or the Barony of Appleby* Kendal: T Wilson
(60) Tithe Map of Appleby Township (St Lawrence's Parish), 1807. County Record Office, Kendal
(61) A Plan of Appleby in Westmorland. From an Actual Survey taken in 1754. Kendal: Public Record Office, Hothfield Papers, WD/Hoth/37
(62) Daniels, R. (2002) Medieval Boroughs of Northern England. Chapter 17 in *Past, Present and Future. The Archaeology of Northern England* ed C. Brooks, R. Daniels and A. Harding. Durham: Research Report 5 of Architectural and Archaeological Society of Durham and Northumberland
(63) Estate Books relating to Burgages in Appleby (Manuscript). In Box 30, Hothfield Papers, County Record Office, Kendal.
(64) Terriers for Appleby St Lawrence and Appleby St Michael. References 9 and 9A, County Records Office, Kendal
(65) Dickinson, J C (1946) The origins of the Cathedral of Carlisle. *Trans C & W A & A Soc, NS*, Vol XLV, pp 134-143
(66) Barrow, G W S (1999) King David, Earl Henry and Cumbria. *Trans C & W A & A Soc, NS*, Vol XCIX, pp 117-127
(67) Richard, Prior of Hexham. *Historia de Gestis Regis Regis Stephani*

References

London: Rolls Series (Ed. Howlett)
(68) Jordan Fantosme *Chronique de la Guerre entre les Anglois et les Ecossais en 1173 et 1174* (Tr & ed Howlett). London: Rolls Series.
(69) Farrer, W (1907) On the tenure of Westmorland, temp. Henry II and the date of creation of the Barony of Appleby. *Trans. C & W A & A Soc, NS*, VII, 100-107
(70) William of Newburgh (ed Hamilton). English Historical Soc.
(71) Ferguson, R S (1894) *History of Westmorland* London: Elliot Stock
(72) Newcastle Society of Antiquaries (1847) *Pipe Rolls for Cumberland, Westmorland and Durham during the reigns of Henry II, Richard I and John.*
(73) Winchester, Angus (2003) Lecture to Upper Eden History Society, October 2003.
(74) Appleby Borough Records. Index, translations of Borough Charters, list of Mayors, County Record Office, Kendal.
(75) Hewitson, W (1891) The Appleby Charters. *Trans. C & W A & A Soc*, XI, 279-285
(76) Washington, G (1959) *Early Westmorland MPs, 1285-1327*. C & W A & A Soc Tract Series, no XV. Kendal: Titus Wilson.
(77) Gibson, E (1722) *Camden's Britannia*, revised edition with additions
(78) Mathews, Canon W A, and Whitehead, J F (1950) *History of Appleby* (second edition). Appleby: J Whitehead & Son
(79) Winchester, A J L (1987) *Landscape and Society in Mediaeval Cumbria* Edinburgh: John Donald
(80) Pennant, T. (1801) *A Tour from Downing to Alston Moor* London: Harding
(81) Noble, Miss (1911) Shap Registers. *Trans C&W A & A Soc, NS*, XI, p. 202
(82) Simpson, W D (1946) Brough under Stainmore: the Castle and the Church. *Trans C & W A & A Soc, NS*, XLVI, 223
(83) Brydson, A P (1913) Notes on the Westmorland Assize Roll of 1256. *Trans. C & W A & A Soc, NS*, XIII, 62-78
(84) Holmes, Martin (1974) *Appleby and the Crown* Appleby: J Whitehead & Son
(85) Clifford, H (1987) *The House of Clifford*. Chichester: Phillimore
(86) Wiseman, W G (1996) The Hospital of St Nicholas, Carlisle, and its Masters. Part 2 – the period from 1333. *Trans C & W A & A Soc, NS*, Vol XCVI, pp 51-68
(87) Appleby in Westmorland Society (2003), Newsletter 4, July 2003.
(88) Plan of Old Gaol, Appleby. Drawing in Record Office, Carlisle: photocopy in possession of Mr L Thwaytes, Appleby.
(89) Carlisle CRO. Machel of Crackenthorpe ms. Card Index ii, D+C.

Information kindly supplied by Mr R Hawkins.
(90) Thwaytes, L. (2001) *St Mary's Priory, Appleby in Westmorland, 1281-1539*. Appleby-in-Westmorland: Barry McKay Rare Books for the Appleby Record Society.
(91) Briggs, Asa (1983) *A Social History of England* London: Book Club Associates
(92) McNamee, C (1997) *The Wars of the Bruces. Scotland, England and Ireland, 1306-1328* East Linton: Tuckwell Press
(93) Sadler, J (2005) *Border Fury: England and Scotland at War, 1296-1568.* Harlow: Pearson Education Trust
(94) Morris, J E (1903) Cumberland and Westmorland Military Levies in the time of Edward I and Edward II. *Trans C & W A & A Soc, NS*, Vol III, pp 307-327
(95) Mason, J (1929) Sir Andrew de Harcla, Earl of Carlisle *Trans C & W A & A Soc, NS*, XXIX, pp 98-137
(96) McNamee, C (1992) Buying off Robert Bruce. An Account of Monies paid to the Scots by Cumberland communities in 1313-14, *Trans C & W A & A Soc, NS*, Vol XCIII, pp 77-89
(97) Barbour, J. *The Bruce*, book xiii, 742
(98) Skelton, J (1522) Why Come ye not to Court? In Henderson, P (ed), *John Skelton's Complete Poems*, London: Dent
(99) Maxwell, H (trans) *The Lanercost Chronicle*
(100) Mosley, C (ed) (1999) *Burke's Peerage and Baronetage, 106th Edition*. Crans, Switzerland: Burke's Peerage (Genealogical Books) Ltd.
(101) Hinchclife, E (1974) *Appleby Grammar School – from Chantry to Comprehensive* Appleby: J Whitehead & Son
(102) Fraser, C M (1966) The Cumberland and Westmorland Lay Subsidies for 1332. *Trans C & W A & A Soc, NS*, LXVI, 131-158
(103) Budden, L (1939) Some Notes on the History of Appleby Grammar School. *Trans C & W A & A Soc, NS*, XXXIX p. 227
(104) Ferguson, R S (ed) (1893) *Testamenta Karlelensia.* C & W A & A Soc, Extra series
(105) Wiseman, W G (1987) The Mediaeval Hospitals of Cumbria. *Trans C & W A & A Soc, NS*, Vol LXXXVII, pp 83-100
(106) Simpson, W D (1959) Brocavum, Ninekirks, Brougham – a Study in Continuity. *Trans C & W A & A Soc, NS*, LVIII pp 68-87
(107) Winchester, A J L and Wane, M (eds) (2003) *Thomas Denton: a Perambulation of Cumberland in 1687-8* Surtees Society, vol 207, p. 40
(108) Rose, A (2001) *Kings in the North. The House of Percy in British History* London: Weidenfeld and Nicholson
(109) Bouch, C M L (1948) *Prelates and People of the Lake Counties* Kendal: Titus Wilson

(110) Welch, D (1975) Three Elizabethan documents concerning Milburn Fell. *Trans C & W A & A Soc, NS*, LXXV, pp 136-149
(111) Barnes, H (1890) Visitations of the Plague in Cumberland and Westmorland. *Trans C & W A & A Soc*, XI, 158-186
(112) Jones, G P (1956) The Poverty of Cumberland and Westmorland. *Trans C & W A & A Soc, NS*, LV pp 198-208
(113) Dr Charles Moseley, personal communication
(114) Dickinson, J C (1986). Three pre-Reformation documents concerning South Cumbria, *Trans C & W A & A Soc, NS*, LXXXVI, p.129-132
(115) James, S E (1996) Sir John Parr of Kendal, 1437-1475. *Trans C & W A & A Soc, NS*, Vol XCVI, pp71-86
(116) Wordsworth, W (1807) Song at the Feast of Brougham Castle.
(117) Skelton, J (1513) Against the Scots, in Henderson, P (ed) *John Skelton's Complete Poems.*
(118) Moorhouse, Geoffrey (2002) *The Pilgrimage of Grace: The rebellion that shook Henry VIII's Throne* London: Weidenfeld & Nicholson/ Phoenix paperbacks.
(119) Harrison, S M (1981) *The Pilgrimage of Grace in the Lake Counties, 1536-7.* London
(120) Hoyle, R W (2001) *The Pilgrimage of Grace and the Politics of the 1530s* Oxford: University Press
(121) Heelis, E A (1909) St Anne's Hospital at Appleby. *Trans C & W A & A Soc, NS.*, IX, p. 192
(122) Leland, J, (1539) *Itinerary*
(123) Winchester, A J L (2004) Reginald Bainbrigg. *In* Oxford Dictionary of National Biography.
(124) Haverfield, F (1911) Notes on Reginald Bainbrigg of Appleby. *Trans C & W A & A Soc, NS,* IX, p 343
(125) Gowling, M (2003) *Kirkby Stephen in 1605* Report prepared for the Heritage Lottery Fund. Kirkby Stephen: Community Centre
(126) Appleby, A B (1978) *Famine in Tudor and Stuart England* Liverpool University Press.
(127) Holmes, M (1975) *Proud Northern Lady* Chichester: Phillimore
(128) Bostwick, Dr David. Lecture to South Lakeland Decorative and Fine Arts Society, 12 October 2004
(129) Spence, R T (1997) *Lady Anne Clifford, Countess of Pembroke, Dorset and Montgomery (1590-1676)* Stroud, Glos: Sutton Publishing
(130) Bouch, C M L (1954) *The Lady Anne, Hereditary High Sheriff of the County of Westmorland and Lady of the Honour of Skipton in Craven* Penrith: Cumberland & Westmorland Herald
(131) Clifford, D J H (ed) (2003) *The Diaries of Lady Anne Clifford. Revised edition.* Sutton Publishing

(132) Salter, M (1998) *The Castles and Tower Houses of Cumbria* Malvern: Folly Publications
(133) Colman, C S (2001) The Paralysis of the Cumberland and Westmorland Army in the First Civil War, c 1642-45. *Trans C & W A & A Soc, Third Series,* Vol. I, pp 123-138.
(134) Shepherd, M E (2004) *From Hellgill to Bridge End. Aspects of economic and social change in the upper Eden Valley, 1840-95.* Hatfield: University of Hertfordshire Press
(135) Heelis, G (2004) The Story of the Moot Hall. In *Newsletter,* Appleby in Westmorland Society, no. 51
(136) Tyson, B (2001) Building a public bakehouse in Appleby in 1615. *Trans C & W A & A Soc, Third Series*, Vol. I, pp 79-87
(137) Churchill, Winston S (1956) *A History of the English-Speaking Peoples.* London: Cassell
(138) McKay, B and McKay, V (2001) *Appleby in Westmorland. An Historic Town Guide.* Appleby in Westmorland: Barry McKay Rare Books
(139) Nicholson, F (1911) The Kaber Rigg Plot, 1663. *Trans C & W A & A Soc, NS,* Vol XI, 212-232
(140) Clarke, P D (1988) The Sectarian 'threat' and its impact in Restoration Cumbria. *Trans C & W A & A Soc, NS,* Vol LXXXVII, pp 160-175
(141) Bouch, C M L (1951) Local government in Appleby in the 17th and 18th centuries. *Trans C & W A & A Soc, NS*, LI, p. 147
(142) Records of the Corporation of Appleby, 1614-1885. County Record Office, Kendal.
(143) Wilson, J (1997) Patronage and Pietas. The Monuments of Lady Anne Clifford. *Trans C & W A & A Soc, NS*, Vol XCVII, pp 119-142.
(144) Whiteside, J (1905) Some accounts of Anne, Countess of Pembroke. *Trans C & W A & A Soc, NS*, V, p 188
(145) Johnson, M H (2002) An Archaeology of Mediaeval to Early Modern in Northern England. Chapter 18 in *Past, Present and Future. The Archaeology of Northern England* ed C. Brooks, R. Daniels and A. Harding. Durham: Research Report 5 of Architectural and Archaeological Society of Durham and Northumberland
(146) Scott, J (ed) (1998) *The 1674 Westmorland Hearth Tax Returns.* Cumbria Family History Society
(147) James, F G (1952) The Population of the diocese of Carlisle in 1676. *Trans C & W A & A Soc, NS*, Vol LI, pp 137-141
(148) Marshall, J D (1975) Kendal in the late 17th and 18th centuries. *Trans C & W A & A Soc, NS*, Vol. LXXV,
(149) Pevsner, N (1967) *The Buildings of England. Cumberland and Westmorland* New Haven and London: Yale University Press
(150) Appleby in Westmorland Society (2003) Appleby New Fair. In *Newsletter,*

Appleby in Westmorland Society, 3/2003, May 2003
(151) Chancellor, F B (1954) *Around Eden.* Appleby: J Whitehead & Son
(152) Gray, T (Transcriber) and Birley, E (editor) (1951) Bishop Nicolson's Diary, 1703-4. Part II. *Trans C & W A & A Soc, NS,* Vol L, pp 110-134
(153) Hewitson, W (1909) The Regalia of Appleby. *Trans C&W A & A Soc, NS,* IX, 166-167
(154) Ferguson, R S (1871) *Cumberland and Westmorland MPs from the Restoration to the Reform Bill of 1867.* London: Bell and Daldry, Carlisle: C Thurnam & Son
(155) Sworn Deposition by Richard Baynes. County Record Office, Kendal. Document D/Lons/Election Appleby 1723.
(156) Oates, J (2003) The last siege on English Soil: Carlisle, December 1745. *Trans C & W A & A Soc, Third Series*, Vol III, pp 169-184
(157) Order to Keeper of Appleby Gaol, 20 December 1745, signed by Prince William, Duke of Cumberland (facsimile in ref (2). A copy kindly made available to the author by Mr & the late Mrs Thwaytes of Appleby bears the Gaolers' receipt for '70 Rebel men & women').
(158) Tyson, B., (2003) Appleby Gaol, Onion Flatt (Waitby) and Robert Fothergill (1693-1779). *Trans C & W A & A Soc, Third Series,* Vol III, pp 139-156
(159) Tyson, B (1996) Some Cumbrian Builders, 1670-1780. *Trans C & W A & A Soc, NS,* Vol XCVI, pp 161-185
(160) Appleby in Westmorland Society (2003) History slot. In *Newsletter*, Appleby in Westmorland Society, 2/2003
(161) Speed, J (1611) *Theatre of the Empire of Great Britain.* Map of Westmorland
(162) Hughes, E (ed) (1961) *Fleming-Senhouse papers.* Cumberland Record Series
(163) Whyte, I (2003) *Transforming Fell and Valley. Landscape and Parliamentary Enclosure in North-West England.* Lancaster: University Centre for North-West Regional Studies.
(164) Swift, F B (1946) The Rev John Barwis and his Journals. *Trans C & W A & Soc, NS,* Vol XLV, pp 67-98
(165) Hinchcliffe, E (1971) The Washingtons of Whitehaven and Appleby. *Trans C & W A & A Soc, NS,* LXXI, pp 151-158
(166) Kelly, L (1997) *Richard Brinsley Sheridan: A Life* London: Sinclair-Stevenson
(167) Hinchcliffe, D (1988) As soon as you can say 'Jack Robinson'. Notes. *Trans C & W A & A Soc, NS,* Vol LXXXVII, p. 248
(168) Bonsall, B (1950) *Sir James Lowther and Cumberland and Westmorland Elections, 1754-1775.* Manchester: University Press (see also *Trans C & W A & A Soc, NS* LXI.)

(169) Beckett, J V (1987) Inheritance and fortune in the eighteenth century: the rise of Sir James Lowther, Earl of Lonsdale. *Trans C & W A & A Soc, NS*, Vol LXXXVII, pp 170-178
(170) Thorne, R E (1986) *The House of Commons, 1790-1820*. London: Secker and Warburg
(171) Hague, W (2004) *William Pitt the Younger*. London: HarperCollins
(172) Barnes, J C F (1990) Freedom and Liberty: Cumbria and the Borders during the period of the French Revolution, 1789-1802. *Trans C & W A & A Soc, NS*, Vol XC, pp 253-265.
(173) Bainbridge, T A (1952) John Wesley's travels in Westmorland and Lancashire north of the Sands. *Trans C & W A & A Soc, NS*, LII, pp 106-113
(174) Gray, T (1769) A Letter to Dr Wharton, October 18th 1769, published in the memoirs of his life by Mr Mason. Article II, Addenda to West's *Guide to the Lakes,* London, 1780.
(175) Gilpin, W (1808) *Observations relative chiefly to picturesque beauty* London: Cadell & Davies.
(176) Hughes, T C (1937) Notes on some Westmorland clock-makers (Part II). *Trans C & W A & A Soc, NS*, Vol. XXXVII, pp 147-151
(177) Mrs Margaret Shepherd. Personal communication.
(178) Newspaper cutting and copy of marriage certificate in possession of Mr L Thwaytes of Appleby: newspaper account also cited in reference 138.
(179) Pollard, S (1952) North-west Coast Railway Politics in the Eighteen-Sixties. *Trans C & W A & A Soc, NS*, Vol LII, pp 160-177
(180) Appleby in Westmorland Society (2004) Appleby's trees. In *Newsletter*, Appleby in Westmorland Society, no. 51
(181) Newspaper Scrapbooks in possession of Mrs Mary George of Appleby
(182) Hinchcliffe, Dorothy (1995) The story of the 'Rock Chapel', now Kingdom Hall, in Bongate, Appleby in Westmorland. Appleby in Westmorland Society *Newsletter* 5, June/July 2002
(183) Appleby-in-Westmorland Society (2004) Newsletter No. 54, July 2004.
(184) Hennell, J (2004) Memories. In *Newsletter,* Appleby in Westmorland Society, no. 52
(185) Appleby in Westmorland Society *Newsletter*, No. 55, September 2004
(186) Cumberland and Westmorland Herald, Saturday 18 June 2005.
(187) Wood, G (Compiler) (1975) *Appleby in the Vale of Eden. Official Guide*. Penrith: Airey and Stephenson
(188) Knowles, M. (2003) Letter to Colonel & Mrs Heelis dated 9 May 1968. In *Newsletter*, Appleby in Westmorland Society, no. 51
(189) Tyson, B. (1985) *Two Appleby Houses in the 18th Century: a Documentary Study,* Trans. C&WA&ASoc, NS, Vol. LXXXV, 193-218.

Index

Aballava, see Burgh by Sands
Abbot, George, Archbishop of Canterbury 136
Abbot Hall Gallery, Kendal 94, 145, 226
Act of Supremacy 119
Adam, Robert 186
Addison, Jane 172
Agricola, Gnaeus Julius 15, 185
Agriculture, prehistoric, 12, 14; Roman, 19, 25; mediaeval, 79, 88, 103, 112, 115, later and modern, 131, 144, 189, 190, 220, 224
Aidan, Bishop of Lindisfarne 24
Alcfrith 24
Al Cluith (Dumbarton) 22, 26
Alexander II, King of Scotland 59
Alexander III, King of Scotland 79
Allerdale 44, 83
Alnwick 45, 49
Alston 16, 19, 46
Ambleside 16
Anglian ('Anglo-Saxon') people 22-25
Anglo-Saxon Chronicle 27, 30, 31, 36
Anandale, Thomas de 100
Annandale 45, 46, 105, 124
Antiquarians 125, 130
Antonine Itinerary 18
Antonine Wall 20
Apple, apple tree, emblems of Appleby 26, 63, 225
Appleby, Arms and seal 63, 64, 183, 224, 225, 233; Assizes 61-63, 83, 104, 116, 135, 154, 157, 170, 187, 219, 226; Borough: foundation, layout 38-43, 50, 53, 56; Borough: growth 54-57, 61, 90, 99; Borough: decline 88, 89, 103-108, 112-114, 144; Buildings, see under respective names; Charters 30, 53-56, 58, 61, 63-67, 107, 129, 144, 155, 164, 165, 170, 212; Churches, see Saint Lawrence and Saint Michael; Civil War and Restoration 144, 154-157; Conflict with Castle 64-67, 106, 194; Corporation 63, 144, 156, 162, 165, 166, 168, 170-172, 182-184, 187, 194, 196, 210-212, 214, 215, 217-220 222; Danish 29-33, 228; Exchequer at 61; Fairs 112, 165, 170, 199, 208, 223, 224; Fee farm 53-57, 62, 66, 67, 88-90, 108, 112-115, 140, 144; Floods 40, 160, 200, 215, 227; Freemen 165, 166, 168, 183, 211; Grammar School, see separate entry; Market 53, 56, 76, 77, 112, 115, 162, 167-170, 187, 190, 202, 207, 208, 227; Mayor and officers 54, 62-64, 67-70, 90, 108, 144, 151, 154-156, 162, 165-167, 172, 181-183, 185, 192, 194-196, 200, 211, 212, 214 (see also under names); Parliamentary representation 69, 70, 88, 89, 115, 151, 152, 56, 161, 181, 183, 192-197, 200, 203; Plague at 102-104, 131, 132; Population 55, 57, 115, 131, 132, 161, 187, 204, 222; Privileges 53, 54, 65-67, 88-90, 108, 112, 167; Roman 18, 37, 229; Scottish rule 45-51, 59; Scottish raids 80, 82, 83, 87-89. 105, 106, 112-114; Setting and prehistory 10-16, 24
Appleby Castle, Roman remains in 18, 37, 229; Earthworks 30, 38; Establishment of 30, 36, 37, 40, 41; Grants of 46, 47, 52, 58, 116, Held by Crown 49, 50, 58, 61; Held by Vieuxponts 58-60; Held by Cliffords 62, 64, 65, 81, 83, 85, 89, 100, 104, 106, 111, 117, 131, 134, 135, 137, 139, 144, 147, 158, 159; Held by Parrs 116; Held by Tuftons 163, 167, 199, 201,

251

213, 214, 225; Buildings of, 37, 38, 40, 50-52, 60, 104, 105, 111, 112, 149, 150, 157, 163, 164, 167, 229-231; Damage and repair 52, 58, 60, 72, 105-107, 111, 112, 131, 147; Castle Park 42, 56, 102, 114, 150, 187, 194, 195; Garrison of 87, 143, 144, 146, 147, 155; Chantry in 100; In Civil War 143, 146-148, 156, 157; Restored and occupied by Lady Anne Clifford 147-150, 158, 159, 231; Reconstruction by Thomas, sixth Earl of Thanet 163, 164, 232; Victorian additions to 163

Appleby Gas Company 204, 218, 220

Appleby Grammar School, Origins of 100, 109-111, 118, 119, 126. 127; Schoolmasters of (see also individual names) 110, 118, 119, 125-129, 144, 191, 201, 203, 216; Curriculum 110, 216, 220; Elizabethan Charter 129; Site and buildings 128, 130, 151, 162, 216, 217, 222, 233; Relationship with Queen's College Oxford 110, 127, 129, 130, 144, 162, 191, 203, 216, 220, 223; Library 129, 130, 131, 235; Alumni 111, 129, 130, 162, 191, 192, 217, 236; Washington family links 191, 192; Rebuilt in Battlebarrow 216, 217, 235; Later development of 220, 223

Appleby and Kirkby Stephen Agricultural Society 204

Appleby, Henry de 81

Appleby, Peter de 68, 69

Appleby Street, Roman road 17, 18

Arms, of Appleby 63, 64, 183, 224, 225, 233

Arthur 20, 21, 23

Arthuret (*Arfderydd*) 22

Asby 27, 32, 159, 220, 221

Ashton, Lt General 146, 147

Aske, Christopher 122

Aske, Robert 120, 122, 123

Assembly Rooms, Appleby 202

Assizes, County, at Appleby 61-63, 83, 104, 116, 135, 154, 157, 170, 187, 219, 226

Association for Preserving Liberty 197

Athelstan, King of England 27, 28
Atkinson, Elizabeth 157
Atkinson, John 165, 182
Atkinson, John, Church organist 205
Atkinson, Captain Robert 146, 155, 157
Auction marts, livestock, Appleby 208
Augustine, Saint 23, 24
Aumerle, William Earl of 45

Badlesmere, Sir Bartholomew de 85, 86
Bailiffs of Appleby 54, 62, 66-69
Bainbridge, Wensleydale 18
Bainbridge, John 168, 171
Bainbrigg, Christopher, Cardinal Archbishop 130; Reginald 125, 126, 128-130, 144, 217, 233, 235; George 150
Balliol, John, King of Scotland 79, 80, 89
Balliol, Edward, King of Scotland 89, 90, 100, 101
Band of Hope 209, 210
Banks, Jonathan 162, 191
Banks Wood and Gardens, Appleby 43, 62, 230
Bannockburn, battle of 83-85
Bard, Sir Robert 84
Barden Tower 118, 147, 152
Barker, Joseph, clock-maker 202
Barlow, Dr Thomas 162, 163, 232
Barnard Castle 84
Barrow in Furness 202, 221
Barrows see burial mounds
Barwis, Rev John 190
Barwise (also Berwys), William de 69, 70, 88; Alexander de 88
Battle of the Standard 45
Battlebarrow, Appleby 57, 58, 74-76, 109, 125, 139, 170, 187, 234, 235
Baynard's Castle 143, 144
Baynes, Richard 185, 193
Baynes, Thomas 201
Beamish Open Air Museum 218
Beamsley 152
Beaumont, Henry 82
Beck, John 121
Becket, Archbishop Saint Thomas 47

252

Index

Bede, Venerable 22, 23
Bedford, second Earl of 131, 134; Francis, third earl of 136
Belatucadrus 20, 21
Bellingham, Alan 127, 157
Benn, Daniel 186
Beresford, Maurice 99
Bernicia, Anglian kingdom 22, 23
Berwick on Tweed 80, 83, 84, 90
Bewcastle 24, 26
Bigod, Sir Francis 123
Bintley, Joseph (County Surveyor) 72, 73
Birmingham 221
Bishopsthorpe 87
Black Death 102
Black Dub 149
Blenheim, battle of 182
Blenkinsop, Christopher 121, 124
Blenkinsopp, Thomas 113
Boece, Hector 33
Boer War 213
Bolton 24, 221
Bolton Abbey, Wharfedale 122, 147
Bolton, Robert 181
Bongate, Appleby ('Old Appleby') (see also St Michael's Church); Boundaries 57, 66, 74, 131, 168; Cemetery 218, 219, 227; Church 29-31, 40, 57, 72, 99, 110, 124, 151, 199-201, 213, 228; Danish settlement in 30, 38; Later village 39, 41, 43, 51, 53, 66, 99, 153, 168, 198, 202, 203, 208, 228; Ford 18, 30, 38, 43, 215, 227, 229; Mill 41, 43, 66, 229; Moor 170, 190; Population 131, 161, 204
Border, Anglo-Scottish 44, 45, 47-49, 59, 80-84, 101, 104-106, 112, 117, 119, 189
Border Regiment 213, 219, 221, 233
Boroughbridge 84, 85, 99
Boroughgate, Appleby; Layout of, 39, 41, 42, 56, 58, 230, 232, 234; Buildings in, 72, 77, 108, 109, 114, 150, 153, 187, 189, 192, 206, 231; Events in, 76, 168, 171, 210, 212
Boroughs, status of 53-55, 90, 99, 103

Borough Stones, Appleby 42, 43, 57, 231, 234
Boscastle 103
Boste, John, Saint 129, 130, 235
Bosworth, battle of 117
Bouch, Canon C M Lowther 161
Bowes 16, 37, 60, 190
Bowness, George, Butcher 168, 169
Brackenber Moor 13, 14, 16, 208, 218
Brampton (near Appleby) 24; Brampton Fair 208
Branby, Thomas de, Vicar 100
Brandon, Eleanor, Countess of Cumberland 131, 132
Bravoniacum, see Kirkby Thore
Breton, John le, Provost 62; Thomas le, Bailiff 68, 69
Bridge ('stanebrigg'), Appleby; Original 39, 40, 50; Mediaeval 40, 72, 73, 75, 76, 100, 104, 114, 209, 214, 234; Gatehouse and Chapel 39, 73, 74, 109, 110, 200; Use as gaol 149, 186; Rebuilt, 1888 215, 234
Bridge End, Appleby 41, 57, 172, 234
Bridge Street (Briggate), Appleby 42, 56, 76, 168, 171, 189, 200, 215, 227, 234
Brigantes 14-16, 19
Briquessart, Ranulf de, see Meschin
British and Foreign Schools Society 203, 218
Britons 20, 24
Broad Close, Appleby 62, 118, 128-130, 217, 222, 233
Brocavum, see Brougham
Bronze Age period and people 12, 13
Bronze metalwork 13, 19
Brough, Roman 15-19, 37; Castle 37, 38, 46, 48-50, 58, 60, 61, 100, 102, 116, 117, 135, 158, 161, 163; Manor and town 29, 32, 39, 58, 65, 83, 84, 103, 105, 121, 124, 126, 127, 132, 152, 190, 191, 199, 200, 228
Brough Hill Fair 199
Brougham, Prehistoric, Roman and pre-Conquest 13-17, 19, 21, 25, 29, 59; Castle 37, 59-61, 81, 85, 87, 100, 101, 105, 107, 115-117, 134-140, 147, 149,

253

150, 152, 156, 159, 161, 163
Bruce (de Brus) family 45, 101
Bruce, Edward 82, 83
Bruce, Robert I, King of Scotland see Robert
Brunanburgh, battle of 27, 28
Burbeck, Thomas 121
Burgages and burgage maps, Appleby 42, 43, 54-57, 99, 108-110, 114, 115, 126, 127, 150, 151, 187, 193-195, 200
Burgdon, John de, Mayor 70, 100
Burgh, Hubert de 59, 60
Burgh by Sands, Roman fort 18
Bull baiting, Appleby 169, 232
Burial mounds 12, 13
Burn, Dr Richard 186
Burneside, Gilbert de 69
Burrells 57, 58, 131, 190
Burrow in Lonsdale 19
Butchers' market, Appleby 168, 169
Butts, Appleby 76, 184, 210, 222, 233
Byland 86

Cadwallon, Prince of Gwynedd 23, 24
Caernarvon 43
Caldbeck 121
Cambridge 57, 132, 197
Camden, William 125, 126, 130
Camden's *Britannia* 55, 125, 130
Carisbrooke Castle 146
Carleton family 165; Thomas 165, 189, 193
Carlisle, Bishops of 87, 101, 159; William Mauclerk 74; Edward Rainbow 159; Thomas Smith 162; William Nicolson 162, 182, 184
Carlisle, City and Land of, Roman 14-16, 19; pre-Conquest 21-24, 26; Norman 30, 35-37, 43, 49; Mediaeval 44, 45, 47, 56, 66, 70, 72, 87, 99, 103; Later 131, 134, 139, 168, 191, 197-199, 206-208, 226, 227; Scottish occupation/attacks 45, 46, 48-50, 80, 82-86, 104, 105, 148, 184, 185; in Pilgrimage of Grace 122-124; Carlisle, Castle 35-37, 46, 122, 156; Cathedral 44; Priory of St Mary 44, 87; Prior 60, 87

Carlisle, Diocese of 33, 44, 88, 100, 161
Carlisle, first Earl of see de Harcla Earls of (second creation) 185
Carlisle, John de, of Appleby 68-70
Carlyle, Alexander 196
Carmelite Order (White Friars) (see also Friary) 74, 75, 100
Cartmel 24
Cartimandua 14, 15, 22
Carvetii, Celtic people 14, 15, 18, 19
Castle Bank, Appleby 229
Castle Douglas 81, 90, 101
Castle Park, Appleby 42, 56, 102, 114, 187, 195, 230, 231
Castrigg, Roman fortlet 16-18
Catterick, Catraeth 22, 23
Cattle, see livestock
Caus, Isaac de 142, 152
Census data, Appleby 204
Ceredig (Coroticus) 21
Cerialis, Quintus Petillius 15, 185
Chantries, in Appleby 64, 72, 78, 99, 100, 108-111, 114; as origin of Grammar School 100, 109-111, 118, 119; suppression of 126; see also under Saint Lawrence, Saint Michael
Chapel Street, Appleby 42, 100, 129, 130, 204, 214, 217, 227, 233
Chapel on the Rock, Appleby 214
Charity Commission 216, 217
Charles I, King of England and Scotland 142-144, 146, 147
Charles II, King of England and Scotland 148, 149, 154-156, 159, 164, 184, 185, 193
Charters, see Appleby
Cheese Company Ltd 224
Chester, Battle of 23; Earldom of, 46
Chivalric revival 152
Cholmley, Sir Henry MP 151
Christianity, in Roman Cumbria 21, 22; in Northumbria 23; Iona and Roman traditions 23, 24
Chronicle of Jordan Fantosme see Fantosme
Churches, see under dedications or places

Index

Churchill, Sir Winston 146
Civil Wars 143-149, 152, 183
Clapham, Christopher MP, 151
Clarendon, Edward Hyde, Earl of 136
Cleveland 33
Cliburn 132
Clifford, family 61, 101, 106, 107, 111, 112, 114, 116, 124, 151; Roger de 61, 64-66, 80; Isabella de 65-67, 80; Robert, first Lord Clifford 80-83, 136; Roger, second Lord Clifford 83, 85, 86, 89; Robert, third Lord Clifford 83, 89, 90, 100; Robert, fourth Lord Clifford 102; Roger, fifth Lord Clifford 100, 102, 104, 106; Maud, widow of fifth Lord Clifford 107; Thomas, sixth Lord Clifford 106, 107, 109; Elizabeth, widow of sixth Lord Clifford 111, 288; John, seventh Lord Clifford 107, 111; Thomas, eighth Lord Clifford 104, 110, 111, 116, 229; John, ninth Lord Clifford ('the Butcher') 116; Henry, tenth Lord Clifford ('the Shepherd Lord') 117-119, 122, 153; Henry, eleventh Lord and first Earl of Cumberland 115, 120-123; Sir Thomas, son of first Earl 123, 124; Henry, Lord Clifford, second Earl of Cumberland 115, 122, 131, 132; Eleanor, Countess of Cumberland 131, 132; George, third Earl of Cumberland 129, 130, 132-135, 140, 152; Francis, fourth Earl of Cumberland 115, 135, 137, 139, 140, 143, 145; Henry, fifth Earl of Cumberland 136, 139, 140, 142-145, 147
Clifford, Margaret, Countess of Cumberland 132, 134, 135, 138, 152; and Westmorland estates 135-137; and Lady Anne's inheritance 136; death and burial 137-141, 151, 159
Clifford, Lady Anne, Countess of Pembroke, Dorset and Montgomery 111, 129, 132, 164, 189, 190, 200, 201, 232; Childhood 134, 135; Education 135; Character 135, 148, 152-154; Appearance 135, 136, 143; Marriage to Richard Sackville 136, 141; Marriage to Philip Herbert 142-144; Interests in Westmorland estates 135-137, 139, 140-145; Travels north 147; Conflicts with tenants 145, 153-155; Conflict with Robert Atkinson 155, 157; Royalist affiliations 143, 149; Great Picture 145, 225, 226; Restoration of castles 51, 52, 111, 148, 149, 152; Builds Appleby gaol 149, 186; Builds Castle stables and 'beehive' 150; Builds Hospital of St Anne 150; Restores churches 150-152, 200, 229; Establishes Temple Sowerby Trust 151, 162; Controls Parliamentary elections 151, 193; Support for local community 153; Celebrates Restoration 155, 156; Life style 153, 158, 159, 161; Accounts 158; Death of 159, 160, 163; Tomb of 139, 159, 160
Clifton Dykes 14-16, 185
Climate changes and impacts 103, 106
Clitheroe 55, 59
Clock-making in Appleby 202, 203
Cloisters, Appleby 162, 163, 169, 210, 232; Public bath in 210
Clyde, River 20, 26
Coach travel 190, 191
Coal, mined on Stainmore 158, 202; Supplied to Appleby Castle 158, 161; Sold in Appleby market 202
Cockermouth 21, 39, 53, 87, 103, 105, 121, 147, 196
Coel Hen, King of Stratthclyde 20, 21
Colby 27, 57, 131, 161, 204
Colby Lane, Appleby 43, 114, 222, 230
Collinfield, Kendal 159
Colte, Maximilian 139
Colyn, William, Vicar 100
Commissions, Appleby 113, 120, 126, 211, 216, 217
Common Council, Appleby 166
Competitors to the Scottish throne 79, 80
Comyn, John 'the Red' 80
Constablewick of Appleby 161; of Bongate 161
Constabulary, Cumberland and

255

Westmorland 212
Constantine I, King of Scots 26
Constantine II, King of Scots 26-28
Cooperative Society, Agricultural 209
Copeland 83
Corbridge 26, 82
Corbrygg (Corbrige), Thomas de, Mayor 70, 108
Corporation of Appleby 63, 144, 151, 162, 165, 166, 168, 170-172, 182-184, 187, 194, 196
Cork, Earl and Countess of, later of Burlington 145, 147, 148, 154
Cornage, tax 107
Corry, Adam de 102
Council of the North 122, 140
Countess' Pillar, Brougham 137, 138, 156, 214
County Courthouse and Gaol, Appleby see also Gaol 181, 186, 200
County Primary School, Appleby 218
County Record Office, Kendal 225
Coupland Beck 104, 203, 210
Court, Royal 122, 123, 132, 134, 158
Courtfield Hotel 213, 229
Crackenthorpe 57, 118, 131, 204
Crackenthorpe, Christopher 125
Cranborne 43
Craven, district 45, 121; Clifford estates in 81, 142, 143, 146
Cromwell, Thomas 119, 120, 122; Oliver 146, 148, 149, 154, 155, 159
Crosby Ravensworth 12-14, 25, 27, 32, 104, 105, 126, 149
Crown and Cushion Inn, Appleby 185
Crumbewell, John and Idonea de 75
Cumberland 25, 31, 33, 36, 44, 52, 81, 101, 104, 105, 107, 120-122, 135, 143-145, 184, 189, 192, 202; Earls of, see Clifford; Prince William, Duke of 185, 190
Cumbria, modern county of 56, 226; Pre-Conquest kingdom of 24, 27, 30-32, 35, 48, 59; region of 11-15, 23, 24, 26, 30, 32, 43, 46, 48, 53, 80, 83, 84, 103, 105, 120, 144, 152, 185, 190, 197, 199
Cuthbert, Saint 21, 24, 26

Dacre 24, 116
Dacre, Sir Christopher 124
Dalston, Thomas 121; John MP 151, 183
Danes, in Northumbria, 26, 28; in Eden Valley and Cumbria 25, 26, 29, 31; attacked by Ethelred 31, 32
Daniel, Samuel 135
Darlington 85
David I, King of Scotland 44-47, 49, 79, 80
David II (Bruce), King of Scotland 88-90, 101, 102
Davidson, A F, Headmaster 217
Dawson, J Ingram 222
Day, John 109
Dee, River 31
Deira, Anglian Kingdom of 23
Dennison, William 187
Dent, George, lock-maker 158; George, official 181; John of Birkdale 169
Denton, Thomas 101
Derby 185
Derwentwater, James Radcliffe, Earl of 184, 185
Despenser family 85
'Devil's Bridge', Kirkby Lonsdale 39, 73, 215
Devon, County 144
'Disinherited', the 88-90
'Distemper' see livestock disease
Dolfin, Lord of Carlisle 35, 49
Domesday survey 33
Doncaster 122, 123
Donne, Dr John 135
Doomgate, Appleby 41-43, 56-58, 114, 169, 171, 172, 187, 230
Dorset, Lady Anne's estates in 141, 154
Dorset, Richard Sackville, Earl of 136, 137, 139-141
Dorset, Edward Sackville, Earl of 141, 142
Douglas, Sir James 84-86; Sir William 101; James, Earl of 105
Drawbriggs Lane, Appleby 57, 234
Dring, Peter de la, bailiff 68, 69
Drovers 199, 208
Drybeck 18, 57, 105, 131, 221, 226

256

Index

Ducking stool 187
Dufton 24, 128, 207
Dumbarton see Al Cluith
Dumfries 22, 24, 46, 80, 87, 124
Dunbar, battle of 148
Duncan, King of Scots 32, 36
Dunmail, King of Cumbria 28
Dunmail Raise 28, 33
Dupplin Moor, battle of 90
Durham 80, 82, 83, 85, 101, 102, 157, 206, 216
Durnford, Mr (of Charity Commission) 216, 217

Eadred, King of England 28, 29
Eadulf, Bishop of Lindisfarne 26
Eamont, river 16, 59
Eamont Bridge 13, 27, 29, 104, 190
Eanflaed, Princess of Northumbria 23
East Ward Rural District Council 220
East Ward Union and Guardians 206, 211, 212
East Ward Sanitary Authority 211, 212
Ecgfrith, King of Northumbria 24
Eden, River 13, 19, 24, 25, 27, 30, 38-42, 48, 57, 58, 66, 72, 74, 104, 118, 125, 160, 171, 199, 200, 209, 215, 229
Eden Valley, prehistory of, 11-14; Roman occupation of 14-19; Anglian and Danish occupation of 24-27, 29-31; Norman occupation of 35-38; Scottish rule in 28, 30-34, 45-49, 59; Scottish raids in, 83, 84, 105, 106; In mediaeval period 44, 59, 83, 106, 116, 132; Later development of 189, 202, 223, 224, 227
Eden Water Board 211
Edgar, King of England 30, 31
Edgar the Atheling 35, 44
Edinburgh 23, 26, 80, 82, 86, 105, 119
Edinburgh and Northampton, Treaty of 87
Edinburgh, Prince Philip, Duke of 222
Edith (Matilda), Queen of England 44
Edmund, King of England 27, 28
Education Act, 1944 223
Edward I, King of England 60, 66, 67, 75, 80, 81, 83, 89, 115, 222
Edward II of Carnarvon, King of England 79-87, 136, 196
Edward III, King of England 63, 79, 87-90, 100, 101, 108
Edward IV, King of England 116
Edward VI, King of England 126
Edward the Confessor, King of England 33
Edward the Elder, King of England 27
Edwin, King of Northumbria 23
Egremont 39, 53, 87, 99
Eirik Haraldsson ('Blood-Axe') 28, 29
Eiriksmal, epic poem 29
Elections, Parliamentary, see Parliament
Electricity in Appleby and District 220
Elizabeth I, Queen of England 103, 129, 131-134, 139, 158
Elizabeth II, Queen of England and Scotland 222
Enclosures of commons, Cumberland and Westmorland 170, 189, 190
Endowed Schools Act 216
England, 11, 59, 79, 102; emergence of, 26, 27; claims on Strathclyde and Scotland 26-28, 31-33, 35, 43, 48, 79, 83, 87, 90, 106; conflict with Scotland 45-50, 81-87, 90, 101, 105, 115, 119, 124; landholdings in Scotland 79, 87-90, 105, 124
Engleys (English) Robert l' 69, Sir William l' 99,110
Erskine, Sir Thomas 134
Ethelberga, Queen of Northumbria 23
Ethelfrith, King of Northumbria 23
Ethelred, King of England 31, 32, 44
Evacuees, Appleby 221
Ewbank, Henry 129
Ewe Close, settlement 14
Exchequer of Appleby 61
Express Dairy Depot at Appleby 220, 224

Fair Hill, Appleby 208, 223, 224
Fairs, at Appleby 112, 165, 180, 208; New Fair 165, 170, 208, 223, 224; at Brough Hill 199

257

Falkirk, battle of 80
Fallowfield, Thomas 113
Fantosme, Jordan 47-49
Farming 12,14, 19, 25, 79, 88, 109, 112, 115, 131, 144, 189, 190, 220
Fee farm rent 53-55, 65-67, 88-90, 108, 112-115, 140, 144
Ferguson, Thomas 198
Fielding, Israel 125
Fiends Fell 13
Fife, Robert Earl of 105
Fines ('gressums') on estates 145, 153
Fire service, Appleby 218
Fleming, Daniel 157, 187, 189
Flodden, battle of 118, 119
Floods, in Appleby 40, 160, 200, 227
Forest clearance 12-14, 19
Foresters, Ancient Order of, 209
Forth, River 20, 26, 90
Fothergill, Edmund 186; Robert 186
France 80, 90, 101, 102, 106, 111, 154, 197, 219, 220
Franceys (Francis) family 71
Fraternity of the Lamp 109
Freemasons, Eden Valley Lodge 209
Freemen of Appleby 165, 166, 168, 187, 211, 212, 219
French Revolution 197
Friaries, bequests to 100
Friary of St Mary, Appleby 58, 74, 75, 89, 100, 110, 111, 120, 124, 125, 127, 222, 235
Friendly Societies 209
Furness Abbey 45, 86

Gale, George 192
Galloway 21, 22, 46, 79
Galloway, Alan of 59
Gallows Hill, Appleby 75, 170, 186, 208
Gaol, Appleby 68, 149, 186, 200, 204-206
Garnett, Richard, Vicar 118
Garth Heads Road, Appleby 57, 214, 222, 234
Gas, in Appleby see Appleby Gas Company
Gatley Toll, see toll

Gaveston, Piers 81, 82
Gibson, Bartholomew, tanner 127
Gibson, E Editor of Camden's *Britannia* 55
Gibson, Edward, Schoolmaster 126, 127, 129
Gilpin, William 199, 229
Gilshaughlin, near Cliburn 132
Girtin, Thomas 8, 72
Glanville, Ranulf de 52, 58, 60, 231
Glasgow 22, 33, 44, 191
Glasgow, Bishop John of 44
Glebe Road, Appleby 43, 230
Goddoddin, the (epic poem) 23
Goldington, de, Appleby family 62, 64, 67-72, 78, 99, 100, 108, 110, 193; Cuthbert 70, 72; Eleanor 69, 71; John II 64, 67, 68, 71; John III 67, 71, 72; John IV 68, 69, 71; Master William 62, 64, 67-7; Robert II 70, 71; Robert III 70, 71, 99; Thomas II 64, 67-69, 71, 72; William II 64, 67-72; William III 67, 70, 71, 90, 99; William IV 70, 71
Goldington Hall, Appleby 72, 77, 108, 109, 231
Gorst, William 167, 168
Gorst, Gilpin 201
Gospatric, Earl of Northumbria 35, 49
Gospatric son of Orm 48-50
Graham, Colonel James MP 183
Graham, Tom, Appleby postman 209
Grammar School, see Appleby Grammar School
Granger, Hugh le, bailiff and MP 68-70
Graveson, John, scavenger 171
Gray, Thomas 199
Great Books of Records, Clifford 136, 152
Great Chesters, Roman fort 21
Great Picture, Clifford family 145, 152, 225
Great Raid, Scots 86, 89
Green, William, MP 70
Gressums, see fines
Grey, Charles, Viscount Howick, later Earl Grey 197
Greystoke 25, 103, 121
Griffith, Moses 138, 141, 201, 229

258

Index

Guadeloupe, HMS 192
Guallauc 22
Guide Books, Appleby etc 207, 226, 228
Gunnhild, 'Mother of Kings'28, 29

Hadrian's Wall 16, 18-21, 130
Halfdan 26
Halidon Hill, battle of 90
Hanson, William 109
Hanson, Thomas 109
Harcla, de, family 71
Harcla, Sir Andrew de, Earl of Carlisle 81-87, 89
Harcla, Sir Michael de 85
Harcla, Michael de 87
Harker, Lt Col G B 221
Harlech 43
Harris, William 218
Harrison, Major General Thomas 148, 149
Hart's Horn Tree 101
Hartley 85, 86, 99, 121, 123
Hartley, John 109
Hartley, Rainold 127, 129, 130
Hastings, le, of Crosby Ravensworth, Amice 67, 68; Christian 67; Nicholas 68; Sir Thomas 67, 68; William 68
Hastings, Lady Elizabeth 191
Hearth taxes 162, 187
Heelis, E A and Mrs 219
Heelis, Thomas 201
Helton, John 109
Henry I, King of England 44-46
Henry II (of Anjou), King of England 46-49, 53, 63, 67
Henry III, King of England 54, 59-62, 67
Henry IV (of Bolingbroke), King of England 107
Henry V, King of England 108, 111
Henry VI, King of England 116
Henry VII, King of England 112, 122
Henry VIII, King of England 108, 119, 122-126
Henry, Prince of England 47, 48
Henry, Prince of Scotland 46, 47
Herbert, George 143
Herbert, Philip, see Pembroke

Hercules, famous hound 101
Hereford, Earl of 85, 86
Heversham 24
Hewetson, John, Bailiff of Appleby 181
Hewitson, William, Town Clerk and Freeman 210, 219
Hexham 26, 45, 82, 87, 105
High Cross, Appleby 153, 156, 169, 186, 193, 214, 231, 232
Highhead castle 87
High Street, Roman road 16, 17
Highways, surveyors of, Appleby 181
High Wiend, Appleby 42, 56, 144, 169
Hilton 24, 57, 130, 131
Hilton family, 108
Hilton, Robert 121
Hiltonne (Hilton), William de 70
Hinchcliffe, Edgar 129
Hobelars 81, 83, 85, 87
Hoff 18, 57, 62, 82, 105, 131
Hog-back tombstone 29-31, 38, 228
Holm Cultram Abbey 46, 86, 87, 121
Holme Farm, Appleby 74, 230, 233
Holme Street, Appleby 40, 233
Holmes, Martin 50, 60
Homildon Hill, battle of 106
Honeywood, General Sir Philip MP 181, 195, 196
Hospital of Saint Anne, Appleby 150, 153, 161, 195, 220, 232
Hospital of Saint Nicholas, Appleby 41, 74, 100, 124, 150, 233
Hothfield, Henry Tufton first Baron 213, 214, 219, 231; Lady 213, 218; John Sackville Richard Tufton, second baron 219-221; Third Baron 225; Anthony Charles Sackville Tufton, Sixth Baron 226
Howgate, Appleby 57, 224
Howgill Fells 11, 46
Huntingdon, Earldom of 45, 46, 59
Hutchinson, John, clockmaker 202
Hutton, Anthony 121

Ida, Anglian founder of Bernicia 22
Industrial Revolution 202
Inglewood Forest 80, 82, 99, 121

259

Inquisitions, Appleby 107, 113-115
Institute of St Michael's Church School 203, 218
Ireland 12, 13, 20, 21, 26, 29, 83, 198
Iron Age, period and people 13
Irving, William 198
Isle of Man 12, 23, 24, 82
Ivy House, school, Boroughgate 206

Jackson, Richard, Schoolmaster 162
Jacobite rebellions, 1715 and 1745, 163, 184-186, 189
James II, King of Scotland 116
James IV, King of Scotland 119
James I, King of England and VI, King of Scotland 115, 134, 139-141, 143, 144, 159
James II King of England (and VII of Scotland) 164, 165, 170
James Stewart, Prince, 'the Old Pretender' 184
Jehovah's Witnesses, Appleby 214
Jenkinson, Charles, first Earl of Liverpool 196
Jenkinson, Robert Banks, second Earl of Liverpool 196
Jennings, William 208
Joan of the Tower, Queen of Scotland 88, 90
John, King of England 53, 54, 58, 59, 63-65, 67, 107, 114
Johnston, Matthew of Stainmore 170
Jordan Fantosme see Fantosme
Jubilee Bridge, Appleby 215, 227
Judges, visiting Appleby 62, 149, 157, 219, 226
Julian Bower 89

Kaber Rigg Plot 157
Karleolo, John de see Carlisle
Keepers of the Lamp 109
Kendal, Roman, Anglian and Norman 16, 24, 26, 36; Barony and castle 33, 116, 143; Scots raids on 84, 86; Development of 99, 103, 126, 127, 132, 144, 162, 187, 190, 197, 206; Cloth industry 158, 187, 203

Kenneth II, King of Scots 30, 31
Kentigern, Saint 22, 33
Keswick 13, 103, 202
'King Arthur's Round Table' 13
King George V Memorial Playing Field, Appleby 100, 128, 217, 222
Kings of England and Scotland, see under individual names
King's Head Inn, Appleby 189, 191, 202, 205, 209, 215
Kirkby Lonsdale 39, 73, 132, 215
Kirkby Stephen, Prehistoric and pre-Conquest 12, 14, 18, 25, 26, 32; Development of 36, 61, 85, 99, 101, 104, 131, 161, 162, 168, 207; In Pilgrimage of Grace 120, 121, 123; Parliamentary loyalties 145, 154, 155; Stocking industry 187; Grammar School 127, 220, 223; Coach and rail transport through 191, 206-208
Kirkby Thore 16, 17, 20, 75, 125
Kirkgate, Appleby 110
Kirkoswald 83, 103
Knaresborough 47, 84
Knock 25
Knole, Kent 136, 137, 141, 152
Knut (Canute), King of England 32

Lady Anne, see Clifford
Lady Garth, Appleby 214
Lady Well, Appleby Friary 75-77, 125
Lake District 11, 16, 22, 24, 25, 33, 198, 222
Lakeland Arts Trust 226
Lamp of the Blessed Virgin Mary 78, 109, 114
Lamplugh, Sir John 121
Lancashire 11, 22, 24, 84, 86
Lancaster, City of 15, 84, 86, 149, 168, 191, 206; Honour of 46, 47; Thomas, Earl of 85, 86
Lancastrian faction in Wars of the Roses 116
Lanercost Priory 80
Langdale 12, 13
Langhorne, Leonard, Schoolmaster 118, 119, 126, 127

260

Index

Langton 24, 57, 88
Langton, Bishop Thomas 110, 111, 127
Langton, Archdeacon Robert 125, 127, 128, 130
Lay subsidy (wealth tax) 90, 99, 108
Lead, mines and products 16, 19
Leather, market in 170
Lee, William 195
Leeds 99
Leith, port of 86
Leland, John 125
Le Meschin, Ranulf see Meschin
L'Engleys, see Engleys
Levens Hall 152, 183
Lewes, Battle of 60
Lewyn, John 112
Leyburn, Roger de 61, 64, 65; Idonea de 61, 65, 67, 85
Library, Bainbrigg 129-131
Lichfield 137
Liddesdale 46
Lincolnshire 36-38, 120, 123
Lindisfarne 22, 24
Literacy, in Westmorland 203
Little Salkeld 13
Liverpool 55, 99, 196, 202
Livestock diseases 88, 106, 170
Livestock trade 199, 208
Local Government, 19th and 20th century 212, 220
Lochmaben 21, 87
Lockerbie 224
Locksmith, William the 62
London, Privileges and status 53, 55, 99; Lady Anne Clifford and 134, 137, 139, 143, 145, 147, 153, 154; Robert Atkinson in 157; Travel from Appleby 190, 191, 199, 207; Trade with Appleby 207; Lord Mayor from Appleby 213, 217; Wartime evacuees from 221
Long Marton 18, 24
'Long Meg and her Daughters' 13
Lonsdale, Viscounts 184, 193, 194; James, first Earl of, 181, 192, 194-197; Earls of, 203, 208, 210, 214, 219
Lord of the Isles 32

Lord's Day, observance of 198
Lothians, district 22, 32, 90, 105
Low Borrow Bridge, Roman fort 16-18, 20
Low Cross, Appleby 156, 169, 186
Low Wiend, Appleby (also Schoolhouse Lane) 42, 56, 100, 110, 118, 215, 216, 222, 233
Lowther 25, 190
Lowther Castle 210
Lowther family 71, 85, 134, 143, 156, 184, 193-196, 201, 204; Hon Henry Cecil, MP 203; Sir James, MP 162; Sir James, 5th Bart, later first Earl of Lonsdale 181, 192, 194-197; Sir John MP 143, 151, 194; Mrs (mother of Sir James) 195; Robert de 89, 90, 196; Viscount 208 (see also Lonsdale)
Lucy, Sir Anthony de 87
Luguvalium, see Carlisle
Lumley, Sir Marmaduke 146
Lune, River and Valley 15, 16, 18, 84, 86, 149
Lyvennet, River and district 16, 18, 21, 25, 27, 149

Macbeth 32, 35
Mace, municipal, Appleby 183
Machell, family 108
Machell, Hugh 118; Hugh 165; Humphrey 50; John 70, 108; Lancelot 155; Lt Col P W 219; Philip 165; Richard 201; Rev Thomas 150, 154, 155
Magnus Maximus, Roman General 20
Maiden Castle, Roman fort 15, 17, 37
Maiden Way, Roman road 16
Malcolm I, King of Scotland 28-30
Malcolm II, King of Scotland 31, 32
Malcolm III (Canmore) King of Scotland 32, 33, 35, 44, 79
Malcolm IV (the Maiden) King of Scotland 47
Malcolm mac Dubh, King of Cumbria 30, 31, 36
Malestang, Thomas de 70, 108
Mallerstang 61, 99, 124, 146, 152, 157

261

Mallory, Sir John 146
Manchester Unity of Oddfellows 209
Manufacturing, in Appleby 187, 202, 203, 224
Margaret, Countess of Derby 132
Margaret, Countess of Thanet, see Thanet
Margaret, Saint, Queen of Scotland 36, 44
Margaret of Scotland, 'the Maid of Norway' 79
Market, Appleby 76, 77, 167-170, 190, 202
Market Place, Appleby 77, 110, 156, 185, 207, 218, 232, 234
Marshall, John, Vicar 109, 110
Marston Moor, battle of 146
Mary, Queen of England 113, 131
Mary, Queen of Scots 131
Mary, Princess, Countess of Harewood and Princess Royal 222
Mathews, Canon 'W A 9, 55, 207, 215
Matilda, wife of King Stephen 45
Mauchaile, see Machell
Maud (Matilda), Empress and Queen of England 45, 46
Mauld's Meaburn 58, 105, 194
Mayburgh 13
Mayors of Appleby (see also individual names) 62-64, 68-71, 90, 99, 108-110, 144, 151, 154, 155, 165, 166, 181, 183, 189, 192-195, 214, 218, 219, 221
Meaburn, Robert de 68, 69
Mechanics Institute, Appleby 204, 209
Members of Parliament see Parliament and under individual names
'Men of the North', alliance 22
Menai Straits 66
Meschin, Ranulf le, Lord of Appleby 36-40, 42-44, 46, 50, 53, 54, 100, 231, 232, 234
Meschin, Ranulf le (II), Earl of Chester 46, 47
Meschin, William le 39, 53
Mesolithic period and people 11, 12
Methodist Church, Primitive 209, 214; Wesleyan 214, 227

Metley toll, see toll
Milburn Fell 102
Militia, Cumberland and Westmorland 184, 185, 208, 233
Milthorpp, John 74
Milward, Edward 201
Mines and mining 16, 19, 46, 158, 187
Montfort, Simon de 60
Moot Hall, Appleby 144, 151,167, 172, 181, 182, 184, 185, 187, 189, 192, 197, 210, 222, 232
Moota Hill 121
Moray, Earl of 83-86
Morcant 22
Morecambe Bay 24, 26
Morland 22, 104, 127
Morland, John de 100
Morreve, John de 84
Morrison, Christopher 201
Morville, de, Norman-Scottish family 45, 49, 50, 59; Hugh de 46, 47, 49, 50, 58, 59, 231
Motte and bailey castles 37, 38
Motorways 13, 223
Mounsey, Robert 121
Mowbray, Roger de 49
Mungo see Kentigern
Municipal Corporations Act, 1882, 212
Municipal Corporations Committee 211
Municipal plate, Appleby 183
Municipal Reform Act, 1835, 210
Murgatroyd, Halifax clothier 154
'Murrain' see livestock disease
Murton 24, 57, 102, 131, 204
Murton View, Appleby 43, 230
Musselburgh 86
Musgrave, family 85, 134, 184, 193; Sir Christopher 165, 182; Edward 165; Nicholas 120, 123, 124; Sir Philip 143, 144, 146, 157, 201; Thomas de 85
Mutual Improvement Society 209

Nanson, Major John 212, 218
Naworth 87
Nelson, Gilbert & Mrs 150
Nelson, Joseph 169
Neolithic period and people 12, 13, 16

Neville family 111, 112, 115, 116
Neville, Ralph, Earl of Westmorland 85, 107
Neville's Cross, battle of 101
New Model Army, Parliamentary 146
Newcastle upon Tyne 45, 99, 146, 191, 221
Newton Garth, Durham 130
Nicolson, Bishop William 162, 182, 184
Nicolson, J and Burn, R, 142, 186, 187, 200, 232
Ninian, Saint 21, 22
Ninekirks, Church and site 21, 152
'Nine Pins', Sir James Lowther's MPs 196
Norfolk, county of 144
Norfolk, Duke of 122-124
Norham 45
Normandy 35, 45, 49
Norman occupation, northern England 30, 35, 36
'Normanization' of Scotland 45, 49
North, Lord 193
Northallerton 46
Northampton 49, 70, 146; Earldom of 45; and Edinburgh, Treaty of 87; James Compton, Earl of 146; Isabella Sackville, Countess of 146
Northumberland 22, 46, 90, 107, 116, 196; Earls of 33, 46, 116, 120, 131; Scottish raids in 33, 35, 36, 48, 49, 59, 80, 82, 101, 105
Northumbria, Anglian Kingdom of 23-25, 43; rule in Eden Valley 24-26, 30; decline of 26; Danish rule of 26-28; English rule of 27, 28, 32
Norton, Sir Fletcher MP 181, 195, 196
Norway, Maid of, see Margaret
Norwegians, colonise Western Isles and Ireland 26, 28; occupy western Cumbria 26, 27, 31

Oerdo, family of Appleby 72, 108; John senior 108; Robert 108; Sir Thomas 108, 109; William, Junior 72, 108, 109
Olaf Guthfrithson 28
Olaf Kvaran 28, 29

'Old Appleby' 30, 39, 65, 66, 228
Old Pretender, see James Stewart
Ormside 121, 190
Orre, Thomas 99
Orton 13, 18, 102, 104, 190, 229
Orton, James, butcher 169
Oswald, King of Northumbria 23, 24
Oswiu, Prince of Northumbria 24
Otterburn, battle of 105
Outhwaite, Thomas 171
Oversleigh, Thomas 68; Nicholas 68, 70
Owain ap Urien, Prince of Rheged 21-23
Owain, King of Cumbria 27, 28
Owain (Eugenius) King of Strathclyde 28, 31
Owain 'the Bald', King of Strathclyde 32
Oxford 146

Pack-horse transport 190
Paley, Rev Dr William 198
Papcastle, Cockermouth, Roman fort 21
Parliament 70, 206
Parliament, Appleby Members 69-71, 89, 151, 181, 183, 193-197, 203; Elections, Appleby 56, 115, 151, 152, 193, 200; Election of 1754, 42, 156, 194-196; Reform, 1832, 203; Westmorland Members 70, 85, 99, 140, 162, 183, 192, 193
Parliamentary party in Civil War 143, 146, 147, 154
Parr, Sir John 116
Parr, Sir William 116
Pathnell, Richard, Priest and Schoolmaster 108, 109
Patrick, Saint 21, 22
Paulinus 23
Pear Tree Garth, Appleby 100, 110, 118, 130
Pembroke, Anne Countess of, see Clifford, Lady Anne
Pembroke, Philip Herbert, Earl of 142-144, 146, 147
Pendragon Castle 61, 85, 87, 100, 116, 117, 132, 135, 147, 152, 161, 163
Pennant, Thomas 58, 101, 125, 138, 141, 199, 200, 201, 229

263

Pennines 11, 13, 14, 16, 24, 25, 83, 84, 86, 102
Penrith 16, 37, 82-84, 100, 101, 103, 104, 107, 112, 121, 127, 131, 162, 184, 190, 191
Penrith, de, family 71
Percival, Bishop John 217
Percy family 74, 80, 112, 115, 116; Sir Henry 'Hotspur' 105, 111
Peterborough, Abbot of 217
Pevsner, Sir Nicolas 163
Philip and Mary, King and Queen of England 113, 126
Pickering, William, Schoolmaster 144
Picts 20
Pike of Stickle 12
Pilgrimage of Grace 120-124, 145, 156
Pipard, Richard, Constable 58
Pipe Rolls 52, 58, 72
Pitt, William, MP and Prime Minister 193, 197, 232
Pitt Club, Appleby 202
Place names, evidence from 16, 25-27
Plague, epidemics of 25, 102-104, 106, 131, 132, 144
Planned towns, see Boroughs
'Pocket' Boroughs 196, 197
Police Station, Appleby 206, 212, 227, 234
Pollen analysis 12
Post Office, Appleby 218
Powley, John and Robert, clock-makers 202
Preston 84, 86, 185, 226
Pretender, Old 184
Pretender, Young 185, 190
Prisons Act, 1865, 206
Protection money, Scots 82, 84
Pullen, Robert 121
Pumps, Appleby 172, 211
Punishments, 18th, 19th centuries 186, 187

Queen's College, Oxford 110, 127, 129, 130, 162, 191, 203, 216, 217, 220

Raids, Scottish see Scotland
Railways, Appleby 206-208, 223

Railway stations, Appleby 207, 208, 214, 223, 234
Rainbow, Bishop Edward 159
Ramsbury 143
Ramsden, Sir John 195
Rayseat Pike, long barrow 12
Red House, Appleby 189, 219
Redlands Bank, Camp 15
Reformation, the 119, 150
Restoration of King Charles II 155-157, 159, 193, 232
Rey Cross 15, 29, 31-33, 35, 45, 49, 83, 106
Rheged 21-24
Rhydderch Hen, King of Strathclyde 22
Richard I, King of England 52, 58
Richard II, King of England 105-107
Richard, Prior of Hexham 45
Richardson, Henry, official of Appleby 181
Richardson, John, Schoolmaster 216
Richmond 33, 55, 60, 83, 84, 99, 121
Richmond, Mr D C 216
Riemmelth, Princess of Rheged 24
'Rising of the North' 131, 135
Rivington, C R 73
Roads, Roman 13, 15-18; on Roman line 37, 39, 59, 104, 148, 149, 185; improvement of, 18th-20th centuries 190, 198, 223
Robert I (Bruce), King of Scotland 80-84, 86-89, 108
Robert II (Stewart), King of Scotland 105
Robinson, Charles, butcher 168
Robinson, Captain Hugh 192
Robinson, John ('Jack'), MP 156, 189, 192, 193, 195, 197, 232
Robinson, Sir John 193
Rognvald, Lord of Northumbria 27
Roman conquest of Cumbria 14, 15; farming 14, 19; forts and civilian settlements, see under modern names 15-19, 37; roads 13, 15, 18; withdrawal 20, 21
Roman Catholic Church, Appleby 222
Roman Catholic faith 119, 129, 131, 156, 184

Index

Romano-British period and settlements 13, 14, 25
Rose Castle 82, 159, 184
Roses, Wars of the 115, 116
Royalist party in Civil War 143, 145-147, 154
Rural District Council, North Westmorland 212, 220, 223
Russel, William 90
Russell, Margaret, Countess of Cumberland, see Clifford
Rutland, Edmund Earl of 116
Royal Commission on Historical Monuments 50, 60, 73, 125, 156, 164, 188

Sackville, Edward, Earl of Dorset 141, 142; Richard, Earl of Dorset 136, 137, 139-141; Isabella, Countess of Northampton 146; Margaret, Countess of Thanet 141, 163
Saint Albans, battle of 116
Saint Anne, see Hospital
Saint John the Baptist, Chapel of 73, 74, 100, 109, 110
Saint Lawrence's Church, Appleby 73, 75, 76, 78, 118, 124, 150, 151, 159, 161, 166, 167, 200, 215, 222, 227; Building work in 52, 72, 109, 114, 232; Chantry of Blessed Virgin Mary 64, 72, 78, 100, 108-111; Chantry of St Nicholas 72, 99, 100, 108-111; Corporation fittings in 183, 233; Endowments and lands 43, 62, 99; Foundation of 30, 40; Organ 162, 233; Parish boundaries 57, 74, 131; Restoration by Lady Anne 150, 151; Restoration, 19th century 213; Tombs in 138, 139, 141, 159, 160, 233; Vicars of (see also names) 100, 110, 118, 126, 129, 198, 207
Saint Mary's Abbey, York 36, 39, 40, 62, 100
Saint Mary's Friary, Appleby see Friary
Saint Michael's Church, Bongate, Appleby 66, 110, 124, 200, 201, 228; Building work in 72, 219; Chantry of Blessed Virgin Mary 99, 110; Conversion to dwelling 213, 229; Founding 30, 40; Hog-back tombstone in 29-31; Parish boundaries 57, 66, 74, 131, 168; Restoration by Lady Anne Clifford 151, 200; Restoration, 19th century 213, 217
Saint Michael's Church School 218
Saint Nicholas, Hospital of, Appleby see Hospital
Salkeld, Christopher 113
Sanderson, Dr Randal 162, 217, 235
Sandford, Sir Richard 181, 195
Sandford, Thomas 113
Sandford Moor 121, 166
Sands, the, Appleby 58, 75, 76, 114, 186, 187, 204, 214, 227, 234
Saxon, see Anglian
Scattergate, Appleby 41-43, 57, 58, 114, 172, 187, 190, 198, 204, 221, 222, 229, 230
Scavengers, Appleby 171
School, Appleby see Appleby Grammar School
Schools in Appleby, founded in nineteenth century 203
School House Close/Gate, Appleby 106, 110, 118, 127, 128
Schoolmasters, see also under names 110, 118, 119, 125-129, 144, 191, 201, 203, 216
Schools Inquiry Commission 126, 216
Scone 26, 79, 80, 90
Scotland 11, 20, 26, 44, 45, 79, 80, 199; claims to Strathclyde 26-28, 31, 32, 44; conflicts with England 27, 28, 36, 45, 49, 50, 59, 79, 80-87, 90, 101, 102, 105, 106, 115, 119, 124; English clams to sovereignty 27, 31, 32, 35, 48, 49, 79, 87, 88, 90; English landholdings in 79, 87-90, 101; in English Civil Wars 146, 148; in 1715/1745, 184; occupation of Lothians 32, 43; raids into England 59, 80-86, 88, 101, 104-106, 112, 113, 116; raise 'protection money' 82, 84; rule over Eden Valley 29-33, 45-49, 59

265

Seascale 202
Sedbergh 18, 127, 150
Sedgwick, George 142, 148, 153, 158, 159, 200
'Seven Sisters' (cannon) 119
Sewell, Hugh, Vicar and Schoolmaster 129
Sewerage, Appleby 211, 212
Shakespeare, William 32, 116, 142
Shambles, Appleby 77, 168, 210
Shameful peace, the 87, 89
Shap 12-14, 86, 104, 105
Shap Abbey 74, 124
Shaw or Shaw's Wiend 42, 56, 72, 230
Shepherd, James P, Freeman of Appleby 212
Shepherd, John 169
Sheridan, Richard Brinsley MP 193
Sheriffs of Cumberland 51, 52, 104
Sheriffs of Westmorland 53, 54, 58, 61, 62, 65-67, 69, 104, 107, 112, 115, 116, 154, 160; 'ship money' (tax) 144
Shire Hall, Appleby 186, 204, 206, 226, 234
Silloth 202
Simpson, Dr W D 39, 104, 112, 163
Siward, Earl of Northumbria 32
Sixteen of the Borough and Church, Appleby 166, 194
Size, Nicholas 32
Sizergh Castle 152
Skelton, John 83, 119
Skipton in Craven 81, 84, 106, 117, 119, 121, 122, 134, 143-148, 152, 154, 163
Smardale 14, 85
Smirke, Sir Robert 210, 232
Smith, Bishop Thomas 162, 217, 232, 233, 235
Smith, Thomas, butcher 169
Smyth, Henry, Vicar 118
Societies, in Appleby and district 209
Solway, Firth and Plain 13-15, 18, 23, 24, 26, 46, 47, 59, 81, 86, 105
Solway Moss, battle of 124
Spanish Armada 132
Spavys, William, MP 70
Spedding, James, butcher 169

Speed, John 187
Spence, Dr R T 132, 135
Spencer, Dr Miles 125, 127, 128, 130
Sproule, J R, Vicar 197
Stainmore 13, 15, 16, 18, 22, 23, 30, 31, 33, 35, 37, 45, 80, 83, 145, 154, 190, 191, 206; battle of, 29, 30; coal mines on 158, 202
Standard, battle of the 46
Stanwick (near Scotch Corner) 15, 16, 22
Stanwix (Carlisle) 19
Station Road, Appleby 74, 125, 214
Stations, Appleby see Railways
Stephen of Blois, King of England 45, 46
Strafford, Thomas Wentworth, Earl of 143
Stewards of Scotland 45. 85
Stewart, Lady Arbella 152; Prince Charles Edward 185; Prince James (Old Pretender) 184; see also Robert II, James II, James IV, James VI and I, Charles I, Charles II, James VII and II
Stirling 80, 83
Stone axe factories 12, 13, 16
Stone circles 13
Strathclyde, Kingdom of 21-24, 26-28, 30-32, 44, 48
Strickland, Walter de 69, 70; William de 69
Surreys, John le, Mayor 69, 70
Surveyors of Highways, Appleby 181
Svein Forkbeard, King of Denmark 31
Swimming pool, Appleby 222
Swine, in Appleby 171
Sword, ceremonial, Appleby 63, 183

Tacitus, Roman writer 15, 18
Taillebois, Ivo 36, 38, 50
Taliesin, Welsh writer 21, 22
Tan Hill 158
Taylor, John of Crosby Ravensworth 170
Tebay 16, 18, 38, 185
Tebay, Thomas 123, 124
Teesdale 33, 34
Temperance movement 269
Temple Sowerby Trust 151, 162, 167, 220
Textile industry in Westmorland 187,

Index

202, 203, 210, 220
Thame 43
Thanet, Earls of, 190, 194-196, 199, 203; John, second Earl 141, 154; Margaret Sackville, Countess 144, 163; Nicholas, third Earl 163; John, fourth Earl 163; Richard, fifth Earl 163; Thomas, sixth Earl 163, 170; Sackville, seventh Earl 181; Sackville, eighth Earl 194-6, 201; Henry, eleventh Earl 213
Thatched buildings, Appleby 42, 76, 82, 218
Theobalds 134
Theodric 22
Thiepval 219
Thompson, Robert, Vicar of Brough 121-124
Thompson, John 201
Thored son of Gunnar 30, 31
Thornburgh, William de, Mayor 70, 108
Threlkeld, John de, Mayor 70; Robert de 72, 99, 110; Sir Lancelot 117; Colin, Schoolmaster, 216, 217
Thurkleby, Roger de 62
Thwaites, Thomas, (governor of County Gaol) 204
Toll Bar, Appleby 190, 229
Tolls, in Appleby 53, 166-168, 211; Metley and Gatley tolls 167, 168
Tories 197
Totnes 43
Tourism in Appleby and district 207, 226, 227
Tower of London 80, 124, 185, 193
Towton, battle of 116
Train Band 184
Tread wheel/mill 204, 205
Treaties, of York 59; of Edinburgh and Northampton 87
Treats, Appleby 166, 182
Tufton, family 144, 163, 193, 196, 201, 213, 219; Sir Richard 213; Thomas, MP 151, see also Thanet, Hothfield
Tufton Arms Hotel 210
Turnpikes 190, 191
Tweed, River 32, 59
Tyne, River and dale 16, 26, 81, 87

Uhtred, Earl of Northumbria 32
Urien, King of Rheged 21-24

Valognes, Thibault de 52
Van Belcamp, Jan 145
Van Dyck, Sir Anthony 143, 152
Venables, Richard 126, 127
Venutius 14, 15, 22, 185
Verterae, see Brough
Vesey, Lord 75
Veteriponte see Vieuxpont
Vicar's Banks, Appleby 43, 62, 230
Vicar's Croft, Appleby 40, 76, 110, 210
Victoria, Queen 135, 205, 212, 215
Vieuxpont, Idonea de 61, 65, 67, 75; Isabella de 61, 65-67; John de 60, 62, 74; Robert I de 58, 59, 64-66, 183; Robert II de 60-62
Vipont see Vieuxpont
Vortigern 20

Wagon Repairs Ltd, Birmingham 221, 222
Wakefield, battle of 116
Waldeve 54
Wales 23, 60, 66, 79, 103
Wallace, William 80
Walls, Appleby 57, 58, 125, 230
War Memorials, Appleby 219, 222, 235
Warcop 121
Warcop (Warcopp) de, family 71, 108, 165; Robert, Mayor 109; Thomas de, Mayor 70
Ward, Anne Jane 205
Ward, Anthony, Mayor 194, 195
Ward, John 201
Warde, William 126, 127
Wardens of the Marches 49, 80-82, 85, 87, 122, 124, 134
Wark upon Tweed 45, 84
Warenne, Earl 80
Wars of the Roses, see Roses
Warwick, Thomas, Vicar 127
Washington family of Westmorland and Virginia 192; Augustine I, 192; Augustine II (Austin) 192; Captain Lawrence 191, 192; John 192;

267

Lawrence II 192; George, President of the United States 192
Water supplies, Appleby 172, 211
Watercrook, Roman fort 16
'wealth taxes', see Lay subsidy
Wensleydale 18, 84
Wesley, John, Preacher 198, 199, 230
'Westmoringas' 25
Westmorland, origin of name 25; pre-conquest 12, 13, 27, 29, 30, 33; Barony 33, 36, 37, 46, 47, 49, 52, 58, 61, 102, 134, 136, 160, 183; Clifford estates 65, 66, 85, 86, 89, 102, 116-118, 124, 135-137, 139, 140, 142, 143, 145, 148, 163; County 33, 44, 45, 52, 59, 81, 83-85, 88, 90, 105, 107, 112, 116, 120-124, 126, 137, 140, 143-145, 154, 189, 190, 192, 193, 202, 208, 209, 212, 213, 219, 220, 226, 233, 236; County Council 212, 215, 219, 220, 226; Earldom (Neville) 107, 111, 131; Enclosures in, 170, 189; Impoverishment of, 52, 88, 90, 107, 144; Literacy in 203; Lord Lieutenants of 140, 143; Militia 184, 185, 208, 233; Officials of 72, 208; Plague in 102, 103, 132; Sheriffs of 53, 54, 58, 61, 62, 65-67, 69, 104, 107, 112, 115, 116, 154, 160, 213
Westmorland County, Virginia 191
Wetheral, Priory of 40, 100, 109
Weyman (or Wemyss), James, clock-maker 202
Wharton 24, 99, 124
Wharton family 108, 116, 124, 134, 185, 193, 194; Sir Thomas, first Lord Wharton 121, 122, 124, 126, 127; Sir Thomas, MP 151
Wharton, Robert, Bailiff of Appleby 181
Wheeler, Sir Mortimer 12
Whelpdale, Gilbert 121
Whigs 197
Whinfell Forest 60, 61, 89, 101, 110, 184
Whinfell, Thomas, Schoolmaster 110, 118
Whitby, Synod of 24
White House, Appleby 189, 193, 232
Whithorn 21, 26

White Friars see Carmelites
Whitehall 143, 147, 152
Whitehaven 186, 192, 194
Whitehead family, Appleby 208; Sir James Bart., 213, 217, 220; Alderman James F, 221, 222, 224
Whitley Castle, Roman fort 16
Wiends, Appleby, see separate names
Wilfrid, Saint 24
William I (Conqueror), King of England 33, 35
William II (Rufus), King of England 30, 35, 36, 43, 49
William the Lion, King of Scotland 47-50, 59, 231
Williamson, Joseph 151
Wilson, Thomas 172
Wilton House 142, 143, 152
Windermere 202
Winton 18, 24, 36, 99, 123
Worcester, battle of 149, 154
Wordsworth, Richard 192
Wordsworth, William 117, 192, 229
Workington 202
World War I 218, 219
World War II 220-222
Wynd, Thomas, Bailiff 68

Yates, Richard, Schoolmaster 191, 200
York, Christopher Bainbrigg, Archbishop of 130; City of, 23, 26, 28, 63, 66, 68, 70, 85, 90, 99, 100, 144, 191; Kingdom of 28-30; Richard, Duke of, 116; Thurstan, Archbishop of 44; Treaty of, 59
Yorkist faction in Wars of Roses 116
Yorkshire 11, 22, 23, 33, 52, 83, 84, 86, 120, 122, 123, 143, 199; Clifford estates in 117, 118, 122, 123, 135, 136, 147, 148
Yorktown, USA 192

A PLAN OF
APPLEBY
IN
WESTMORLAND
From an Actual Survey taken 1754.

The North East VIEW of the CASTLE.

The whole Quantity of Ground in the Castle
Park including the Castle, the Gardens Stables,
&c. is 212 Acres and 8 Perches.

The Quantity of Ground in the Castle Park included
between the Park wall and Wotten Lane is
4 Acres and 37 Perches.